SOMALI REP.

RUANDA-URUNDI

NYASALAND

MALAGASY REP.

KENYA

ZANZIBAR

TANGANYIKA

SWAZILAND

BASUTOLAND

UGANDA

MOZAMBIQUE

Indian Ocean

REPUBLIC OF THE CONGO

N. RHODESIA

S. RHODESIA

REP. OF S. AFRICA

CONGO

GABON REP.

ANGOLA

BECHUANA-LAND

SOUTH-WEST AFRICA

S. CAMEROUNS

CAMEROUN

RIO MUNI

SIER

South Atlantic Ocean

THE NEW FACE OF AFRICA SOUTH OF THE SAHARA

THE NEW FACE OF AFRICA

South of the Sahara

THE NEW FACE
OF AFRICA

South of the Sahara

by

JOHN HUGHES

AFRICA CORRESPONDENT OF
The Christian Science Monitor

LONGMANS, GREEN AND CO.
NEW YORK · LONDON · TORONTO
1961

LONGMANS, GREEN AND CO., INC.
119 WEST 40TH STREET, NEW YORK 18

LONGMANS, GREEN AND CO., LTD.
48 GROSVENOR STREET, LONDON W 1

LONGMANS, GREEN AND CO.
137 BOND STREET, TORONTO 2

THE NEW FACE OF AFRICA

PUBLISHED SIMULTANEOUSLY IN THE DOMINION OF CANADA BY
LONGMANS, GREEN AND CO., TORONTO

FIRST EDITION

LIBRARY OF CONGRESS CATALOG CARD NUMBER 61-14962

PRINTED IN THE UNITED STATES OF AMERICA

FOR LIBBY

For too many years, Africa in the minds of many Americans has been regarded as a remote and mysterious continent which was the special province of big-game hunters, explorers and motion picture makers. For such an attitude to exist among the public at large could greatly prejudice the maintenance of our own independence and freedom because the emergence of a free and independent Africa is as important to us in the long run as it is to the people of that continent.

RICHARD M. NIXON

To those peoples in the huts and villages of half the globe struggling to break the bonds of mass misery, we pledge our best efforts to help them help themselves for whatever period is required—not because the Communists are doing it, not because we seek their votes, but because it is right. If the free society cannot help the many who are poor it can never save the few who are rich.

JOHN F. KENNEDY

Acknowledgments

The writing of this book was compressed into a relatively short time. But most of the material was gathered during six years of African travel and reporting as Africa correspondent of *The Christian Science Monitor*. I should like to thank the *Monitor* for the many opportunities and experiences it has brought my way.

In particular I should like to thank Joseph G. Harrison, of Boston, and Stanley Uys, of Cape Town, for reading the manuscript and for perceptive advice.

Mr. John L. B. Williams, of Longmans, Green, has offered a number of helpful suggestions.

Thomas Nelson and Sons, of Edinburgh, and the Public Affairs Press, of Washington, have kindly given me permission to quote President Nkrumah and President Nasser from *Ghana, the Autobiography of Kwame Nkrumah*, and *Egypt's Liberation: the Philosophy of the Revolution*, respectively.

Finally, there is my wife, who has shaken more African dust out of her hair, sat out more African crises in various African hotel rooms, and exhibited more fortitude during the writing of this book, than any other full-blooded American girl of my acquaintance.

JOHN HUGHES

Acknowledgments

Contents

Contents

THE NEW FACE OF AFRICA

South of the Sahara

CHAPTER I

Africa: Bursting the Bonds

BY THE TIME this book is published, the United States or the Soviet Union may well have fired a man at the moon.

In Africa, however, are many men for whom a journey into another world is nothing new. They are the black Africans who in a few brief years have been catapulted out of the primitive world of tribal Africa into the flashing, clanging wonderland of the twentieth century. This for them is a journey tinged with all the fantasy and adjustment of a flight to the moon for other men.

Swiftly and suddenly, a dramatic revolution has swept across their continent. Today we are confronted by an entirely new Africa.

This revolution is a many-sided one.

It is economic, plucking Africans out of their leaves and loin-skins, and dumping them down as miners and mechanics and bulldozer operators and factory hands making everything from nylon stockings to bicycle bells.

It is social, ripping into both the white man's color bar and the African's own background of tribal custom and superstition.

Above all it is political, as Africans ride a rocket to self-rule in a shower of political pyrotechnics.

Nonwhite nationalism which freed Asia from colonialism fifteen years ago has leapt the oceans and gone crackling through Africa like a bush fire, touching off an African freedom drive from Algiers to Cape Town.

Until 1957, European colonial powers like Britain, France, Belgium and Portugal ruled the bulk of Africa. In the few

1

intervening years, one African state after another has shrugged
off foreign rule and marched out to independence. At the end
of 1961 there were just a few colonial blobs on the African map
awaiting the inevitable. Most of Africa is under black African
rule and the political revolution against colonialism is virtually
over.

Thus there is a crop of brave new African flags fluttering on
the flagpoles outside the United Nations in New York. Inside,
able African foreign ministers and delegates, many of them
reared in mud-and-dung huts, suavely debate Laos and the H-
bomb and whether they should admit those Communist Chinese.

From sovereign African states, finance ministers with gorgeous
robes and unpronounceable names come knocking on the doors
of Wall Street and the World Bank for money for hydroelectric
dams and universities and soil conservation projects.

African leaders of a stature to parley and parry with Washington and Moscow are bustling about the world with diplomatic
secrets. African premiers breakfast at the White House and sip
tea with Britain's Queen Elizabeth II.

Their black African subjects are learning to pilot ships and
high-speed air liners, becoming sculptors of royalty, winning
prizes at the Olympic Games and handing down erudite supreme
court judgments.

There is an African poet so versed in the culture of France
that Frenchmen seek him out to hear him speak. There are Africans who sparkle in donnish debate on Kant and Nietzsche,
Thoreau and Emerson. These are the new intellectuals and educated elite of Africa, sparing a moment now and then to reflect
wistfully on the cheese-tasting evenings back at Harvard, or those
Sunday afternoons with the tutor at Oxford.

Often their transition from steaming African village life to
languid student days with Shakespeare beside the rivers Charles
or Cherwell has been remarkably swift. There to prove it sometimes, above the old school ties knotted with careless pride, are
the cheeks scarred with tribal tattoos and patterns inflicted by
knife during childhood.

Most of today's leaders in Africa were reared in goatskins or
less against a simple tribal background. Few of their parents were

educated. Tanganyika's Julius Nyerere, an impressive African
leader with a master's degree from Edinburgh University, likes
to startle his primmer white visitors thus: "I don't know how old
I am. We never kept any records. My parents were illiterate, you
know."

During Ghana's independence celebrations of 1957, I saw a
dramatic sight. African drummers and dancers, festooned with
all the regalia of tribal Africa, pounded away on the ground in
one of their centuries-old rituals while the latest jet planes of
Britain's Royal Air Force screamed overhead. This in a way
symbolizes the leap which Africans are trying to take from what
in many cases was the Stone Age into the modern world of education and technology.

.   .   .

Although it has become trite to say it, it is so strikingly accurate
that it is necessary to say it again: Africa is a continent of the
most incredible contrasts.

Thus, although many Africans have made the leap, millions
more remain in a vacuum of poverty and backwardness. As yet
there is no African middle class, and the gap which exists in its
place is a wide one. There is impressive progress, yet much of
Africa still teeters by on peasant agriculture. For the African
villager this is agriculture at the backbreaking subsistence level,
scratching no more than a bare living from the parched soil.
Across the length and breadth of Africa, countless women haul
all the water they need in buckets and gourds atop their heads
from the nearest stream sometimes several miles away.

Africa is one of the world's richest and poorest continents all
rolled into one.

From Africa come all the world's diamonds that matter, most
of its gold and huge slices of every important mineral. Yet half
the mineral production of the entire continent comes from just
one country, the Republic of South Africa. This is the only state
in the continent with a reasonably industrialized economy. There
is an economic backlog in every other African nation.

Africa has enough untamed roaring river water to light up
the whole world with electricity. Every crop under the sun will

grow in one part or another of the continent. There are literally mountains of valuable ores. It has the largest man-made forest in the world and great resources of timber. There is every major mineral here. There is even oil.

Of course, major development is afoot. The Kariba Dam, bringing hydroelectric power to the Rhodesias, is backing up the Zambezi River into the biggest lake in the world made by man—175 miles long. The Volta scheme will light up Ghana. At Lake Victoria in Uganda, engineers have trapped the Nile at its source. They were not the first with the idea, however. Fifty years ago an East African traveler by name of Winston Churchill, then Under Secretary of State for the Colonies, declared delightedly: "What fun to make the immemorial Nile begin its journey by diving through a turbine."

Schemes like Kariba are literally changing the face of Africa. When the lake is filled, cartographers must redraw their maps of Central Africa. Scientists are trying to trap the African sun's energy for solar cooking and heating. Others by rain-making experiments are trying to control the fall of the African rains. All this is changing the lives of millions.

Yet Africa is so unimaginably huge that its surface has barely been scratched. Many of these resources are only potential wealth. While revolutionary change swirls across the continent, it remains basically underdeveloped from an economist's point of view.

. . .

Africa is a continent so big that when a London newspaper published a map of it some time ago it was able to superimpose upon it the whole of the United States, all of Communist China, plus Tibet, India and Pakistan, and leave room enough around the edges for a half dozen of the smaller European countries. You could squeeze the United States into Africa nearly four times.

This is a continent of gasping, waterless desert wastes, but also of dripping tropical jungles and steaming swamps and great green rivers like the Congo and Limpopo.

For hundreds of miles the veld shimmers off into endless flatness. But in Africa too is mighty Mount Kilimanjaro, and the

Ruwenzori, the Mountains of the Moon, and snow enough to ski on not far from the equator.

Africa still exists in the raw. Till recently it was not unusual for your inward-bound aircraft to circle Nairobi, in Kenya, until they cleared a rhinoceros off the runway. The East African game plains extolled by Hemingway are still there, with the tang of the untamed and wild, and echoing to the thunder of galloping herds of buffalo and elephant. But there are great tracts so un-African that Hollywood cameramen have gone home in frustration to film their African shots in California. Then there are the modern cities, big and brash like Johannesburg, belching factory smoke as thick as Pittsburgh's.

Africa is home to 230,000,000 people, only 5,000,000 of them white. The nonwhites speak up to a thousand languages among themselves and are often as diverse as Spaniards and Scandinavians. They range from the giant Watusi, who measure up to eight feet in height, and whose high-jumping surely will cause a stir if ever they get to the Olympic Games, to the little pygmies, four feet high.

All these people hail from the same continent, yet there are differences among them as great as between an Arizona cowpoke and a man in a New York gray flannel suit. For all they have in common, one of Johannesburg's jazzy juveniles-in-jeans might as well be a man from Mars to the arrogant Masai tribesman in Tanganyika, spearing lions to prove his manhood, and living on a diet of milk and blood siphoned from the veins of his living cattle. Yet both are "Africans."

A particularly important contrast is that which exists between the Arab or North African lands and the Negro or black African lands lying south of the Sahara Desert. This separates the continent into two distinct worlds.

To the north of the great desert barrier lies Egypt, and the Libyan battlegrounds of World War II, and Tunisia and Algeria and Morocco, strung out along the shores of the bright blue Mediterranean. These are part of the African continent, yet Egypt, for example, is at the heart of the Arab world. The other Mediterranean countries look more to the Middle East than they do to black Africa. None of these is an African state in the black

African sense of the word. Thus, while their interest in black Africa will be mentioned from time to time, there is no special section for them in this book, the topic of which is black Africa south of the Sahara.

There are of course some broad ties between Arabs and Africans. There is Islam, which has spread south to parts of West and East Africa and rippled down the eastern coast beyond Zanzibar to Mozambique.

Then of course the Arab and African and Asian lands have a strong common bond in their opposition to colonialism, where it lingers, and imperialism and racial discrimination.

In recent years the Arab countries of North Africa have begun to participate in various pan-African conferences and organizations.

Nothing has stimulated North African interest in Africa more than the Congo crisis. Morocco, Tunisia and the United Arab Republic sent troops to the Congo and have played a prominent role in international negotiation over this troubled land both in the Congo itself and at the United Nations in New York. There have been persistent charges that the United Arab Republic supplied arms direct to the Lumumba camp in the Congo. Thus in one way or another the Congo has drawn these North African countries into black African affairs.

President Nasser, of the United Arab Republic, has long expressed a general interest in Africa. His radio stations beam propaganda at black Africa, and in his book, *Egypt's Liberation: the Philosophy of the Revolution,* he writes: "We cannot, even if we wish to, in any way stand aside from the sanguinary and dreadful struggle now raging in the heart of Africa between 5,000,000 whites and 200,000,000 Africans. We cannot do so for one principal and clear reason, namely, that we are in Africa. The people of Africa will continue to look up to us, who guard the northern gate of the continent and who are its connecting link with the outside world."

Friendship there may be, but black Africans do not look to President Nasser for a lead. After Ghana's independence, Dr. Nkrumah struck up a friendship with President Nasser, and Dr. Nkrumah's wife is Egyptian. Yet the Ghanaian president has quietly but firmly resisted attempts to make Cairo the center of pan-African affairs. Black Africans need no prompting or guidance from Cairo in black African politics.

Thus, although they exist on the same continent, there are major differences of interest and character between the Islamic arc of lands and the countries of black Africa which are separated from each other by the ageless impassive sands of the Sahara.

. . .

Negro Africa has lain dark and unknown for hundreds of years.

Exploring sea captains made their mark along the coastline of course, and the slavers who carried away millions of African slaves pushed into the coastal belt. Then at the southern tip of the continent whites have been settled for more than three hundred years.

Nevertheless it was only a hundred years ago that Livingstone and Stanley, Burton, Speke and the other giants of exploration made their arduous journeys through the heart of Africa.

After them came the missionaries who have been responsible for most of Africa's elementary education, and the hunters and traders and adventurers. In the latter half of the 1800's began the scramble for Africa by the European powers. In thirty years they had carved the continent up. Britain, France, Belgium and Portugal won the biggest colonial empires. Italy and Spain, together with Germany, gained African colonies too, but, with the exception of a few existing slivers of Spanish African territory, they were later edged out of the continent.

Thus as recently as sixty and seventy years ago many African territories saw their first waves of white colonial administrators and settlers.

Africa slumbered on in remoteness until World War II. Suddenly it became important. Its minerals were vital. Warships sped down to South Africa on secret missions to hustle gold back to the United States and Britain. The Allies demanded industrial diamonds for their tank factories and munitions plants and the furnaces of war. Uranium for the Hiroshima and Nagasaki atom bombs came from the Belgian Congo's mine of Shinkolobwe.

Africans made contact with the outside world. Massive Allied convoys ploughed around Africa to the Middle East. Thousands of British and other troops swarmed ashore at African ports. There were campaigns in East Africa and Ethiopia. The Free French set up operations in West Africa.

Then came the Americans, with chewing gum and new ideas, bulldozing airstrips out of the equatorial jungles for the planes they were ferrying from the United States to West Africa, then on across Africa and up into Egypt.

Thousands of Africans were themselves recruited for military service and had their eyes opened to a new and equal way of life in foreign lands from Britain to Burma.

After the war, foreign geologists came hunting new minerals and fuels. Businessmen came looking for new markets. Colonial governments stirred and began development programs, nudging roads and railways through bush and swamp. Then came new airfields, and lately the big modern ones to handle the jet air liners which link New York and London with Johannesburg in about twenty hours.

While white men flew in to size up Africa, the flow of African students began to the world outside. Off they went to study public works in Blackpool and ball-bearing-making in the American Midwest and to enroll in universities in California and Scotland, in India and Egypt, and also in the Communist lands.

Cheap radios and new African magazines and increasing African literacy all helped to bring the outside world closer. Now there is television with its vast capacity for bringing light to the former Dark Continent.

It was the great awakening. Africans struck out in search of their own African "personality," as Ghana's Dr. Nkrumah calls it. The wind of change went buffeting across the continent and in a few brief years the political map had been turned upside down.

Six years ago, my wife and I flew into the Kenya capital of Nairobi to begin a newspaper assignment. We bounced down on a sad little airstrip and clattered out through the old army huts which served as an airport terminal into a colony still riven by the effects of the Mau Mau rebellion. White feelings ran high. Sunburned young settlers strode the streets with revolvers slapping at their thighs. Votes for Africans? African farmers in the "white highlands"? No prospect of this. The whites seemed firmly in control again.

Yet when I flew out of Nairobi recently, this time from the new jet airport built by Mau Mau prisoners, Kenya politics had turned somersault. Now there was an African majority in parliament and Africans saw independence around the corner. Such was the speed of change.

At the end of World War II there were only two nonwhite independent states in Africa south of the Sahara. They were Liberia and Ethiopia. Until the brink of the 1960's, most of Africa lingered under alien rule. Now, however, the white man as a political master remains only at the southern end of the continent. There the Portuguese and the white South Africans and the Rhodesians have thrown up the barricades against the African advance.

Has it all been too fast? Would some states have benefited from longer white tutelage? Interesting questions, but academic ones in the 1960's, when the anticolonial revolution is all but over, the campaign is done and black men sit at the power-steering. There are those important exceptions at the continent's southern tip, but otherwise white man's rule in Africa, like Aunt Agatha's aspidistra or the Charleston, is a quaint and archaic reminder of a forsaken age.

This does not mean the white man is no longer welcome in Africa. There are more whites in Ghana today than ever there were in colonial days. Ghana, like other African states, needs the white man's skills and is anxious to get them. But the terms are different now. Today the white man stays as an equal, not as a political master.

This is the new Africa. This is black man's country.

WEST AFRICA

CHAPTER II

Ghana: Pioneer of Free-DOM

GHANA IS THE HEART of the new Africa.

This may not always be so. Already there looms the challenge of Nigeria, whose 35,000,000 people may build their nation into the most powerful in Africa, overshadowing Ghana's influence.

There is the restless ambition of Guinea's President Sekou Touré, whose dreams range far beyond the horizon of his country's present, tottery union with Ghana.

There are the tough new young nationalist leaders like Tom Mboya from Kenya. As African lands shrug off their colonial ties and taste the heady atmosphere of independence, there are challengers aplenty for the leadership of emergent black Africa.

Yet for the moment these clammy cocoalands on the underside of the West African bulge are astir with new-found importance. There is, in the Ghanaian (pronounce it Ga-nay-an, with the emphasis on the second syllable) capital of Accra, an air of bustle and excitement which indicates that it still is the pole of attraction and stimulus for much of the African world.

Accra itself is an unrestrained, riotously colorful African city. It is set on the sea and looks out over white, palm-fringed beaches cluttered with gaily painted dugout canoes and fishing nets and naked, coal-black little African boys, onto the Gulf of Guinea and the sparkling blue South Atlantic beyond.

The boys must be the friendliest in Africa. Elsewhere Africans are sometimes shy, and occasionally resentful, if photographed without their permission. But in Accra, whenever I set up my camera to photograph the long, curving beaches, I would look

13

down into the viewer to find it crammed with laughing little black boys, all strutting and posing and anxious to be photographed. Thus I brought away very few pictures of the beaches, but a whole series with every corner of the photograph filled with these cheery chaps.

Although one is being finished at Tema, sixteen miles to the east, Accra itself has no harbor. Ships anchor half a mile out and their cargoes, and sometimes passengers too, come skidding in with a fine flurry and sputter of spray in surfboats manned by thickset African paddlers.

These boatmen, I was told, are recruited from the same coastal villages which have supplied them year after year. Their technique is passed down proudly from father to son like that of an old-time English blacksmith or one of the disappearing trades preserved at Williamsburg, Virginia.

However, even these experts make their occasional slip, and when they do one of the heavy surfboats goes tumbling over broadside-on in the breakers and some consignee gets a damp and dismal crate of corn flakes, or whatever the cargo may be that is rescued from the sea.

If passengers or cargo have still farther to travel, one of the jolliest forms of transport is by "mammy waggon." Mammy waggons are the trucks and open-air buses owned by the market "mammies," or women traders. Daubed with an exotic range of slogans from SATCHMO'S CHARIOT and SAMSON AND DELILAH to HEAVEN OR BUST, these rumble up and down the coastline and up to four hundred miles inland to Ghana's northern border.

By Africa's enormous standards, Ghana is small. Its area is about 79,000 square miles, and that is only about three times the size of Scotland.

It is shaped a little like a top-heavy layer cake. For its base there is a 60-mile-wide coastal plain. Then comes a forested belt up to 170 miles deep. It is capped by a broad layer of open savannah, scoured by the harmattan wind which blows in off the great deserts to the north.

The population throughout the country is now nearly 6,700,000 but of course it is Accra that throbs with most of the activity.

Downtown in the capital the streets teem with noisy, boisterous

Ghanaians. Many wear Western dress of lightweight slacks and sports shirts for the sticky climate. But a delightfully large number still wear the sandals and gorgeously hued robes, cut toga-style off one shoulder, which are traditional costume.

For special occasions, wealthy Ghanaians wear robes of kente cloth. This is expensive material woven with gold thread and infinite patience into long strips about four inches wide, which then are sewn together to make a gown. Such a gown may cost more than three hundred dollars.

By day the raucous market mammies carry on their full-throated business and hundreds of ever-honking cab drivers add to the confusion.

Then when darkness comes, the night clubs blare out West Africa's own distinctive jazzy "High Life" music.

The night spots are simple affairs with just a few tables and chairs set around a slab of concrete open to the African stars. Admission is rarely more than twenty cents. At the start of each dance, couples trot off together but soon break to wiggle and waggle their separate ways, still in time to the brassy music, often to opposite ends of the dance floor. Both men and women wear the same type of ankle-length robes and one sometimes wonders whether they always do find their own partners again to end the dance.

Clearly then, Ghanaians have an awful lot of fun. Of course the city council is bulldozing imposing new boulevards through the ramshackle tenements and the higgledy-piggledy side streets. The corrugated iron and whitewash with which Britain has left its mark on tropical Africa is being steadily replaced by magnificently sober and solid new buildings. But it will be quite some time before all this awesome municipal respectability smothers the Ghanaians' built-in exuberance.

. . .

Accra these days is something like an African Grand Central Station. It is a major West African terminal whether you fly in from New York, or from London over the Sahara, rippled by row upon row of rounded hills like the pattern of the sea upon the sand.

It is a meeting place and lobbying spot for visitors, both African and non-African.

There in a corner may be an emissary from Algeria, here a group of political refugees from South Africa, there that mysterious figure from Angola who flits from one African capital to another.

Stay long enough and you probably will see every important African nationalist and politician from Guinea's Sekou Touré, turning on the charm or withdrawing into frigid aloofness depending on his mood, to little Basutoland's Ntsu Mokhehle, looking like an African Spencer Tracy.

Ghana's President Kwame Nkrumah encourages all this. Whatever the future may bring, for the moment he has established his country as a cornerstone of the African revolution and a hub of pan-African activity.

An ardent proponent of African unity, he has made Ghana host to a string of African conferences and gatherings and to attract more he plans an international conference hall of ambitious magnificence, equipped for simultaneous translation of delegates' speeches into many languages. The cost? Nearly $3,000,000.

Another $3,000,000 is being spent on the "Voice of Ghana," a powerful radio station which will beam Ghana news, views and other programs to Africa and beyond in English and French initially, then later in Arabic, Swahili and the West African language of Hausa.

Meanwhile, ask a man the time in the foyer of Accra's principal Ambassador Hotel and he may reply in Russian, Arabic or French. He may be a Communist trade delegate, or an American blues singer on a tour for the U. S. Information Service, or a Swedish agronomist from the UN, or a North Country Briton selling boilers with a Lancashire twang.

Since independence in 1957, the Israelis have launched Ghana's shipping line, but the Egyptians have been training Ghana's police dogs. The Canadians planned the "Voice of Ghana." The Americans are drilling boreholes and building dams under the economic assistance program.

Scandinavians are coaching the leading Ghana football teams, for, despite the tropical climate and as in most of black Africa, soccer is the favorite sport.

Meanwhile, everyone has sent a trade mission to Ghana—the Yugoslavs, Czechoslovakians, Poles, Soviets, East Germans, West Germans, Egyptians, Israelis, Dutch, British and Americans.

The Communists have not been left behind. Prominent at the independence festivities, they have kept up the pressure. Once when the Ghanaians held a scientific conference in Accra and opened it to delegates from around the world, the Soviets swamped it with an unannounced delegation of more than twenty. The startled Ghanaians had themselves sent only two men to the meeting.

Significantly too, of the three permanent foreign correspondents based in Accra when last I was there, one was the man from *Pravda*, and the other from the New China News Agency. The third was the man from the British Reuters agency.

All these visitors have not dropped in for the tourist season. Accra may have plenty of cheerful color, but it still is short on the attractions which might distract the crowds from Miami Beach and the Mediterranean Riviera.

The pilgrimage which all these foreigners have made to Ghana is recognition of this little country's influence in many parts of the continent as a champion of African nationalism and a pioneer in the business of independence.

Liberia, of course, existed before the old British Gold Coast became Ghana, but Liberia had been settled by Negro slaves from the United States and was never colonized by the white man. Thus Ghana was the first of the really black African lands to shed colonial rule for independence.

. . .

The man who swept the Gold Coast to independence, and who today as a reward holds power tightly in his hands as president of Ghana, is a shrewd, able, controversial crusader by name of Kwame Nkrumah.

Born in 1909 the son of a simple and illiterate African goldsmith, Nkrumah trod the same difficult mud-hut-to-president path as most of the African leaders who today hold political responsibility.

Nkrumah went to school at Roman Catholic missions, although he describes himself as a "nondenominational Christian." Then he taught elementary school himself in the simple schools of the neighborhood. But his own thirst for more education was not assuaged. He set his sights high—a university education in the far-off United States.

He stinted, saved, borrowed some of his fare, and at last in 1935 arrived in New York for studies which were to keep him in the United States for the next ten years. He won a bachelor's degree in philosophy and theology at Lincoln University, a master's in philosophy and education at the University of Pennsylvania, and part of the time lectured in political science at Lincoln.

Each vacation he joined in the familiar American custom of finding a student job to help pay his way.

But Nkrumah carried Africa with him in his thoughts. His was a key role in the organizing of other African students at American universities, many of whom now are the educated elite of West Africa. Endlessly they debated the exciting new political theories they were learning, and their application to Africa.

Nkrumah decided he must steep himself in a knowledge of the law before his return home. He detoured via London on his way back to the Gold Coast, but did not get far with his law studies. There was far too much exciting political activity among the African students there. Once again his flair for organization came to the fore and he became a central figure in the politicking of the student basement rooms and the cheap restaurants behind the British Museum and around London University.

By now his fame had spread to his homeland. He was hustled back to become full-time organizer of the United Gold Coast Convention (UGCC), the Gold Coast's prime political party under the British colonial government.

Organize it he did with a flurry of energy, and an attention to detail in the remotest branch offices. Many of the campaign methods he applied he had learned overseas and so brightly painted loud-speaker trucks soon were rumbling with the party's propaganda through the length and breadth of the country.

Here controversy clouds the record. Embittered founders of the

UGCC claim Nkrumah organized the party right out from under their noses to form his own new Convention Peoples Party(CPP). Nkrumah's lieutenants affirm that he broke with the UGCC after a policy split with its conservative leadership, and that many of the UGCC rank and file followed him into the new CPP.

Whatever the case, Nkrumah now was on the road to the premiership. He organized, toured, campaigned, endlessly. He was one long thorn in the side of British colonial authority. Eventually they locked him up for a year for incitement and Nkrumah won the martyrdom of many another nationalist leader jailed for his beliefs.

While their leader was making fish nets behind the bars of Accra's James Fort Prison, CPP supporters, so the story goes, would tramp past the prison walls singing, to the tune of "John Brown's Body": "Kwame's body lies a-moldering in James Fort Prison, But his work goes prospering on." Nkrumah's work certainly did prosper on under the hand of his faithful and astute aide, Komla Agbeli Gbedemah, now minister of health and a possible contender for leadership in the unlikely event that Nkrumah should relinquish power in the next few years.

While Nkrumah was in jail, the authorities held the Gold Coast's first general election. Nkrumah, as a convict candidate, romped home with a huge majority. So did his CPP.

In a realistic decision, but one tinged with courage too, the British released Nkrumah and he stepped from prison cell to become leader of the Gold Coast's new CPP government. As prime minister, Nkrumah kept up the ceaseless pressure for independence and on March 6, 1957, he led his nation to its sovereignty.

Thus ended the history of Europe in the Gold Coast which had begun sketchily as far back as the fifteenth century with its discovery by Portuguese seamen. In the seventeenth and eighteenth centuries, however, the Portuguese were edged out by the slave traders from other countries.

Over three centuries more than 12,000,000 African slaves are believed to have been shipped off to the West Indies and America, and from them one in ten Americans claim their Negro ancestry today. The old slavers' forts still exist along the West African coast and President Nkrumah himself has lived in Christiansborg

Castle, built by Danish slave traders in the 1660's. (Perhaps here, to avoid confusion, it should be explained that Prime Minister Nkrumah became President Nkrumah in 1960 when Ghana adopted a new constitution making it a republic within the British Commonwealth. The post of prime minister was abolished at that time and Kwame Nkrumah became president, retaining political power.)

With the slave trade quelled in the nineteenth century, European interest in the Gold Coast fell off. It was left to Britain to arrange treaties among the chiefs, a so-called "Bond" which whittled away their power. Eventually the Gold Coast became a British colony and remained so until the Union Jack was hauled down for the last time in 1957, 113 years after the signing of the Bond.

. . .

Independence for the Gold Coast marked not only the birth of a new nation, but also of a new era in which millions of black Africans would wrest political control from the European colonial powers and emerge as a significant new force.

Clear recognition of this was the dispatch of high-powered delegates to the independence celebrations. The United States sent Vice-President Nixon. To represent Britain's Queen Elizabeth II came the Duchess of Kent. Mr. R. A. Butler, Lord Privy Seal, was there for the British government. More than seventy nations sent representatives.

Communist lands sped in their array. There was a minister from the Soviet Union and a vice-premier from Communist China. With the Communists came Soviet film men and reporters from *Pravda* and the New China News Agency.

Distinguished guests included Dr. Ralph Bunche and—a human touch—Dr. Nkrumah's old landlady from his London boarding-house days.

Accra was crammed. The government requisitioned the luxury Ambassador Hotel for diplomatic guests and quartered other visitors as guests of officials and resident diplomats around town. It hustled the two hundred foreign newsmen who had arrived to cover the ceremonies into a new wing of the university college even as builders hammered the last tiles onto the roof.

For distinguished visitors it had imported a fleet of gleaming new American limousines and British Jaguars. Mr. Nixon got a cream Jaguar flying the Stars and Stripes. The bill for the celebrations topped $2,000,000.

The streets were gay for miles with bunting and banners and shields with molded elephant heads and eagles and the insignia of guest countries. The new flag of Ghana, red, gold and green in horizontal bands overprinted with a black star, fluttered everywhere.

Thousands of happy Ghanaians, many of them with three weeks' advance pay in their pockets, had clogged the streets for days before March 6. Many wore print robes emblazoned with life-size heads of Dr. Nkrumah, specially printed and imported from Manchester. Some had "Independence" or "Freedom and Justice" daubed in white paint on their foreheads. From the country, the mammy wagons came swaying in fully laden for the fireworks and excitement and high jinks.

From the shops open to the dusty sidewalks blared calypsos like "Well Done Ghana," "Good Luck Ghana" and—yes—even "Gha Gha Ghanaaaayikoo." Everyone blew a hooter, threw a streamer, waved a flag.

On independence eve the minutes ticked steadily away toward midnight. The crowds grew noisier and noisier. Inside the floodlit parliament, Dr. Nkrumah made his last solemn speech to the legislature of the Gold Coast. Nkrumah and his cabinet had come wearing their little round white prison caps. Embroidered with the initials "PG" for "Prison Graduate," these were a last sly reminder of their imprisonment by the British, and of the struggle for freedom.

At midnight the clamor of sirens and hooters blended with a great roar from the waiting mobs. Dr. Nkrumah was whisked bobbing on the shoulders of his supporters to a platform on the old polo ground. It was a neat piece of symbolism that this pukka symbol of British rule should be trampled into dust by thousands of Africans that night, though with an amity and good humor which gave Britons or any other whites safe and friendly passage through the densest part of the throng.

There in an incredibly moving scene, sweat from the photographers' floodlights running together with his streaming tears as he broke down and sobbed with emotion, Kwame Nkrumah called for the national anthem of the new nation and the new state of Ghana was born.

The celebrations went on for days. During them there were many delightful incidents. There was the time, for example, when Vice-President Nixon made a short safari to a little village about thirty miles from Accra.

About one hundred newsmen accompanied the Vice-President and Mrs. Nixon. About one hundred subchiefs and headmen were waiting to greet the Nixon party. The chiefs decided that all we reporters, despite our perspiration and crumpled suits, must be Nixon aides. Politely but firmly the hundred of them insisted on shaking hands with each of us. That made something like ten thousand handshakes. The resulting melee, with Mr. and Mrs. Nixon in the middle of it, must be one of those occasions the accompanying secret service men prefer to forget.

The same village produced the only frown on Mr. Nixon's face during a hot and exhausting tour. With the Nixons installed on tribal thrones under huge umbrellas there began an exchange of courtesies between Mr. Nixon and the village senior chief through an African interpreter.

When conversation began to flag, the chief contributed in his own language: "You are not the first American to visit us." "Oh really?" replied Mr. Nixon with polite interest. "No," said the chief, "we had one some months ago. He was a Mister . . . Mister . . . Mister Adlai Stevenson."

Mr. Stevenson apparently had visited the identical village and sat in the very same chair as Mr. Nixon just some while previously.

As a footnote to the whole affair, we later learned that the chief whose comments were translated so laboriously from his own language spoke excellent English and had a son at the University of California.

Meanwhile, the Nixons with good humor bowed to the cameramen's demands to dance with the chief, and to "just sit the little African baby on your lap, Mrs. Nixon," and to "now just do the whole thing over again, Mrs. Nixon."

Even when seating arrangements at the main state banquet

upset some members of the American delegation, Mr. Nixon remained imperturbable. The American delegation was not seated at the head table and some members maintained that it should be, representing a major power. Mr. Nixon explained carefully to inquiring reporters, however, that the seating had been arranged alphabetically and that a nation like the United States, starting with the letter U, was assigned to a side table, as it happened, alongside the U.S.S.R. This placed Mr. Nixon next to Soviet Farms Minister, Ivan Benediktov. "We talked about soya beans most of the evening," said Mr. Nixon diplomatically. "It was most interesting."

So the festivities drew slowly, and for the Ghanaians reluctantly, to a close.

The highlight was the glittering state ball. Prior to this, Dr. Nkrumah had been one of the "world's worst dancers," according to one British official. Thus for some days previously he had been quietly taking lessons in the modern dance from Mrs. Louis Armstrong, wife of the famous Negro American trumpeter. Mr. Armstrong is a friend of Dr. Nkrumah's and it is said he claims his great grandparents came from Ghana. He had been unable to make the trip for the independence celebrations but had sent his wife along nonetheless.

In a short while, Mrs. Armstrong had given the prime minister a sort of concentrated Arthur Murray course.

On the great night, as protocol demanded, an African prime minister in flowing African robes thus took into his arms the Duchess of Kent in a gown of glistening white to circle the ballroom floor.

Nobody cared very much about the prime minister's dancing. It was a picture flashed instantly around the world, for it was acceptance at this high royal level of the African's new stature and dignity.

CHAPTER III

Ghana: After the Party

THE PUBLICITY which greeted Ghana's birth did not cease in the first years of independence.

As the first of the African colonies to win self-rule, and the first African member-state of the British Commonwealth, Ghana came to be looked upon as a yardstick of the African's ability to run his own affairs.

Many onlookers seemed to regard Ghana as a sort of experimental laboratory. The results from it might yield a formula to gauge African capacities throughout the whole continent.

Perhaps this was inevitable. It was not very logical. As we have noted, African peoples are tremendously diverse among themselves. From country to country they are at varying stages of political, cultural and economic progress, and often have widely different problems. Thus, while Africans thousands of miles away from Ghana drew inspiration from its example in achieving self-government, there was no particular reason why they should pattern their own political systems and rates of progress after Ghana's.

In addition, all this attention was hard on the Ghanaians, whose early fumblings and stumblings were bathed in the glare of international publicity as Japanese TV crews and American columnists and a host of other visitors flew in, then out again to spread their impressions.

The impressions were mixed ones, and they still are today.

Thus the cynic about African rule can tour Ghana, list a dozen instances of corruption, maladministration and autocratic rule, and write the whole country off as a failure.

24

The enthusiast, however, can list a separate dozen instances of stability, achievement and greater economic development than under colonial rule, and interpret Ghana as a great success.

Some of Ghana's well-wishers may tend to gloss over trends such as the erosion of political opposition and the drift to one-party rule.

The critics, on the other hand, sometimes set their sights inordinately high, judging by lofty standards not always present in their own countries.

Ghana does have its graft. There is political patronage and detention without trial and perhaps intimidation of the opposition. However, the United States has its own television quiz scandals. An old democracy like Britain can have on its conscience the clubbings to death of political prisoners at Hola Camp in Kenya. Hundreds of Africans have been detained without trial in the Rhodesias and in South Africa.

The London *Daily Telegraph's* Ian Colvin, who was arraigned in a much-publicized Ghana court case for one of his dispatches, wrote afterward that he would "rather be tried in a Ghana court than in Yugoslavia or Russia, where, to use the common parlance, 'Europeans' administer justice."

Nevertheless it was obvious soon after independence that Ghana was to become overnight neither the kind of de luxe Disneyland which some of its less sophisticated citizens had envisaged, nor would it be patterned after the well-ordered world of British Whitehall, with African civil servants scurrying to the office each morning in bowler hats and clutching neatly rolled umbrellas.

Some Ghanaians I talked to before independence had bizarre ideas of what it all would mean. One market mammy assured me the police would be abolished once the British left. A barber confided that the reserve funds of the state-controlled Cocoa Marketing Board would be shared out. His own allocation, he had worked out, would come to $4,068.40.

Independence did not, of course, replace the rattling mammy waggons with purring American limousines. Ghana did not become a fairyland of Cadillac coaches and gingerbread houses. To many, independence has not yet brought the down-to-earth houses they need to replace their tin shanties.

More enlightened Ghanaians such as the students at the university college up on Legon Hill were aware of problems ahead, particularly in the economic sphere.

Ghana's economy is keyed to cocoa, of which it is the largest producer in the world. The economy is thus vulnerable to fluctuations in prices on the world cocoa market and, to swing his country away from dependence on this single export crop, Dr. Nkrumah is working hard to diversify and industrialize.

This takes time and money and in the meantime his government is confronted by the need to produce some tangible fruits of independence for the electorate.

At the moment, Dr. Nkrumah is riding the crest of the wave and is extremely popular among the masses in his own country. Yet the challenge in the future may come from the thirty to forty thousand young school-leavers each year. For them independence will be an established fact surrounded by little of the glamour which it holds for the present generation. Their loyalty to Dr. Nkrumah may depend upon his ability to provide jobs and opportunities.

Already, to occupy some of Ghana's younger men, Dr. Nkrumah has formed a "Builders Brigade." Its members live in camps under a kind of military discipline. Some critics charge there is an ulterior motive to the scheme and that the brigade could swiftly be converted into a band of government-supporting shock troops. But they are unarmed at present and the government says its aim is simply to train school-leavers in various trades before they are turned loose among Ghana's competitive labor force.

Center of Dr. Nkrumah's dreams for an industrial revolution in Ghana is the Volta River hydroelectric scheme. This is a vast dam and power unit to cost many millions of dollars. The American Kaiser Corporation has done the preliminary work on the site and the World Bank has conditionally promised a loan of $40,000,000, the United States government one of $30,000,000, and the British government a third loan of $14,000,000. Ghana must itself find a similar amount from its own resources.

The essential part of the scheme, however, is the development of big bauxite (aluminum ore) deposits near by. Ghana wants foreign aluminum companies to invest in a big smelting plant for the production of aluminum. The plant would be a major consumer of hydroelectric power and justify the dam's existence, but there would be power enough too for other new industries.

The scheme is part of Ghana's current and breathtakingly ambitious five-year plan. In six years of British rule immediately prior to independence plus two successive years as a sovereign state, Ghana spent $330,000,000 on development. Now in five years to the end of 1964, Dr. Nkrumah plans to spend three times as much, $957,000,000. However, items in the plan are rated with different priorities and some will be dropped out if capital is not available.

.   .   .

Ghana's more publicized problems lie in the political sphere. Within a few months of independence it was clear the new state was not to become, at least in its early years, the well-oiled democracy for which some of its Western friends had hoped.

There are grounds for arguing, of course, that Ghana was not much of a democracy during most of British colonial rule. One prominent Ghanaian, taxed by a Briton over his government's actions against some of its political opponents, replied with a smile: "But, my dear fellow, that's what *you* did to *us* when you held power."

However, Dr. Nkrumah's action in sanctioning the deportation of a string of critics and opponents in the early months of independence was much publicized outside Ghana. One of the deportees, a disillusioned ex-fan of Dr. Nkrumah's by the name of Bankole Timothy, was assistant editor of an Accra newspaper. Later the Nkrumah government was engaged in a number of wrangles with newspapermen and has deported some and barred entry to others.

All this was climaxed by the Offences Against the State (False Reports) Act, providing for penalties up to fifteen years in jail for the dispatch of "false reports" out of Ghana. Eager to allay foreign criticism, Information Minister Kofi Baako announced that only Dr. Nkrumah himself would act under the new legislation. Dr.

Nkrumah, said Mr. Baako, "is very jealous of free speech and freedom of the press and the Act will under no circumstances be used to interfere with legitimate press freedom."

However in 1960 Dr. Nkrumah took powers of censorship in a new Criminal Code Amendment Act and, despite protests from the International Press Institute, barred the country's sole opposition newspaper, the *Ashanti Pioneer,* from publication without censorship of its contents by the Information Ministry. Later the newspaper announced tersely that it would henceforth support President Nkrumah.

Considerable adverse criticism of Ghana was undoubtedly stirred by the actions and comments of a tough little party organizer, Krobo (swiftly nicknamed "Crowbar") Edusei, whom Dr. Nkrumah had appointed minister of the interior. Responsible for police and security matters, Mr. Edusei stumped the country uttering dire threats to the government's opponents. Of course, they were cabled overseas. Eventually Dr. Nkrumah reshuffled his cabinet, moving Mr. Edusei to another post within it, but he remains a forceful character.

With the passing of a new Preventive Detention Act providing for detention without trial or appeal for up to five years, foreign suspicions of an authoritarian trend in Ghana were considerably heightened.

A few months after the Act was introduced there came the real sensation of Ghana's postindependence years to date when the government swooped on more than 40 of its opponents, including two members of parliament, and clamped them into jail where they still languish without trial under the provisions of the Act. The government charges that the detainees "conspired in an attempt to kill or capture the prime minister and to overthrow the government by force."

Although the government has consistently refused to bring these alleged traitors to trial, it did, perhaps bowing to foreign criticism, order a public inquiry and publish extracts from the resulting report.

The three-man inquiry, headed by a British judge of the Ghana appeal court, found that the two arrested parliamentary opposition members had been engaged "in a conspiracy for an unlawful purpose revolutionary in character." The chairman differed with the two other commissioners, however, on their finding that the plotters had actually conspired to assassinate the prime minister and stage a *coup d'état*.

The opposition United Party retorted with a 37,000-word statement claiming the inquiry had in fact exonerated the accused. Except for the unfortunate men in prison, the affair ended on an inconclusive note.

The opposition charges that in the years since independence, Ghana has passed "from the oppression of imperialism to the injustice of despotism."

Part of all this tough action by the Nkrumah government has been designed to smash tribalism. Like many another African nationalist leader, Dr. Nkrumah sees tribal diversity and jealousy as the most dangerous threat to national unity. He is dedicated to the concept of strong central government. It is one of the reasons he backed so vigorously the Lumumba camp in the Congo against its opponents demanding a federal structure.

In many parts of Africa there is this clash between feudal traditional rulers and the ambitious young nationalists who seek to sweep them off their thrones. In Ghana, opposition to the Nkrumah government has been rooted in the Ashanti region inland which has long been the stronghold of the Ashanti kings and chiefs. Dr. Nkrumah was determined to neutralize the power of these rulers, and, though many of them still occupy their thrones, or "stools" as they are called in Ghana, they are now only nominal rulers, for their influence has been steadily undermined and restricted by a variety of Nkrumah tactics.

But whatever the reason for them, all these authoritarian measures against political opponents in Ghana have inevitably stirred some thoughtful questioning about the prospects of democracy in the new Africa.

Dr. Nkrumah himself clearly foresaw that he might have to take tough measures after Ghana's independence for he wrote in his autobiography: "Even a system based on social justice and a democratic constitution may need backing up during the period following independence by emergency measures of a totalitarian kind. Without discipline true freedom cannot survive."

At this stage, leaders like Nkrumah and Guinea's Sekou Touré are committed to "centralized democracy," or one national party within the framework of which there is room for discussion and dissent. Certainly the CPP in Ghana has on occasion had more trouble from its own back-benchers than from the opposition party.

Those who justify the Nkrumah standpoint make various points. The first is that colonial rule was not democratic. The second is that the two-party system is quite foreign to Africans only just emerging from tribalism. Decisions were taken within the framework of the tribe and opposition to the chief's rule was usually of a treacherous kind. The new states of Africa then, goes the argument, in these first days of independence need strong central governments to override tribal leanings, draw together the diverse groups confined within artificial national boundaries, and stimulate the economic development which is the key to national progress. Certainly in many of Africa's new little states there has been a steady drift toward one-party rule.

In Ghana, Nkrumah's lieutenants charge that the political opposition has adopted unorthodox and nonparliamentary methods. In bloodcurdling eagerness to underline their point, they declare that the Ashantis have a warlike background and that they themselves engaged in the slave trade in ancient times, capturing and selling their fellow Africans at the coast. Then there are grim stories of past Ashanti punishments, such as the thrusting of a sharpened stake through cheek, tongue and cheek.

Meanwhile the fact is that the Nkrumah government has steadily whittled down the parliamentary opposition. There have been further arrests of opposition supporters under the Preventive Detention Act. The opposition's parliamentary leader, Dr. Kofi A. Busia, a sociologist whom some observers considered to be a misplaced intellectual in the role of politician, has fled the country and now teaches in a Dutch university.

After Ghana became a republic, the government abolished the terms "government side" and "opposition side" in parliament and instead seated all members in a U-shaped chamber. To many this abolition of a formal parliamentary opposition seemed but recognition of the political fact of one-party rule.

.   .   .

If this be despotism, however, it appears to be despotism with the consent of the majority of the populace rather than by force.

Nobody can deny the vast popularity of Kwame Nkrumah among the masses, nor the probability that in free elections tomorrow he would romp back to power again. Even his opponents, who talk wistfully of an ultimate change in the political climate, concede this. During the republican referendum of 1960, Dr. Nkrumah swung more than 1,000,000 votes for himself as president, against only 124,000 for his only opponent, Dr. J. B. Danquah. Dr. Danquah was the man who brought the young Nkrumah back from London to organize the old United Gold Coast Convention party. An Accra lawyer, he now is an embittered foe of the man who, as he sees it, supplanted himself.

Much of Nkrumah's strength stems from the fact that he and his ruling CPP guided Ghana to independence. Thus there is about him a glamour and stature which will likely command the grateful respect and support of his people for a number of years to come.

The Nkrumah mystique is one which he himself has done much to further. Dr. Nkrumah is a master at the art of publicity. In his early days as a politician he was affectionately known by the nickname of "Showboy." Now his people call him by the rather more dignified title of "Osagyefo." Pronounced "Osah-jefo," this means broadly "Victorious Leader." Despite the change he keeps them entranced with a variety of events and diversions.

Thus it may be some exciting new conference in Accra, bringing African leaders or important visitors from the ends of the earth to the Ghanaian capital. Or perhaps a dramatic new announcement of union with Mali. Or a foreign tour by Osagyefo from which the pictures are rushed back of him shaking hands with the American president, or in the embrace of President Nasser, or arm in arm with the Duke of Edinburgh.

All this is exciting stuff for Africans who have long been condemned to inferiority and who now are anxious to assert their own importance and ability. Sometimes it distracts attention from basic problems at home such as the breakdown of the water supply system which caused drinking water to be shipped all the way from England in ocean tankers.

Also it helps contribute to the personality cult which has grown up around Dr. Nkrumah. His head has replaced that of the Queen's on Ghana's coins and postage stamps. Roads and traffic circles are named after him with lights which flash his name on and off at night. His picture is nailed to hoardings and trees along the sidewalks. His activities dominate the press.

Outside parliament his statue commands the approaches with the inscription cut into its base: "Seek ye first the political kingdom and all other things shall be added unto it."

His critics say this is but the satisfaction of his power-drunk ego. Nkrumah aides, on the other hand, say that after independence the opposition began a clandestine campaign to smear Nkrumah as a stooge of the British. The opposition, so the story goes, whispered that Ghana was not really free, that Nkrumah did not really rule. To counter the slander, say Dr. Nkrumah's supporters, he had to assert himself. He ordered his own head printed on stamps, coins and so forth, in a positive demonstration that a black African ruled Ghana.

Whatever the truth, it has all put Dr. Nkrumah beyond the threat of any serious challenger to his position. From within his own party the two most likely candidates as a successor are Health Minister Gbedemah and Kojo Botsio, currently minister of agriculture and minister of state for parliamentary affairs. It is conceivable that without Nkrumah's unifying presence, a struggle for power between these two could split the CPP.

At present, however, the party has the country buttoned up politically. As might be expected with Nkrumah at its head, it is expertly organized. It spends money freely and its opponents tell hair-raising tales of how that money is acquired which are impossible to check. Certainly it believes in political patronage, a system not entirely unknown outside Ghana. It has extended its control over trade unions, farmers, the press and women's organizations.

The CPP indeed has paid particular attention to its organization among the influential market mammies and the women of Ghana who perhaps make up 50 per cent of the electorate. Nkrumah, it might be said, is the man who decided that the woman's place is no longer in the hut. Significantly in the new republican constitution he reserved ten special seats in parliament for women.

Some of Dr. Nkrumah's close friends maintain that his long bachelorhood was motivated partly by political considerations. They believe his appeal to women voters was greater while he was unmarried. Certainly he was fond of declaring: "Every woman in Ghana is my bride." Friends also say that his selection of a wife from Egypt was to circumvent jealousies which might have been roused among Ghanaian women had he chosen one among their number for his bride. While this is all a fascinating study in political psychology, there is no certainty that Dr. Nkrumah was motivated by such ideas.

Meanwhile, whatever all the critics may say about its shortcomings, the machinery of government ticks steadily over in Ghana. The administration has not collapsed under African rule. The jungle has not crept back. If anything, there has been more progress and development and expansion than under colonial government.

When, on one of my visits, I was interviewed by Ghana Radio, a Ghanaian interviewer conducted the session, a Ghanaian recorder made the tape, and Ghanaian technicians who were running the station put the whole thing over with practiced efficiency. This was a tribute to the British Broadcasting Corporation men who trained them and perhaps to the other Britons who have done much for Ghana, including the training of a splendidly disciplined and drilled police force and army.

One of the most heartening aspects of postindependence Ghana is the friendliness of the Ghanaians to whites of both British and other nationalities. Many more white men live in Ghana today than before independence, and the government is recruiting more for specialized jobs for which Ghanaians are as yet unavailable.

There is no color bar, and blacks and white mingle freely on the beaches, in the swimming pools, in the hotels and restaurants and movie houses. For the white man who accepts equal status with the black Ghanaian whose home this is, and who seeks no especial privilege on account of his skin alone, there is no disability or friction to living among more than six million Africans.

Of course there are petty trials. I remember the *Life* photographer who had some altercation with a new Ghanaian customs officer who wanted him to open up some precious, undeveloped film! But it might just as well have been an African photographer put through the hoop and there was no especial racial antagonism.

For Britain as a nation there is considerable respect and affection. I have heard a black Ghanaian police officer with Ghana's forces attached to the United Nations in the Congo quietly lecturing an Indian journalist on how much both Ghana and India owe to Britain.

Dr. Nkrumah has welcomed members of the British royal family to Ghana, as well as Britain's Prime Minister Harold Macmillan. The Duke of Edinburgh has ridden arm in arm with Dr. Nkrumah through the streets of Accra. The Ghanaian president has been a guest at the Queen's country home at Balmoral and holds an honored appointment as one of her select privy councilors. When Dr. Nkrumah decided that Ghana should become a republic instead of a monarchy with the Queen at its head, he elected to keep his country within the Commonwealth on the friendliest of terms with Britain.

For Dr. Nkrumah, foreign affairs are primarily African affairs, and this friendship does not preclude his strongly attacking Britain for its last lingering vestiges of colonialism, nor other Western nations like the United States when they take a line on Africa with which he disagrees.

The basis of his foreign policy in Africa is closer union between African states. This has not been particularly successful to date, of which more later. In addition, Dr. Nkrumah has incurred the enmity of some African states which are rivals for influence or which resent what they term Ghana's "meddling" in other nations' affairs.

Over-all, Nkrumah is pledged to a policy of "positive neutralism," or nonalignment between Western and Communist worlds. Thus he accepts aid from, and criticizes, both sides.

In the first years of independence Dr. Nkrumah talked privately as a good friend of the West. While the United States built a big wooden Teahouse-of-the-August-Moon-ish embassy on stilts in Accra, Dr. Nkrumah stalled Soviet requests to open an embassy. While he has visited both Washington and London on a number of occasions, he has not yet been to Moscow or Peking. Both his long years as a university student in the United States, and American involvement in the Volta scheme, give him special ties with the United States.

Of course, the Soviets are now represented in Accra and are forging closer links with Ghana. Moscow has given Ghana a $40,000,000 long-term credit to help fund a program boosting agriculture and industry. The Soviets have sent a team to Ghana to assist in mineral prospecting, building industrial plants and minor hydroelectric dams, and organizing model state farms.

Ghana is buying machinery, steel, petroleum products, building materials and chemicals from the Soviet Union in return for Soviet purchases of Ghanaian cocoa, coffee, copra, skins and hides, rubber and fruit. Ghana Airways has bought eight aircraft from the Soviet Union. Less happily, there have been shipments of Communist arms to Ghana recently.

All this has seemed alarming in some circles and been interpreted as a dangerous Ghanaian flirtation with the Communists rather than a move, in line with Nkrumah's declared policy of neutralism, to balance his earlier close association with the West.

It may be, of course, that if Dr. Nkrumah becomes disillusioned with Western policies, particularly in Africa, he may lean even more toward the Communists. But if all his philosophy of African nationalism and assertion of the African personality mean anything, he is no man to turn Ghana Communist. Suggestions in the past by prominent American spokesmen that Ghana is "drifting toward the Communist camp" have been regarded by many African specialists as major diplomatic blunders.

Thus then, in a few years of independence, Nkrumah's dynamism and imagination have carved out a remarkable niche for Ghana. Nobody doubts he has serious problems and rivals ahead. But "Showboy," "Osagyefo," Mr. President, call him what you will, Kwame Nkrumah is no man to write off as a future influence in Africa.

CHAPTER IV

Guinea: A Cheerless Birth

AFTER GHANA, GUINEA. This little-known French West African colony was the next of the African lands to gain independence.

Guinea's birth could hardly have been more different from Ghana's.

In Ghana, or the Gold Coast as it then was, the British had groomed Africans for nationhood with a certain enthusiasm. They built them a university college, hustled other bright young Gold Coasters off to Britain for training, installed the machinery for African government, and generally, once the principle of self-rule was conceded, did their best to fit Africans for their coming responsibilities.

For Ghana's christening, Britain threw a wing-ding independence party, invited friends from far and near for the festivities and stood clucking with motherly pride in the background. To launch the baby on its way, Britain bestowed gifts, blessings and promises for the future. And though British control was clearly at an end, well, everyone guessed that in time of trouble Ghana could go home to mother for at least a little sympathetic advice and Britannia would see the fledgling nation through.

Guinea, however, was dumped on the world's doorstep like a child its disgruntled French motherland would really rather not have spawned.

There was no christening party, no kind word from Paris, no motherly pride, and the new state was cut off without a franc to its name.

For the French, Guinea's offense was that it had been born already grown up, so to speak, with an independent mind of its own. Without waiting for childhood and tutelage, Guinea had elected to pack up and leave home.

When General de Gaulle returned to power in France and started planning a new relationship between France and her overseas territories, he probably recognized that one day these colonies would grow to nationhood and independence. But clearly he expected them to live for some years as one big family under the same roof, and all dominated by the quiet influence of the motherland.

Guinea alone among the territories spurned this relationship, elected immediate independence and moved out from under the family wing. "Ingratitude," cried the French. More seriously, Guinea's departure might give other territories ideas about leaving.

So France decided to play the hurt parent, make the severance with Guinea a brutal one and thus quietly underline for other French African lands the disadvantages of breaking with France.

The abruptness with which Paris cut off relations shocked even Guinea. The French stripped the country of everything they had put into it and that they could carry away. They took the desks and the typewriters and the electric light globes. They took the telephones and the telephone directories and some of the telephone wiring too, according to the Guineans. They took maps and records and receipts, and when the Soviets arrived two years later to rebuild the Conakry railroad, they claimed the French had taken the maps and working drawings of that too. French officials and their families poured homeward by plane and boat, and government departments collapsed like deflating balloons behind them.

Desperately alone in the world, and as youngsters who feel themselves misunderstood sometimes will, Guinea fell in with a new, fast-talking bunch of friends who appeared suddenly on the scene. They seemed to understand. They offered sympathy and help. They were the emissaries of international communism.

Now Guinea is a little like a teenager swept along by its razzamataz friends for the ride. Aghast at these new non-U friends, old family friends of France like the United States and Britain have hastened to hold out the worried hand of friendship. France itself has softened some. They all would like to see Guinea in safer company.

There are signs that Guinea itself is aware of the dangers. But then its new friends are generous with their presents. And so, defiantly, Guinea declares it really is friends with everybody and that it can step out of that Communist automobile any time it wants.

The West has seen confident little nations carried off by the Communists before. It fears that if Guinea is not beyond redemption, it nevertheless may get taken for a long, long ride.

.   .   .

Before it broke its links with France and won prominence, Guinea was an unremarkable little corner of France's African empire. Its population is only about 2,500,000, living in a country about the size of New Zealand, but which, unlike New Zealand, has a tropical climate far different from that cool green land's. Guinea owns impressive resources in the shape of bauxite (for aluminum) and iron ore, but despite infusions of French development capital and some foreign investment it has remained primarily a backward and underdeveloped country.

The French, nonetheless, have a flair for beautifying even the remotest parts of their domain chopped out of the African bush. Thus with a white corniche here, a few tropical palms there and a dash of pastel paint they turned the dusty little village of Conakry into an attractive tiny capital set upon the sea. There is a modern hotel with a circular dining room almost overhanging the ocean's breakers, and in each of its bedrooms one complete wall a huge, pivoting slatted shutter which swings open to a view of a pretty little bay with a twinkling lighthouse and to the cool breezes off the South Atlantic.

As a finishing touch, the French set out a series of neat, tree-lined squares, dominated by the statues of French governors and other French notables.

A week or so after independence, African workmen under orders from the new government set about a special task. Carefully they prised all the statues from their pedestals and carried them away to a government store. There, visitors with a taste for a

French governor in the hall or the garden back home, could acquire some excellent French statuary at bargain prices, I was told. Meanwhile the last time I was in Conakry, the empty stone bases which had carried the statues were still bare and embarrassed-looking. Perhaps by now there are new statutes of African administrators and notables.

The story of the statues is in a way symbolic of the revolution which overtook Guinea when it elected for independence in 1958. This was not a violent upheaval in which rioting mobs pulled down and smashed statues offensive to them, but a peaceful one wrought by the ballot, after which workmen quietly removed symbols of the old government.

When France, in 1958, called upon de Gaulle to return and lead the nation in peace as he did Free France in war, the French overseas empire was offered a new deal. Territories could vote "Yes" in a referendum and thus forge a new type of association with France. Or, although de Gaulle gambled they would not, they could vote "No" and become independent of France with all the implications of that decision.

Came polling day and eleven of France's twelve states in West and Equatorial Africa voted "Yes," later becoming states within the new French Community enjoying autonomy in domestic affairs.

The one state which rebelled and voted "No," thus automatically voting itself out of the Community, was little Guinea.

If a rebellious vote from Guinea was inevitable, the man who made it so is its present leader, President Sekou Touré. For years Sekou Touré had been dedicated to making trouble for the French administration. He delights in claiming descent from an old-time Malinke tribal leader, Samory, who for many years harried the French on the field of battle as effectively as did M. Touré on the political field in the years before Guinea's independence.

Like most of Africa's prominent leaders, Touré got a simple start in life. Though today he is poised and urbane as occasion demands, he had only a few years' schooling before entering the French colonial administration as a clerk. But his curiosity was intense. He read everything he could lay his hands on, studied and questioned with relentless energy.

His ambition directed him to trade unionism. He organized his fellow workers, clashed frequently with the French administration and eventually came out fighting on top of the Guinea branch of the Communist-controlled French Confédération Générale du Travail (CGT). Here he attracted the attention of the Communists and came back from union gatherings in Warsaw and Prague inspired by the new seed of Marxism. But later he broke with the Communists to form Guinea's own first trade union.

The road from unionism to politics was a short one. Touré became mayor of Conakry, a deputy in the French Assembly in Paris and a spellbinding orator and ruthless organizer. By the time de Gaulle visited Guinea on his prereferendum tour, Touré had the people solidly behind him. Even before independence he had smashed the influence of tribal leaders and chiefs.

For de Gaulle, Guinea was the jarring note of the tour. Touré, in the tradition of hardened African nationalists elsewhere, told the French leader bluntly Guinea preferred freedom in poverty to captivity in riches. De Gaulle stamped off in anger.

Then M. Touré called upon his people to vote for independence. In the referendum they responded with a fantastic 95.4 per cent poll backing up their leader. There are some observers who believe that if M. Touré had called upon them to vote the other way, they would have done so with a similarly decisive vote. This perhaps underlines one of the lessons of Africa today, that the inclination of the electorates in many countries is to vote for a personality rather than a policy.

As the results of the referendum in other French territories came tumbling in, M. Touré may have been staggered by the loneliness of his position. He perhaps had hoped that at least neighboring Senegal with its big and prosperous seaport of Dakar would have joined him in his daring rejection of France. But all except Guinea voted for continued ties with France, and the economic and other aid which went with them.

France lost little time in underlining Guinea's loneliness. French technicians were shipped home. With them, as we have seen, went equipment, files, arms and ammunition, everything that could be moved. French banks turned off the credit tap. French capital was siphoned off home.

With the withdrawal of key French officials, the administrative machinery all but collapsed. There was a serious shortage of teachers. There were grave financial problems. Guinea looked in bad shape.

With characteristic energy, M. Touré set to work. He made a meteorologist minister of public works. A shopkeeper became minister of commerce and a radio technician minister of information. Guineans studying overseas were recalled in the middle of their studies. Some sympathizing Frenchmen were induced to stay on.

At the beginning, officials worked without salaries, sharing secretaries, desks and the government's single list of telephone numbers. M. Touré himself handled a mass of desk work, tied to his office for fifteen and sixteen hours a day.

With improvisation, the Guineans discovered they could keep the machinery of government grinding along at least in bottom gear.

But to fill the vacuum left by France's precipitate withdrawal, there soon appeared the agents of communism. Moscow and the other Communist lands were the first to recognize Guinea. Their diplomats were soon speeding into Conakry. To some extent, the ground was laid for them by French Communists already in the administration who stayed on when their colleagues left, and by others who moved in to fill vacant posts.

One of the guides which the Information Department attached to me when I visited Guinea soon after independence was a Communist journalist who had worked for a French Communist newspaper and who made no secret of his political sympathies.

Within weeks of independence, Guinea was the object of a Communist campaign of intensity. One after another the missions from Eastern Europe flocked in. Conakry's principal hotel was cluttered with members of an East German trade mission in *lederhosen* and checked shirts, and Poles and Russian-speaking Bulgarians. One day a plane swooped down to unload an eighteen-man Czechoslovakian military mission, headed by a full general. So blatant was it all that at one stage even the Communists seemed concerned and decided to distribute some of their number rather less ostentatiously in private lodgings around town.

Struggling to raise the American flag in the face of all these Communist battalions was one American chargé d'affaires with a young assistant. For some months they worked from their hotel rooms before acquiring an office in the corner of an American oil company's premises. Elsewhere in Africa, and from a source other than these two officers, I learned that even this humble beginning was nearly postponed because there was no financial provision for a post in this area.

Meanwhile the Communists were busy offering culture, trade, aid, arms.

Within a short while, Guinea had signed away some sixty per cent of its agricultural exports in a series of barter agreements with the Soviet Union, East Germany, Poland and Czechoslovakia. Today Hungary and Communist China are also on the list.

The Communists offered bursaries for university study in Communist lands and the Czechoslovakians soon set up a trade fair from their country in downtown Conakry. Included in the display were small arms. Soon after, the West was startled by the arrival of bulk shipments of these Czechoslovakian arms.

The first shipments contained between eight and nine thousand rifles, with pistols, machine guns, a few armored cars and something in the way of light artillery and antitank guns.

The amounts were not spectacular but the West was concerned, nonetheless. The Guineans had a simple answer: France stripped our 2,000-man army before leaving. We need arms. We would take them from the West but the West has not obliged. The Czechoslovakians offered them to us with no strings attached. We could not turn down so useful a gift.

Guinea's increasing contacts with the Communists took place against a background of general sullenness among the country's leadership over Western tardiness with aid and assistance. There lingered the suspicion that France was pressuring the United States and Britain to go slow with recognition and help. In Conakry, Western officials were often treated with discourtesy and left uninvited to official parties and receptions. The government made an insultingly abrupt cancellation of a tour which M. Touré was due to make of the United States, although the tour later took place with considerable success.

Government spokesmen, however, declared that Guinea was friends with everybody, open to the aid it needed from all comers. President Touré himself told me in an interview that he was eager for Western assistance. He particularly wanted the West to build Guinea's big Konkouré Dam project. Like Ghana's Volta River plan, this is a scheme for generating hydroelectricity for use in an aluminum smelter. Like Ghana, Guinea has substantial deposits of bauxite for aluminum production and, like Dr. Nkrumah, President Touré believes he will spark an industrial revolution if he can get the project operating.

President Touré affirmed that the Communist world had offered to help fund the $300,000,000 project. In return, the Communist nation or nations involved, which he refused to specify, wanted a blanket mineral concession over Guinea's bauxite and iron.

Frankly, said the president, he would prefer the West to do the job of dam-building. For the moment he had turned the Communists down, but if the West could not help, well, he might be forced to reconsider.

Had the Communists really offered to help with the dam or was M. Touré engaged in the tiresome old business of trying to play the West off against the Communists? Would the Communists really become implicated in such a major project in a remote West African country of only 2,500,000 people? On the face of it, it seems unlikely. But the enigma of Guinea today is that one can never be quite sure. Who, for example, should pop up later as the Soviet Union's ambassador to Guinea but Mr. Daniel Solod, Moscow's man in Cairo who wooed President Nasser, who had much to do with events leading up to the Suez crisis, and a diplomatic big gun for little Guinea.

Despite all the protestations of neutrality and nonalignment, Guinea has snuggled much closer to the Communists in the ensuing months.

It has won a $35,000,000 loan from Moscow and another of $25,000,000 from Peking. Eastern European advisers are in every government ministry. The Czechoslovakians are training the army and the police force and the East Germans are building a great printing plant and perhaps a radio station too. The Hungarians are training Guinea's footballers who perhaps will one day play in a 25,000-seat stadium which the Soviets have promised to build, along with a cement plant, a timber mill and a shoe factory. The Soviets are also rebuilding the railway.

Hungarian buses rumble along Conakry's streets and Czechoslovakian Skodas are swiftly replacing the old French Peugeots and Renaults. The cement comes from the Soviet Union and the shoes from Czechoslovakia. The Communist Chinese, whose achievements are much admired by M. Touré, have opened their first embassy in black Africa in Conakry. They plan a pilot rice-growing scheme which might bring many more Chinese into the country.

M. Touré himself was given a magnificently organized reception in Peking and a warm welcome in Moscow. But, of course, he has also visited Washington and London.

Then again, although Guinea receives substantial assistance from East Germany, M. Touré moved swiftly to deny diplomatic relations with East Germany and to soothe West Germany's ruffled feelings when the West Germans threatened to sever relations in 1960.

Toward the end of that year Guinea signed an agreement with the United States for economic and educational aid to Guinea, and, when he attended the same session of the UN General Assembly as the shoe-pounding Mr. Khrushchev, M. Touré criticized both the West and the Communists at various stages.

Thus M. Touré seems to be walking a swaying tightrope between Western and Communist worlds, while spectators guess whether he can keep his balance.

A key question is the degree of "Africanization" of the Marxism which he absorbed during his visits to Eastern Europe. He himself says he has "adopted Marxism to the extent that it is valid for Africa." He says he has rejected "the principle of the class struggle" and "substituted the anticolonial struggle for the class struggle." This, he says, does not make him a Communist.

For all this, Guinea has developed many of the trappings of an Eastern European state.

Here, as in Ghana, we see "centralized democracy" at work within the framework of one political party. But this is a much more blatantly one-party state than Ghana, ruled rigidly by

Touré's Parti Démocratique de Guinée, which has established 4,000 local committees throughout the country, one for every 600 men, women and children. This is the "dictatorship of the people," as Touré calls it, which brooks no opposition or questioning from outside the party.

Real power in the "People's Democracy" which Touré is building is vested in the "Politburo." This is the central organization of party leaders which makes the decisions and hands them on to the National Assembly for rubber-stamping. This role has been underlined by Assembly President Diallo Saifoulaye, who is also political secretary of the PDG. He has said: "The party is above all. Is this party dictatorship? Yes, over its responsible officers, members and militants who have freely accepted its discipline and placed their confidence in the PDG. To the party, and not the government, belongs the heavy task of education of the masses and reconversion of their minds and methods."

Meanwhile, President Touré has left the citizens of the republic in little doubt of their fate in the event their individual interests clash with that of the party. "In our republic," he has said, "individual liberty is placed within the framework of its practical utility to our society."

His regime has cracked down fiercely on corruption and crime, using tough new legislation and threatening public executions to combat the latter. The government has imposed capital punishment for armed robbery and theft by night. It automatically exonerates from punishment a man who kills a burglar in self-defense.

Commenting on the introduction of these regulations, M. Touré declared: "These measures must be related to the revolutionary concept of our party, which is that everything is only a means to serve the people, that nothing can be justified except with relation to the people's interests.

"Therefore if the people's interests were to require that 1,000 or 2,000 persons should be killed, we would do it without hesitation in order to permit the masses to live in happiness, honor and dignity."

M. Touré's admiration of Communist China extends in particu-

lar to the Chinese concept of collective labor. In Guinea there is
a collective labor system already in existence and Touré has
talked of his people building the Konkouré scheme "with their
own hands" if outside assistance is lacking. Philosophizing on the
upliftment of the peasant, M. Touré has declared: "For the
Guinea people, only rationalized, collective work will be able to
make their experience of value." He is enthusiastic about manual
labor. Again: "A total reconversion is necessary in our country
to honor and encourage manual and skilled labor. At the moment,
office workers are twice as well paid as carpenters and plumbers.
We are resolutely determined to change this unjust situation."

All this atmosphere of tense endeavor has left its mark on Sekou
Touré. In the old days, say his friends, he was a gay, fun-loving
man always with time for a dance and the social whirl. A handsome and still relatively young man, he still is capable of flashing
charm from time to time. But for many of today's visitors he
strikes a brooding, almost Napoleonic pose, high in his office
overlooking the sea. Some Western diplomats speak of the difficulty of achieving any rapport with him and complain of his lack
of warmth.

Since Guinea shed French rule, problems and responsibilities
have come tumbling about Sekou Touré's shoulders.

For the ordinary Guinean, times have changed too. For them
there have not been the titillating postindependence events as in
Ghana. Instead, Touré offers them forced labor, sacrifice and perhaps unwelcome agricultural reforms. Clearly their temper must
be watched.

Always there is the threat of a challenger for power among
his henchmen. There are enemies beyond Guinea's borders, jealous of his head start in French Africa with independence, and
anxious over his burgeoning stature. In Conakry there are rumors
of plots and intrigue and already nineteen "plotters" have been
sentenced to death.

Looming over everything is this question of Guinea's dalliance
with the Communists. Is Sekou Touré a Communist? Or is this a
dangerous oversimplification? And if it is, does it matter, if he
ends up doing what the Communists want him to do? Or are

Communist successes in Guinea the result of a Western failure to gauge the pace and feel of African nationalism? These are the questions which complex Guinea poses.

And if one cannot produce all the answers, there nevertheless are a few facts one can bear in mind. Firstly, Sekou Touré is an African nationalist. Like all African nationalist leaders he is jealous of his country's new-found independence. He is not eager to surrender it voluntarily to either Communists or capitalists.

Touré is determined, able, politically ruthless. So are the Communists. He believes he can handle them. There is always a possibility that he can.

CHAPTER V

Nigeria: A Touch of Texas

NIGERIA IS the Texas of Africa.

Of course there is not much resemblance between the sprawling shanty suburbs around the Nigerian capital of Lagos and the buildings of modern Dallas. Nor, although both have a certain flamboyance in their own ways, is there much similarity between the gorgeously gowned Nigerian and the average Texan.

Nevertheless against a purely African background, Nigeria stands out as a stimulating land of wide-open spaces and big ideas. With 35,000,000 of the friendliest people in Africa, cheerfully confident that their country is going places, it has a population bigger than any other state on the continent. It brims with opportunity and potential. This may very well become the strongest voice out of Africa.

Nigeria is a big land, much of it arid, and almost half as large again as Texas.

It grows cotton and groundnuts and Nigerians are no end amused when they read from time to time that their own groundnuts are giving tough competition on world markets to peanuts from Florida, Alabama, Georgia and, yes, Texas too.

Nigeria even has oil wells, down among the coastal swamps where Shell-BP have made one of their rare strikes in black Africa after pouring in millions of dollars for exploration. Current output of oil is about 10,000,000 tons a year, but by 1965 this may be 15,000,000 tons, earning the Nigerian government more than $40,000,000 annually in royalties and taxes.

Since Nigeria became independent of British rule in October, 1960, the oil company has announced it will build a $33,000,000 refinery, and, with other plans for textile plants and flour mills and cement and bicycle factories, foreign capital is pouring in.

Bicycles always have been good business in Nigeria. In five years before independence, the Nigerians imported nearly a million of them, worth $30,000,000. The country is flat, bicycles are cheap, and so the Nigerian takes to them like a Hollander.

Often the bicycle takes the place of a beast of burden. Bicycles in the palm-oil-producing areas are laden with cans of oil weighing up to three hundred pounds. On occasion the cargo is a live chicken or goat, sometimes even a small pig, wrapped up in a straw mat and strapped firmly, if squealingly, to the rear carrier.

Nigerians have their idiosyncracies just as much as any other race and thus Nigeria is among the biggest buyers in the world of red rubber surgical tubing. The Nigerians use it to decorate their bicycles, wrapping it around various parts of the frame.

With all this air of bustle and development it is perhaps not surprising that Nigeria should be the first country to bring the light of television to the dark continent. Much of the material used initially has been old canned film imported from the United States. Thus Negro Africans sit raptly watching Laurel and Hardy in one of their custard-pie fights, or some now-ancient cowboy hero pinking yet another bad man with a slug from his six-gun.

Yet only recently is the name of Nigeria creeping into the headlines. Its steady movement over the years toward independence was not marked by the riots or explosion of violence which attract the attention of the world's press. Then even though it was Britain's biggest African territory it was overshadowed by the earlier emergence of Ghana, and perhaps by Dr. Nkrumah's international activities, and of course later by strife and chaos in the Congo which dominated world attention at the time of Nigeria's emergence into sovereignty. Thus till recently publicity for Nigeria has been confined to the odd spectacular event, perhaps a visit by a member of the British royalty, marked by one of those ceremonial durbars in Northern Nigeria when hundreds of wild-looking horsemen come thundering down at full gallop to rear up their horses in salute just a few feet from the royal dais.

Now interest in Nigeria is growing. Within hours of independence Nigeria had sent its troops to join the UN force in the

Congo in a swift reaction to the demands of international responsibility. Its prime minister, Alhaji Sir Abubakar Tafawa Balewa, has declared Nigeria's viewpoint on a string of issues from the Congo to South African apartheid. Already Nigeria is emerging as a force which may counter the influence of Ghana's President Nkrumah. Certainly it is a nation to watch.

．　．　．

Like most new African states, Nigeria has its problems. The main one is that of internal differences among its diverse regions and tribes. There are some 250 of these separate tribes within the boundaries which Britain drew around Nigeria. They are spread across three "regions," called logically enough the North, the East and the West. As Nigeria is a federal state, there is also a fourth, minute region of federal territory, twenty-seven square miles in area, which contains the federal capital of Lagos.

The Northern Region is by far the biggest of them all and its 19,000,000 people outnumber the population of the rest of the country combined.

This is Moslem country, bordering the harsh desert wastes of the Sahara and deeply sensitive to French atomic testing there, despite France's reassurances on fallout danger.

Kano, once the terminal for the trans-Saharan camel caravans from Tripoli, is the best-known city of the North and perhaps the most romantic in all Nigeria. Now it has a new $1,500,000 airport and is the first port of call after the desert crossing for many of the big jets on the Africa run.

Occasional camel trains do still sway in and out of Kano with loads of peanuts from the neighboring territories. Sometimes, when they are silhouetted against the setting sun and the palms and the pyramids of the city, there is a breath of the Arab world about the scene. But the pyramids are not built of stone. They are enormous pyramids built meticulously with bag upon bag of peanuts which are awaiting shipment by rail to the south and foreign lands.

One famous and much-photographed camel bears a wizened little Hausa man in turban and ankle-length *kaptani* to the airport each day. Long ago, in the airfield's primitive early days, he was hired for a simple little job. Whenever an aircraft arrived or left he had to blow a tremendous blast on a fifteen-foot-long silver horn to warn pedestrians or animals off the unfenced runway.

American pilots and servicemen will probably remember the character of the old airfield well from the days when they used it as a refueling stop on the World War II ferry run from the United States to West Africa and then on up to the North African battlefields.

But of course all that is changed now and the airport has long since lost its frontier look. The little Hausa man, like many another government servant, has made himself unfireable, however. Still he greets every aircraft with a terrifying, but now quite unnecessary, noise on his king-size bugle. And as well as a salary he collects hush money from the visitors. He and his camel are perpetuated in photograph albums all over the world belonging to passengers who at one time or another have passed through Kano.

From one point of view, Kano is an air traveler's delight. It must hold the world's record for drip-dry shirt-drying. It has a searing hot dry climate like that of a blast furnace. Though this may crumple the passenger a little, he can get his shirt bone-dry and ready to wear again only five minutes after taking it dripping from the sink.

Despite all the modern aerial bustle, however, there still was a Graham Greene-ish touch or two about Kano the last time I was there. There was a bus service rumbling grandly off across the whole desert breadth of Africa every month or so with Nigerian Moslems making the trip to the Red Sea and Mecca beyond. It was the sort of adventurous journey one feels it would be fun to take one day if one had the opportunity and a couple of months to spare.

Then there was the hotel with its revolving overhead fans, and the wooden slatted windows, and the lizards which dropped on to your head when you slammed the door of the mosquito-netted porch too hard.

Somehow you always expected to see Peter Lorre around the next corner, perhaps whispering mysterious instructions to another sinister screen crony before slipping away with the smuggled diamonds on the next plane to Macao.

But of course there were just the Englishmen, of whom there are still plenty in Nigeria, sitting splendidly isolated twelve feet away from each other at separate tables in the dining room, and carefully avoiding each other's eyes lest even here, in the middle of Africa, they be forced to talk to each other without being introduced.

Africa is vulture country but only in Kano have I eaten breakfast with thirty of them peering in at me from their perch on the corrugated iron roof of the kitchen near by.

Within the mud walls of Kano is the biggest market in Africa, its alleys cluttered for mile upon mile with little shops and stalls selling calabashes and camel blankets and spices and peppers.

The Northern Region is dominated by the proud, tough Hausas and has long been the preserve of powerful Moslem emirs, sultans and other traditional rulers, magnificently built men in handsome robes, dominating their courts.

For many of the old-school British colonial officers stationed in Nigeria before independence, these Northerners were their favorites. Perhaps they felt a type of upper-class affinity toward the horse-riding, hunting and shooting Nigerian aristocrats who may be the nearest African equivalent to England's landed gentry and country squires and masters of foxhounds. The British and the Northerners worked well together and many Northern noblemen have been given British knighthoods and other titles. Some British officials have retired to England to find no interests there and have returned as private citizens to live in the arid north of Nigeria which they have come to love.

The Northern rulers, clinging to their pattern of medieval aristocracy, dispensing feudal justice with a flick of the finger or nod of the head, are wary of influences which might topple them. Maybe for this reason the North alone has refused its women the vote.

The North is also the most backward and underdeveloped of the various regions and, although its leaders profess a contempt for the regions to the south, they are suspicious of the middle-class prosperity in this non-Islamic southern belt, particularly among the Yoruba tribesmen.

The Yorubas dominate the Western Region and are an industrious, go-ahead people. It was in the West that television was first introduced. It was the Western Region's leaders who startled the electorate by first using the helicopter for political campaigning in Nigeria. The West has hired a firm of American public relations consultants to manage its publicity. The West claims it is the most efficient of Nigeria's regions and at least one of its political leaders used to tell the British slyly: "You may not like us as much as your precious Northerners. But you must admit, we do our homework."

Nevertheless, although their election campaigns are perhaps the best organized, the Western Yorubas have not been able to win victory in national elections. Numbers are against them and in addition to hostility from the North there is the antagonism between the Yorubas and the Ibo tribesmen who dominate the Eastern Region. The Ibos are poorer than the Yorubas but sharp and eager and coming up fast.

Each region has its own government, administrative machine and prime minister, all in addition to the federal government located in Lagos.

Until a year or two before independence, politics were fought largely on a regional basis, but this was while Britain exercised over-all control. With the prospect of Britain's withdrawal, Nigerian politicians recognized that the federal government would become a powerful factor and no longer be a weak spot in the chain of government. Thus began an intensive campaign to capture it and Nigerian politics have become more centralized.

For a short course in Nigerian politics, there are three main parties and four main politicians to remember.

The principal political party in the North is the Northern Peoples Congress (NPC).

The West is the home of the Action Group (AG), while the National Council for Nigeria and the Cameroons (NCNC) dominates the East.

Perhaps still the most powerful figure in Nigerian politics is the premier of the Northern Region, Alhaji Sir Ahmadu Bello, Sardauna of Sokoto and head of the NPC. The Sardauna is a big, regal man whose American limousine speeds him about his beloved North in a commanding flurry of dust. He has not plucked for himself the federal premiership which would cause him to live in Lagos, 600 miles to the south. For the moment he pulls many political strings from the North, and some people say his ambition lies in becoming Sultan of Sokoto, and thus spiritual ruler of the North.

The Sardauna, however, is well aware of the importance of the federal government and the federal legislature which Northern members dominate. The Northern nominee to the federal premiership is the second on our list of key politicians, Alhaji Sir Abubakar Tafawa Balewa.

Sir Abubakar is a dry aesthetic Moslem whose voice has the deep resonance of booming Big Ben before the BBC newscasts from London. Besides the resonance, he has the immaculate accent of a BBC announcer, and once, while a student in London, he did in fact read a BBC script over the overseas service to Nigeria.

An impressive man to meet, he nevertheless came to politics without a particularly dynamic background. He was a compromise candidate for the federal premiership when first the post was created under British rule. Born in 1912, he had become a schoolteacher and education officer and was thrust into politics because of the North's lack of well-educated men.

Later he became Minister of Transport. In 1955 he visited the United States to see how American experience with river transport on the Mississippi and Ohio rivers could be applied to Nigeria's own river giants like the Niger and Benue. Proudly, he remembers his honorary citizenship of New Orleans.

Then, as a rare politician acceptable to all regions, he graduated to the position of federal premier when it was created in 1957.

Sir Abubakar will talk freely of the reservations and reluctance which he brought to his new job, and of his own doubts about Nigerian unity. But he will also discuss what he believes to be his own growth in his position and his conversion to dedication in the task of building and preserving a united Nigeria.

Nigeria has swept to independence in a relatively gently way. Sir Abubakar has not had to be the fiery nationalist, tossed into jail by a colonial government. He has not had to pound the independence road with inflammatory oratory. At one stage before independence, this had some British officials worried. They felt he would be good for the country after independence but felt his national following might be lagging. Thus one official, so the story goes, told him: "I say, sir, you'll have to be a bit more vicious towards us if you want the crowds behind you."

Nevertheless, Sir Abubakar did lead his party to victory in the preindependence elections. He did it in his own right, has much increased his stature both within and without the country, and now is far from being the mere nominee of the North which he once was. Some people see in him the man to begin the democratization of the North, believing he may develop a Nehru-like capacity for reforming Northern feudal rule.

Meanwhile, he is respected in all regions as efficient and quietly incorruptible. Sometimes he is called the "Silver Voice of the North" and his skill as a mediator, calming and coordinating diverse factions, is of immense worth to the new nation.

Leader of the Western Region's Action Group, which is the parliamentary opposition in the federal parliament, is Chief Obafemi Awolowo, who has sensed the change overtaking tribal leaders and thrown himself into the political fray to become a popular elected leader. Bespectacled and solid, Chief Awolowo's speeches seem dull at times but behind him there is the well-oiled machinery of his party. Formerly prime minister of the Western Region, he now has moved into federal politics to become leader of the opposition.

Finally there is the Eastern Region's Dr. Nnamdi Azikiwe, or "Zik," as he is better known. Dr. Azikiwe is probably the best known overseas of all Nigeria's politicians. Educated at Storer College, West Virginia, then Howard, Lincoln and Pennsylvania universities, he returned to West Africa to establish a chain of fiery newspapers and become a leading figure in the nationalist politics of both Gold Coast and Nigeria.

His lithe long frame of a basketball player has ranged across various capitals since, vocal in his demands for African self-rule. To many foreigners he has become the symbol of Nigerian nationalism. Yet, ironically, Dr. Azikiwe has not been able to establish the national following which would give him political control of the country. Like the West's Action Group, his NCNC in the East is vastly outnumbered by the overwhelming North.

The best that Dr. Azikiwe could extract from Nigeria's pre-independence elections was a pact between his own NCNC and the North's NPC which put them in alliance against the West.

In the elections the NPC won more seats than any other single party, but not enough to outnumber all other parties combined. Therefore it rules in a loose coalition under which NCNC men hold a number of ministerial posts.

For Dr. Azikiwe there was only the presidency of the Senate out of the deal initially. Then with independence and the retirement of Britain's Sir James Robertson, he succeeded him in the ceremonial post of governor-general. In East Nigeria one of his own former cabinet ministers, Dr. Michael Okpara, succeeded him as prime minister.

In his new post as governor-general, Dr. Azikiwe is bringing all his charm to bear. There is a lively atmosphere to the governor-general's garden parties in Lagos now. Is this the end of "Zik" as a political figure? Some observers suggest that Dr. Azikiwe is quietly creating a national image for himself as governor-general and might yet re-emerge in politics. If Nigeria should follow Ghana's example in becoming a republic, Dr. Azikiwe might be a contender for role of head of state with executive powers. Time and Dr. Azikiwe will tell.

Now with the independence celebrations long over, and Nigeria's green (for agriculture) and white (for peace and unity) flag fluttering over parliament, Nigeria is on the march.

There are obstacles enough to be removed before unity is a reality and Nigerians can sing with complete confidence the words of their new national anthem:

> Though tribe and tongue may differ,
> In brotherhood we stand,
> Nigerians all, and proud to serve
> Our sovereign Motherland.

Of course Nigeria could burst at the seams and go flaming

down in Congo-like chaos. Tribal diversity and antagonism was one of the root causes of disaster in the Congo. Yet with this was coupled a complete lack of training for political responsibility and government.

This is where the situation in Nigeria is different. From 1900, when the British government took over administration of Nigeria from the Royal Niger Company which had been trading there, until after World War II, Nigerians themselves had little say in their country's affairs. With constitutional changes beginning in 1946, however, Africans were drawn more and more into the machinery of government, learning its intricacies although ultimate authority always rested in British hands till independence.

Thus they have operated the arms of government themselves, they have hammered out compromises and deals between their various regions at one constitutional reshuffle after another, and they know that if Nigeria is to achieve its promised influence in African and international affairs their country must remain united. Many Nigerian leaders look with dry skepticism on Dr. Nkrumah's plans to set Ghana at the head of a pan-African union, for example, but they recognize that Nigeria's power to either thwart or support Dr. Nkrumah's ambitions lies in the strength of its 35,000,000 people joined in one strong nation. There is a shrewd awareness that it is in Nigeria's interest for its peoples and regions to stick together.

Other problems loom. Although it is retaining key white specialists, and has higher numbers of its own skilled and university-trained Africans than many other countries, Nigeria still is short of teachers and engineers and all the other specialists it needs for development.

Although its economy is buoyant by some other African standards, millions of its people are peasants and Nigeria needs foreign capital for economic stimulus.

This is already flowing in. Lagos itself is a center of international activity as new embassies spring up and trade and other missions move in. The city is set on an overcrowded island, steamy and tropical, and joined to the mainland by Carter Bridge, which spans the waters of a coastal lagoon. Heart of the island is Tinubu Square, a teeming focal point around which the banks and the big commercial houses and the oil companies are throwing up imposing office blocks in a gesture of their confidence in Nigeria's future.

Big business, and the oil companies in particular, have very often been far swifter than governments to note the trends in Africa and, thus, in Nigeria the oil companies have long been "Africanizing" their staffs and managements, and encouraging bright young Africans, giving them university training, and generally creating a sympathetic atmosphere for their continued operations in an expanding African market.

Meanwhile, the United States is subsidizing harbor development, Britain has forged strong trade ties and is training Nigeria's army officers, and, remarkably in a country with a broad Moslem belt in the north, the Israelis are active with various projects in the south, while student teachers and engineers from the Northern Region are studying at universities of the United Arab Republic.

The West Germans have offered to train Nigerian planners in the completion of slum-clearance schemes originated by the British. For many years, Lagos was pocketed with slums, incredible hovels of sacking and paper and rusty tin, all crisscrossed with a network of slimy, open sewers, which must have been among the worst in Africa. Gradually they are being razed and their occupants rehoused in attractive flats and semidetached villas on the mainland.

Amid all this, Sir Abubakar is emerging as Nigeria's principal spokesman and a politician of increasing power and influence. A warm friend of Britain's, he is frequently on record with his expressions of appreciation for British achievement and assistance in Nigeria, though icily contemptuous of specific British officials who he feels exploited Nigeria and did not pull their weight. He is cautious of Communist overtures and Nigeria has kept a sharp eye open in the first months of independence for Communist influence.

This of course does not preclude Nigeria from sharp words to the West from time to time, particularly as Sir Abubakar may wish to establish Nigeria as a thoroughly "African" country in the eyes of other African nations in the first year or so of independence.

And then, if its problems are surmountable, Nigeria may very well become the giant of Africa.

CHAPTER VI

French Africa: The Quiet Revolution

IN WORLD WAR II, a friend of mine who was a British navy flier was given an unusual chore. From the air he had to make a photographic record of various stretches of the African coastline under the French and British flags.

"You could always tell whether you were flying over British territory or French," he says with a grin. "If it was British down below, the towns would be all corrugated iron, and terribly neat and efficient. If it was French, it would be all higgledy-piggledy, but with promenades and pretty little villas perched over the sea as attractive as the Riviera."

Anyone who has made the journey from British Africa into French will recognize that there is some truth in this story. With no disrespect to Britain's achievements in Africa it can be said, as we have remarked once before, that the French have developed a capacity for making the attractive best of their situation even in rugged Africa.

This is especially remarkable, for from the start the French did not get the best parts of black Africa to administer. In the early days, they were edged out of the glorious country down around the Cape of Good Hope. They never gained a foothold in temperate Central or East Africa. One wonders what they might have made of Cape Town's Clifton beach, or the romantic coast of East Africa with the warm Indian Ocean lapping at its golden beaches, had they had the opportunity.

Instead, the French were left with a lot of the steamy tropical coastline of West Africa, and an arid hinterland merging with desert. Without the discipline of the British, or the wealth which the Belgians extracted from the Congo, they nevertheless have imposed an air of Gallic charm along much of the coast at least.

Thus today, for example, for all its governing Africans in French-cut suits and shoes speaking impeccable French, there still is a flavor of metropolitan France about a city like Dakar. There are gay awnings, and window boxes bright with flowers, and sidewalk cafés engulfed from time to time with the exhaust smoke from battered Peugeots stuttering and honking through the cobbled streets.

Above the sea, the French chiseled out a winding marine drive to set upon it pastel-colored villas smothered with climbing blooms. There too clubs and commercial firms built week-end chalets for boating and swimming and table tennis, and for dancing to a concertina under the soft sky at night.

There are still Frenchmen in Dakar, businessmen and lecturers at the university, and employees of the new African government. The gay berets of French seamen still bob along the streets from time to time.

Outside the city there is a magnificent hotel which rises sheer and slender like the United Nations building in New York, just the width of one room so that every one has a glorious view over the ocean.

The cooking is French, and down on the beach the hotel provides bathing cabanas and bright beach balls and Hawaiian surf boards and sun umbrellas. With all this and the handsome young men with the movie-star smiles, and the well-bronzed young ladies in bikinis, one wonders whether it is not just a waste of holiday money going on to Cannes or Juan-les-Pins.

All this French influence in Africa south of the Sahara may come as a surprise to many readers. The history of French rule in Algeria, Tunisia and Morocco is well known. But perhaps few realized that till recently France also ruled a Negro African empire extending from Dakar, at the westernmost tip of Africa, in a great arc through 2,800,000 square miles of West and Central Africa to the steaming banks of the Congo River.

Now a string of sovereign independent states, this is home to more than 25,000,000 Africans as diverse as the tough Senegalese who gave the French army some of its top fighting men, and the primitive tribesmen of Ubangi-Shari, slotting big metal discs in the lips of their womenfolk. They are spread from the waterless camel lands of the Sahara to the forested world of Dr. Albert Schweitzer at Lambaréné in Central Africa and the dripping, flamboyant jungles at the equator.

Twelve colonies made up the empire. In French West Africa, administered from Dakar, there were Senegal, Mauritania, Sudan, Guinea, Ivory Coast, Upper Volta, Niger and Dahomey. Then in French Equatorial Africa, ruled by Paris via a French administration in Brazzaville were Chad, Ubangi-Shari, Gabon and the Middle Congo.

Further, until they became independent in 1960, France administered such assorted territories as the United Nations trusteeship territories of Togoland and the Cameroons, as well as the Indian Ocean island of Madagascar, 300 miles off the African coast. The French tricolor has continued to fly over French Somaliland at the eastern horn of Africa.

Today the empire has disintegrated as the colonies have moved one after the other to independence. These French African lands have been swept by one of the swiftest but quietest revolutions in the whole of Africa. It is a political revolution which they have wrought almost in partnership with their former rulers, and by the ballot box instead of by bullet and bayonet. Guinea's early break with France strained relations between the two, but for the most part the other states which have followed Guinea to independence enjoy a cordial association with France.

．　．　．

Perhaps the start of the revolution was the call which went out in 1958 from Paris to a little French village named Colombey-les-deux-Églises. This was the message to the home of General Charles de Gaulle, summoning him from years of lonely glory to political power once more.

It is de Gaulle who has played a key role in the transition of French black Africa. Interestingly enough, it was he, fourteen years earlier, who played a prominent part in the first cautious steps toward liberalization of France's African policy. Africans in French territory had rallied to the flag of Free France in World

War II. In 1944, de Gaulle summoned a conference at his African wartime headquarters in Brazzaville to debate their future. There was advanced a new policy of equality between France's white and African citizens, designed to change the spirit of France's administration in black Africa.

Africans elected representatives to the French parliament in Paris and eventually acquired territorial assemblies in the colonies themselves. But power was centralized in Paris. There was no move to bestow real legislative authority upon Africans in their own areas.

By the time de Gaulle came again to power, African nationalism was stalking the continent. A crop of African political parties had bloomed in the French territories. Men like Sekou Touré were disrupting the political calm. Many of France's African subjects did not want to become "good Frenchmen." They wanted to become good Africans, holding political power in their hands like Ghanaians and other Africans around them.

Constantly in de Gaulle's thought, and indeed the reason for his recall to the political scene, was the haunting problem of Algeria. Clearly, France could not afford a repetition of Algerian strife in its black African colonies. Nobody can say how much this factor alone influenced de Gaulle to give the African lands their choice.

In a referendum of September, 1958, the overseas territories were required to decide whether they should retain links with France in a new French Community to replace the old French Union, or whether they should become independent and cut themselves adrift.

Quietly they were reminded that France had poured more than $2,000,000,000 in grants and loans into its black African colonies in the ten years preceding the referendum. Sparsely populated and economically retarded, they could ill do without it. And now, a vote to remain in the Community would keep it all flowing in. This was the carrot dangled before their eyes, which de Gaulle gambled they would snatch.

As we know, only Guinea plunged past the carrot and on to independence at that time. The other eleven states in French West and Equatorial Africa became republics within the Community, autonomous in internal affairs, but virtually subject to French control on certain stated issues like foreign affairs, defense, currency, finance and so on. Two of the Equatorial African states, Ubangi-Shari and the Middle Congo, changed their names to the Central African Republic and the Congo Republic respectively.

But the wind of change had not stopped ruffling through the French Community. Although French aid was attractive, so too was the complete independence which Ghana and Guinea were enjoying, with seats at the United Nations and the prestige in Africa which enabled them to look down on the republics of the Community, tied to Mother France's apron strings. The republics were envious.

Clearly, their status as semiautonomous republics within the Community could not satisfy them. Thus there followed a remarkable transformation of the Community into something closely resembling the British Commonwealth, with fully independent nations joined in voluntary association.

Incredible as it may seem against the background of France's early hauteur with Guinea for seeking independence, the republics began amicable negotiations for their own independence, one after another in a string ending with freedom for Mauritania in November, 1960. France has not turned off the pipeline which keeps technical and economic aid flowing in. Initially at any rate the new states retained their links with the Community, but a Community whose concept had undergone a drastic expansion. While de Gaulle may have privately admitted its ultimate possibility, few could have forecast that change would occur so swiftly.

The winds of change are still swirling throughout what used to be French Africa. There is fluidity and uncertainty and its final shape is far from clear.

Even as independent states, some of the new nations have continued to smart under the jeers of other African lands for their support from time to time of French policy in Africa. M. Félix Houphouet-Boigny, for example, who ironically has long been one of France's closest African friends, sitting in French cabinets in Paris, has led his own Ivory Coast together with Upper Volta,

Niger and Dahomey, out of the Community altogether. Already grouped together in what they term the Entente Council in a bid to achieve unity among themselves, this is intended as a dramatic assertion of their independence.

Thus, while most of these former French African states retain cordial relations with France, they are not necessarily members of the Community. The ultimate shape, and fate, of the Community is not clear.

Even before attaining independence, Senegal and Sudan had attempted to fuse their quite separate personalities in the Mali Federation. So named after a fourteenth-century kingdom spread across part of West Africa, they had hoped to include Upper Volta and Dahomey and perhaps other territories later.

One of the federation's principal architects was Léopold Sédar Senghor, Senegal's outstanding poet-professor-politician from Dakar. Unlike Sekou Touré, who demanded that French African states should first win independence and then negotiate union among themselves, M. Senghor was a proponent of "primary" federation. He believed the states should seek unity among themselves before claiming independence as a single bloc.

M. Senghor's dreams have not fared well. He could corral only his own Senegal and Sudan as founder-members of the Mali Federation. Even these have since parted after a violent quarrel and the Mali Federation has been quietly buried. Sudan has assumed the name of the Republic of Mali under the presidency of Modibo Keita, its former prime minister, and has since announced its decision to join the loose union which already exists between Guinea and Ghana.

Further shuffles and changes loom. Senegal eyes Gambia, the little British enclave within its borders which can hardly hope to stand alone as a nation. Mauritania, one of the poorest of the former French states but which, after exploitation of vast iron ore deposits with the aid of a $66,000,000 loan from the International Bank, may become one of the wealthiest, has border disputes on its hands with Mali and Morocco.

Then the Congo Republic headed by Abbé Fulbert Youlou on the northern banks of the Congo River dreams of fusion with parts of the former Belgian Congo across the river which would reunite men of the same tribe spread along both river banks.

Clearly then, politics in former French Africa can prove every bit as mercurial as in France itself.

There are strong arguments on economic grounds alone for continuation of the association which these assorted republics enjoyed when colonies of France. Some of them are barely viable entities by themselves and would stand to gain much from pooled transportation, postal and telegraph services, customs and so on.

Yet even though the uniting thread of French tuition and the French language runs through them, there are clearly immense difficulties hindering their reunion. There is the clash of personalities alone, for Sekou Touré and Senghor and Houphouet-Boigny and Modibo Keita, although all graduates of colonial rule by the French, are separate poles of political influence, each with their own strategies and policies.

The failure to date to achieve unity even with France's former African territories underlines the difficulties implicit in formation of any wider African union of diverse states. This is probably a suitable moment to pause and consider this over-all pan-African unity movement.

. . .

When you fly along the west coast of Africa there is a deceptively uniform look about it from the air.

Follow the curve of the West African bulge down from Dakar and the coastline is one of endless tropical beaches all run together. The great green rollers of the South Atlantic come crashing in with a spatter of foam on the white sands. There seems hardly an interruption except for a little fishing village here and there, its dugout canoes pulled up under the coconut palms.

This looks like one great country, but, as we know, it is carved up by a network of international boundaries into a string of separate nations.

Try and motor along it and you may have to produce passport and papers at half a dozen international checkpoints in two or three hundred miles.

Most of the borders were drawn artificially by the various

colonial powers which staked out the area and bear little relation to tribal divisions. Like Ghana, much of West Africa is made up of layers of horizontal, east-west terrain with tribes strung along them. But the colonial borders drawn by the pioneering whites penetrating inland from the coast run north-south.

Ludicrous anomalies are the result. The Ewe tribe finds itself strung out across three separate countries, Ghana, Togo and Dahomey. Thus an Ewe may live in one country, work his lands in another, and yet have to cross to a third to visit his relatives. In theory, he would have to go through all the rigmarole of an international journey each time he crossed one of the borders.

In colonial times the lines of communication from these territories ran back to the respective motherlands, and not from one West African country to another.

Thus it still sometimes happens that when you send a cable from a former British colony to a former French colony a hundred miles up the coast, it must be routed back over thousands of miles to London, then across to Paris, and back to your West African neighbor.

What prospect is there for the United States of Africa, of which some African leaders dream, which would sweep away all these divisions and bring Africa forth as a massive united force?

Once it was a Briton, the ambitious and restless millionaire-politician, Cecil John Rhodes, who dreamed of a United States of Africa, and painted British red on the map stretching from the Cape to Cairo, or at least to East Africa.

If a United States of Africa emerged today, it would clearly be one created and controlled by black Africans, but if we are ever to see it a string of momentous problems must be overcome.

At the center of the united Africa campaign is Ghana's Dr. Nkrumah. Ghana is small in size and population and unless it can somehow gain more prestige, as at the head of an African union, Dr. Nkrumah's influence is threatened by that of bigger African nations now finding their feet. Aside from this, Dr. Nkrumah sees many advantages for Africans in the economic and other types of cooperation which would come with closer association, and he is steeped in the theories of pan-Africanism which he absorbed in his student days.

Thus he has seized the initiative and been instrumental in summoning a series of pan-African conferences designed to further African unity.

His most tangible success to date has been a "union" between his own Ghana and Guinea. Soon after Guinea's independence, when that country was still in serious financial difficulties, President Touré flew to Accra to see Dr. Nkrumah. After some discussion the two leaders emerged to drop their bombshell: "Inspired by the example of the thirteen American colonies which, on attainment of their independence, constituted themselves into a confederacy which ultimately developed into the United States," they had decided their countries should unite "as a nucleus of a union of West African states."

To seal the deal, Ghana announced a loan to Guinea of $28,-000,000 to help tide over the first frail years of independence.

Nobody at first knew what the union really meant. It appeared to have been announced with little prior thought and no consultation with other countries. The British Foreign Office and Commonwealth Relations Office met queries with embarrassed ignorance. Some British newspapers exploded that Ghana intended bringing a "foreigner" uninvited into the British Commonwealth of which Ghana already was a member. The French saw a diabolical plot in it, designed by Britain to sneak France's African territories away and into the Commonwealth.

Nobody need really have been that distressed. The union to date has been so vague that it has raised no constitutional problems.

There have been protestations of brotherhood and the Guineans are teaching English in their schools and the Ghanaians French in theirs. But there is no written constitution, no common currency or judicial system or parliament or flag or army and few concrete examples of fusion. There is nothing like the seriousness with which Egypt and Syria have joined to form the United Arab Republic, for example.

Some Ghanaian leaders like Health Minister Gbedemah are disappointed with results to date. They hoped for a much tighter association with a written constitution than has yet emerged. President Touré conceded to me that there was a division of opinion over the union. Guinea, he said, favored a much looser union than Ghana, a "broad confederation, not a federation." This would permit other nations like Liberia to join without losing their identity and sovereignty.

Some cynics claim that once President Touré had secured his loan his enthusiasm for unity began to cool. Both Dr. Nkrumah and M. Touré are genuinely dedicated to pan-African unity, however. What is evident is that they differ on strategy and interpretation and perhaps on the ultimate form of the unity for which they are working.

Undoubtedly M. Touré casts hungry long looks at the rest of what used to be French black Africa. He has rivals and enemies in these territories and we have already traced the difficulties hindering the prospect of unity among them. Nevertheless, it must be a tempting prospect to strike out for leadership of former French Africa rather than become a subordinate in an association with ex-British and other colonial countries with which he has less in common.

Of course Mali has since joined this vague union of Guinea and Ghana and between them they may induce more states of various colonial ancestries including French and British to rally to their at present nonexistent flag. The union may grow and flourish and confuse the skeptics.

Nevertheless these major differences of viewpoint exist and underline the formidable problems to be shouldered aside if a specific union of African states is to become a reality.

Meanwhile, both Ghana's neighbors of Togo and the Ivory Coast have rebuffed Dr. Nkrumah's overtures for a grouping of their countries, or parts of them, with Ghana.

Although there were several reasons for Dr. Nkrumah's persistent backing of the Congo's controversial Patrice Lumumba, one of them was Nkrumah's obsession with pan-African unity. As the Ghanaian leader saw it, Lumumba was the most likely of the Congolese leaders to bring the vast Congo into a union with Ghana and other countries. There are grounds for believing that Ghana had already put out feelers for such union in the early days of the Congo's independence, and before Lumumba was arrested and eventually killed.

Lumumba had visited Ghana before the Congo's independence, and drew much of his nationalist inspiration from Dr. Nkrumah. The Ghanaian president appears to have regarded Lumumba as a political protégé, sending him back to the Congo with advice and perhaps even cash to assist his political campaign.

Of course, President Nkrumah regarded Lumumba as the most genuinely nationalist of all the Congolese leaders and the Congo's rightful leader. Further, Lumumba stood for strong central government in the Nkrumah mold, in the face of opponents demanding a federal-type constitution. But this prospect of Lumumba's agreeing to the Congo's inclusion in an African union must have been another attractive reason for Nkrumah's support.

. . .

Although African union is off to a shaky start, there is no gainsaying the many impressive arguments in its favor, particularly in the economic sphere.

Many international economists view with apprehension the prospect of Africa's "Balkanization" into small and nonviable states. They point to the vast benefits to be gained from pooling of resources, standardization of transport systems and so forth. There is much in all this. Almost every state in West and Central Africa has its own hydroelectric project planned. There are many instances of duplication which it would be in everybody's interests to eliminate. Many nations would benefit by abolition of inter-African trade and other barriers. But economic cooperation and unity is still a long step from a politically instituted United States of Africa.

Of course, the revolt against colonialism has wrought a kinship among Africans of many different backgrounds. At pan-African conferences or at the United Nations the African states often speak with impressive unity in condemnation of the last lingering outposts of colonialism. But the unifying factor is the struggle against colonialism and that is almost done. One wonders whether the unanimity will last now that Africa is virtually free and the goal achieved.

There are still some issues with cementing influence among

the African nations. There is their opposition to racialism, and particularly South Africa's apartheid policy.

But for all that, the strains have begun to show as more and more states reach nationhood and have their say. The republics of the French Community side with France and against Ghana and Guinea from time to time. Nigeria growls a disassociation from Ghana. Recognition of Cameroun divides the African bloc.

African nationalism is common throughout the continent and black men 3,000 miles away in South Africa may reverently pin a picture of Kwame Nkrumah on their battered walls. Yet unity on specific emotional issues is far from union, a pan-African union spelled out in a written constitution.

Even within their own borders African leaders are sometimes hard put to maintain unity. To preserve Ghana as it is, Dr. Nkrumah has resorted to tough measures. Nigeria's principal concern is to avoid the cracks of secession. There are strong separatist factions in half a dozen African states. The Congo is a ghastly example of disunity and factional dissent.

With all this it is easy to understand the differences which hinder union between complete nations, divergent as they are with differing tongues, and all at their own stages of cultural, economic and political development.

Regional groupings are perhaps more feasible than any continent-wide union. The three East African territories of Uganda, Kenya and Tanganyika may find federation under African rule which eluded them under white. Africans in central Africa might hammer out a new association. Even Dr. Nkrumah's West African union might harden into something more concrete. But of course neither a West African nor any other wider union makes much sense without the most populous country of Nigeria as its pivot. As yet, the 35,000,000 Nigerians exhibit little enthusiasm for submerging their own proud new identity in a West African union.

"Look, old man," one of their shrewdest politicians exclaimed. "Joining in a common struggle against foreign rule is one thing. Surrendering the power you have just won for a merger with other states, even though they all be under African rule, is quite another."

While Dr. Nkrumah declares Ghana is prepared to surrender

its sovereignty for union with other African states, they are less ready. Liberia's President Tubman, for instance, has reasoned he ought to get on the unity band wagon. But the unity for which he is carefully calling is a meaninglessly vague one which would leave Liberia's sovereignty intact.

All this is not to say that we will not see great changes in Africa. There are strong pressures for the straightening and realigning of boundaries and for the reunification of certain tribes mentioned earlier. Few African specialists would care to forecast the shape of the continent's political boundaries in ten years' time.

But in the interim, African politicians are as capable of ambition and ruthlessness and wariness and suspicion as any others. For the overwhelming majority of them, independence still has the fresh new scent of spring about it. It is something they intend guarding jealously.

CHAPTER VII

West African Finale

GHANA, GUINEA, MALI, NIGERIA. These are the names which spring first to mind in West Africa. Such lands as these are the most prominent, the probable headline-makers of the future.

Yet there are others we cannot neglect.

There is Liberia, for example. Some readers way wonder that Liberia, the oldest independent Negro African state on the continent, should be left to a roundup of smaller West African states.

But despite its long history of independence, Liberia has not emerged as a dynamic force in Africa. There seems little of the drive or energy here which characterizes today's Ghana or Guinea. Inspired young nationalists in other African lands may seek to include Liberia in a united Africa, yet often they can barely conceal their contempt for what they see as a forlorn and stagnant corner of Africa.

All this may come as a shock to many Americans, for Liberia has the closest association of any African land with their own bustling United States.

In 1822 an American expedition sponsored by the American Colonization Society and the government of President Monroe (from whom the Liberian capital of Monrovia got its name) marked out a slice of the West African coast for the repatriation of American Negro slaves to their own home continent.

Technically speaking, Liberia never was a colony. But in fact it was colonized by these Americo-Liberians, as they are known, who came from the United States to exert much the same sort of control over the local African populace as did white colonists in other parts of the continent.

74

The number of American Negroes who settled in Liberia was not large. Today their descendants make up something like 1 per cent of the population, although this is a guess, for the population has never been counted and may range between one and two million. Nevertheless it is from this Americo-Liberian aristocracy, or upper class, that Liberia's rulers have primarily been drawn.

Bonds with the United States are still strong. The American embassy in Monrovia is one of the biggest in Africa. American aid missions are dotted about the country.

There is a superficial overlay of American mannerisms and dress and even accents about the citizens of Monrovia. The creased and crumpled uniforms of the military and the police are styled after those in the United States. The police race down the main street in an American-style prowl car with lights flashing and siren screaming.

The government uses American terminology and its various departments in their tumble-down, moss-covered, wood-and-iron bungalows are fancifully termed "Bureau of this . . ." and "Division of that. . . ." There is a Capitol. The currency is American dollars and cents. There is even a county called Maryland.

For all the chewing gum and juke boxes and the fourth-rate American cowboy films which pack the movie houses, there is little evidence, however, that American imagination and drive have been transplanted here.

There appears to be nobody in Monrovia to repair an air conditioner. Most of the commerce is in Lebanese and other foreign hands. When I was there, a balcony which had collapsed alongside the wall of the presidential mansion had been left where it was with its reinforcing girder work trailing sloppily to the ground. Within the mansion, an expensive report recommending a central air-conditioning system had been rejected in favor of a scheme utilizing individual units. Thus workmen chipped holes for the installation of these units and marred the exterior with scores of air-conditioning units spattered across the building. The sidewalks a few steps from the president's mansion are dotted with cavernous uncovered manholes.

Most of the important public works, from the airport at Robertsfield to the electricity system which flickers and sputters throughout the night because of overloading, have been built by foreigners, notably the Americans during World War II. Robertsfield is fifty miles from the capital and for some extraordinary reason there is a forty-five-minute difference in the times observed between the two. There is no bus service, nor even a telephone, connecting the capital with the airport.

Robertsfield is the international airport used by the big planes such as fly in from New York, but there is a tiny airstrip in Monrovia itself which can take smaller aircraft operating along the coast. When I landed there it was to face the most hysterical display of inefficiency by immigration and customs officials I had witnessed anywhere in Africa, including the Congo at the peak of its chaos.

A bawling Liberian immigration man snatched passengers' passports from their hands at the foot of the aircraft steps and disappeared to a remote office within the airport buildings. Passengers had to find him there and unscramble their documents from the chaos he had made of them. In the baggage hall, customs men screamed and ranted and ripped luggage apart.

When I left Liberia from the other airport at Robertsfield I traveled out in a taxi with an American businessman who had been physically bundled off a departing plane the previous week because he did not have an "exit permit." He could only get this, said Liberian officials, fifty miles back in the capital. And with the lengthy application form he had to produce identity photographs. For this mistake he was stranded a week until the next available plane. The final straw, after all this delay, came when immigration officials demanded a $4.50 "head tax" from him before he could leave.

There are grounds for believing there is a serious corruption problem. Certainly at these lower levels there is some appalling corruption, confusion and disorganization. Often it is coupled with an arrogance toward the white visitor which one does not find, for example, in friendly Ghana. Perhaps this is because of a suppressed sense of inferiority, or is a bluff attempt to hide Liberian shame over the atmosphere of dilapidation and preserved decay which hangs over the city.

However, it is not surprising that, despite the honeyed words of some American embassy officials who are charged with maintaining good relations with Liberia, many American businessmen leave the country muttering frustratedly that the American aid for which their taxes help pay ought to be cut off forthwith. This may be short-term thinking but it is perhaps understandable against the background of indignities they may have suffered.

All this is the most depressing side of Liberia. As always, there are two sides. It is perfectly, if ironically, true that Liberia has "suffered" by not having experienced European colonial rule. Liberians claim that what they have done, they have done with their own resources. While there have been infusions of American economic aid, it is correct that Liberia has not had a steady flow of development and loan capital as have other African lands from their administering colonial powers.

There are numbers of Liberians sensitive to their country's shortcomings. Prominent in the movement for change is Liberian President William V. S. Tubman who has ruled with benevolent autocracy since 1944. Every four years the country goes through the motions of an election. Tubman's last opponent offered himself "in response to the ardent desire of Dr. Tubman for fair and friendly competition." But as he pointed out, he was "not particularly opposed to the continuation in office of President Tubman," and neither, apparently, was the electorate, for Tubman got more than 350,000 votes against his opponent's 41.

Under Tubman's rule, annual revenue has climbed from less than $1,000,000 in 1944 to more than $20,000,000 today. He has built roads and schools and welcomed foreign investors to provide the economic stimulus lacking at home.

One of the backbones of the economy is the Firestone Rubber Company, which has thousands of acres of plantation under rubber trees. A new big project is development of a mountain of iron ore at Nimba in the interior by a Swedish-American company. The company is spending $200,000,000 to extract some 200,000,000 tons of ore via a 170-mile railroad and a new port, both of which it is building for this express purpose. Production will start late in 1962 and is expected to reach 10,000,000 tons a year. Liberia has a half-share in the profits and this might double present government revenue.

In the political sphere Mr. Tubman has launched a "unification" program. This is designed to bring Liberia's twenty-eight main tribes together and draw them into the government which has till recently been monopolized by the Americo-Liberian aristocracy. Mr. Tubman says he wants to "agglutinate and unify our population—to graft in all the principles of devotion to this their country as their only native land."

Tubman is a shrewd political boss and it perhaps is not a coincidence that the program has been of benefit to his ruling True Whig Party. It is intended to forestall political frustration among the masses and the leaders who have been brought into government have just happened to support Mr. Tubman's own party.

To effect the program, Mr. Tubman went sweating through the hinterland by canoe, jeep and light plane to talk to tribal leaders as no other president before him.

The same shrewd appraisal of trends which caused him to launch the unification program at home has also caused him to vitalize Liberia's foreign policy.

As a lone black independent state in Africa, Liberia achieved little prominence.

From time to time President Tubman would steam up and down the West African coast in the presidential yacht. A vast foreign-owned shipping fleet registered in Liberia because of its sympathetic tax laws carried the Liberian flag to the ends of the earth. But the fleet was not Liberian and meant nothing really. About the president's foreign travels and exotically uniformed entourage there was a sadly comic air.

With the emergence of tough new nationalist leaders like Kwame Nkrumah and Sekou Touré, Tubman's complacent isolation took a jolt. These were men who would go to jail for their convictions and who would not rest until they had turned all Africa upside down and made it free.

Thus Tubman has joined the melee of pan-African politics. He has called for an "association" of independent African states which would carefully affect nobody's sovereignty. His ambassadors are moving out to new African posts. Liberia's name appears more and more at African conferences. Tubman does not want to be left out of the new Africa.

For all this, Liberia has far to go still before it shakes off its unfortunate label of lethargy and political inconsequence.

.   .   .

Unique upon the map of West Africa is little Gambia. This alone of British territories here has failed to win independence. This is not due to any particular reluctance on Britain's part, but simply because nobody quite knows what is to become of Gambia. It is a tiny territory, clinging to the river of the same name, and cannot possibly seem to exist as an independent country without a built-in overdraft from Britain or some other source.

Scene of a disastrous British egg and poultry scheme after World War II, it has never picked up any economic momentum and lives on a razor's edge of peasant agriculture subsidized heftily by Britain.

The whole country pokes into Senegal, which surrounds it on all sides except for its tiny front to the sea, and many observers believe its future lies in absorption by that country. Now that Sierra Leone has become independent, Gambia lingers as Britain's last responsibility in West Africa. Indeed, with the exception of the little enclave of Portuguese Guinea, it is the last colonial territory of any kind in this part of the world. A decision on its future can hardly be postponed much longer.

Meanwhile, Sierra Leone won its independence in April, 1961.

Sandwiched between Guinea and Liberia, this was a much bigger British colony than Gambia, with a population of some 2,250,000. But it also is backward and underdeveloped and is without either the political ambition of Ghana, or the strength and size of Nigeria, Britain's other former possessions in West Africa.

Founded by Britain, in much the same way as Liberia was to be developed later by the United States, as a home for freed slaves in 1787, Sierra Leone was made a crown colony in 1808. And as Liberia had its Americo-Liberian aristocracy, so did Sierra Leone develop a Creole upper class descended from its first Negro "settlers" and a handful of white London prostitutes shipped to Sierra Leone about the same time.

The most spectacular facet of Sierra Leone's contemporary history, however, is diamond smuggling. This is primarily an agricultural country but there are substantial deposits of diamonds inland which have been netting the country a substantial income from taxes on diamond mining and sales.

However, illegal mining and smuggling have reached such proportions that the territory has been losing up to $28,000,000 worth of diamonds a year and it is estimated that losses totaled some $125,000,000 in the five years preceding independence.

Top British detectives have tried to stop the drain and pink-kneed English policemen in shorts kept a sharp eye on every shady character when they controlled the country before independence. Thus there was an air of tropical drama about the capital of Freetown, where visitors come and go by air, or by sea from the great harbor which saw big assemblies of convoys in World War II. This is the setting of Graham Greene's diamond-smuggling saga, *The Heart of the Matter.*

There has been some success in the antismuggling campaign but the security men are confronted by large-scale and extremely brazen gangs at the open diamond fields. Gangs of up to four hundred men would slip through the barbed wire protecting the mining company's concession under cover of night to plunder the diamond-bearing ground. Incredible though it may sound, they would sometimes prepare the ground over several nights before making their final haul. And on occasion there have been "digging wars" between gangs excavating at night, and company bulldozers filling in the ground by day.

Diamonds stolen in this way are still smuggled out of Sierra Leone in quantity and, against an over-all background of underdevelopment requiring substantial sums in outside assistance, it is clear that Sierra Leone's principal postindependence problems lie in the economic sphere.

.   .   .

Finally we come to two slices of Germany's short-lived empire in Africa, the republics of Cameroun and Togo.

At the end of the nineteenth century the Germans staked out an area known as the Cameroons. The Germans ruled the territory with stern efficiency and there are still *schlosses* and other buildings of stony solidarity hidden in the bush today as mementoes of their presence.

But one by one, Germany lost its colonies in World War I, and at war's end they were parceled out to its wartime enemies as mandates from the League of Nations.

The Cameroons were split in two. A smaller sliver alongside Nigeria went to Britain, and France got the major portion. After World War II the territories lingered on under British and French administration respectively as United Nations trust territories.

But in 1960 the French portion became the independent republic of Cameroun. In 1961, the southern portion of the British Cameroons elected to reunite with Cameroun after long years of separation. In the interim the two areas had developed separate economies and administrations and even languages, and the exact details of the reunion probably will take some time to iron out. The northern sector of the British Cameroons, meanwhile, elected to become an integral part of Nigeria.

Cameroun lies at the crook of the right-angled turn made by the West African coastline as it changes direction and flows down and on along the central African trunk of the continent. With typical African spaciousness, Cameroun stretches one long finger more than 700 miles northward to Lake Chad and the barren Sahara, and another corner southward and eastward to the steaming Congo.

An obscure country of only 3,000,000 people, although now to be swelled by the addition of up to 1,000,000 from the British Cameroons, the Cameroon Republic achieved independence in sensational circumstances.

A sputtering internal guerilla war which had dragged on desultorily since 1955 flared anew in the months prior to independence. In the middle of the actual independence program, terrorists opposing the government of Prime Minister (now President) Ahmadou Ahidjo staged a bloody massacre.

Terrorism has been attributed to an underground, ultranationalist wing of the Union des Populations Camerounaises (UPC), a political organization which fought French rule, and later that of France's protégé, M. Ahidjo, on grounds he worked in suspiciously close concert with the French. At the start of terrorism in 1955, France outlawed the UPC and its extremist leader, Dr. Félix-Roland Moumie, was exiled.

Dr. Moumie drifted between Cairo and Conakry and any other sympathetic capital. He sought aid for his campaign to overthrow M. Ahidjo in Moscow and Peking. This led to French charges of Communist influence behind terrorism in Cameroun and of accusations that the terrorists were receiving arms from Czechoslovakia and other Communist lands.

Dr. Moumie and his wing claimed that it was from them that the original impetus for independence had come. They pointed to M. Ahidjo's cordial relations with France and his retention of French troops to combat terrorism as evidence that he was a French puppet. They never recognized Cameroun's independence, maintaining that France was still its actual ruler.

Late in 1960, Dr. Moumie died of poisoning in suspicious circumstances in a Swiss hospital. It has been alleged that he was killed by an extreme right-wing organization operating in France.

Whether Dr. Moumie's influence in exile was as great as he believed is a moot point. He was a leader of only part of the UPC. When M. Ahidjo legalized the UPC again shortly after independence, the more orthodox faction of the party became a legal opposition party where it has taken an antiterrorist line.

It is doubtful whether even all the terrorism was performed by guerillas responsive to Dr. Moumie's influence, for there are groups antagonistic to the Ahidjo regime for other reasons. Here, as in other African lands, there is a problem of tribal diversity and the motivations for violent opposition to the government are more varied and complex than might at first appear.

Meanwhile, a country which achieved its independence in a more peaceful atmosphere than Cameroun was Togoland. Now known as the Republic of Togo, this is a narrow finger of a country 300 miles long, squeezed between Ghana on the west and Dahomey on the east.

Like the Cameroons, Togoland was colonized by Germany and ruled by Germans till World War I. Like the Cameroons, Togoland was split between France and Britain after the war, a western sliver going to the British and the eastern to the French as mandates from the League of Nations and ultimately as United Nations trusteeship territories. And again, like Cameroun, Togoland marched to independence in 1960.

British Togoland, however, had previously been absorbed into the British Gold Coast which became Ghana in 1957. Thus Togo has a common border with Ghana.

Events along this border are worth watching. Dr. Nkrumah wants Togo integrated with Ghana. Ghanaian pressure for integration has been warming up. Togo contemptuously dismisses Ghana's overtures. Sparks may fly.

Togo has only about 1,000,000 people strung along its length from the Gulf of Guinea to its northern savannah lands. Nkrumah's argument is that fusion of these with Ghana's own population of more than 6,000,000 would strengthen both groups. There would be economic advantages and such fusion would partly reunite the populous Ewe tribe which is strung out across these countries and Dahomey.

On the Togolese side of the border there is a supporting desire for Ewe unification. But to many of the wary Togolese, Ghana looks like a big cat to their own country's little mouse. Ewe unification they want, but not at the price of being eaten up by Ghana.

The Togolese have never forgiven Dr. Nkrumah for encouraging the incorporation of British Togoland into Ghana. They feel British and French Togoland should have been united as one country first and then, with a little more strength behind their unity, should have opened negotiations with Ghana for some form of association.

Jealously watching over Togo's new independence is an able and engaging African named Sylvanus Olympio, who is well known at the lobbies of the United Nations where he pressed Togo's claims to freedom year after year.

In UN-supervized elections crowning his campaign, M. Olympio and his party came romping home to power, and ultimately he led Togo to independence.

M. Olympio is a successful businessman in his own right. After three years of study for a Bachelor's degree at the London School of Economics, he joined the Unilever Company in Togoland and swiftly rose to become its chief executive in the country.

He switches from French to English or German with complete fluency and has a delightful capacity for subtle humor in each.

He is probably the only president in Africa, perhaps in the world, whom you might catch riding to work on a bicycle. Of course he has an official car, but he refuses to use it for private business. Once when his own car was being repaired he hopped onto a bicycle to keep his engagements, and from time to time he uses one still. This is an expression of independence in keeping with the character of this Togolese leader so watchful of his country's freedom.

And so we leave West Africa and the heartlands of the African revolution. Here the campaign against colonialism is ended. This is the postrevolutionary aftermath. Often it is dominated by new problems like trade and aid and new schools and factories and hydroelectric dams and exports.

Of course, there are the problems of inter-African unity and inter-African rivalry. There is expansionism and jousting for power and border trouble, just as there has been among nations elsewhere for centuries.

Yet the fact is that in four brief years, starting with Ghana in 1957 and ending with Sierra Leone in 1961, more than 80,000,-000 Africans have been swept to independent power and influence by the dramatic revolution which has washed across West Africa. Mostly it has been accomplished with remarkable stability. The flaming chaos of the Congo is the exception rather than the rule. Here in West Africa there has not been that kind of misery, nor the bloodshed of Europe's wars and revolutions.

Obviously, the future is far from clear. There is confusion, as the political and economic debris of upheaval is cleared away. But then revolutions, whether peaceful or violent, are rarely tidy affairs.

CENTRAL AFRICA

CHAPTER VIII

Congo: Prelude to Disaster

THE CONGO is the scene of the greatest colonial disaster in Africa.

This is the grand letdown, the point at which the African revolution has exploded into violence and sensation.

Throughout the great sweep of West Africa, change has come without bloodshed. The Congo is the grim contrast which has brought tragedy to thousands, plunged the United Nations into its biggest-ever military and salvage operation, and brought the major protagonists in the Cold War growling to the brink of intervention.

Crisis in the Congo has put Africa on the world map. Over breakfast tables from Anchorage, Alaska, to Sarasota, Florida, and Bombay to Bonn, has poured out the daily jumble of news about Katanga and Kasavubu and Kasai and Gizenga.

Yet the sensational story from the Congo has overshadowed the quieter, more constructive, course of events elsewhere in Africa. Nations like Nigeria, with a population three times the size of the Congo's, have moved peacefully to independence with hardly a fanfare. In the Congo itself there are 13,000,000 people and only a minority of these are involved in actual violence. Outside the Congo, more than 80,000,000 Africans have gained orderly independence in two or three years, and the population of the whole continent is more than 230,000,000.

Nevertheless it is the Congo's chaos which has impressed itself on the outside world, and sewn seeds of doubt and disillusion about Africa in some circles. Anarchy in the Congo has done more than any other single event to harden white opinion in the Rhodesias and South Africa. Aside from the tragedy for the Congo itself, the Congo's explosion is one which is costing all Africa dearly.

Physically, the Congo is a Hollywood script-writer's idea of darkest Africa. With the exception of the Sudan, it is the largest country in the whole continent, about as big as the eastern third of the United States. Here are the dense jungles ablaze with brilliant birds and screeching parrots. Elephants and gorillas and other wild animals crash, or slink, through the bush as is their wont.

There are primitives with bows and arrows and poisoned darts, and little pygmies who hunt with nets strung through the forests to catch buck and other wild animals. Sometimes they creep up behind an elephant, slash the tendons of its rear legs, and finish it off with poisoned darts while it is disabled and unable to charge.

This is a land of steaming swamps and red, muddy rivers, and the Congo, the greatest river in Africa for many, which meanders 3,000 miles across the country, shrugging off crocodiles and hippopotami along its banks before it roars over falls and cataracts until it reaches the port of Matadi, where the borders of the country narrow to a little neck of land leading to the sea.

The Portuguese first made contact with African tribes at the mouth of the Congo river in the fifteenth century. From then on into the nineteenth century, slave traders shredded the population along the coast of what is now the Congo and Angola. Several million Africans were captured and shipped as slaves across the Atlantic in crammed boatloads during this period. Most of them went to Brazil. Meanwhile, Arab slavers began their penetration from the east in the early nineteenth century, seizing their share of slaves from the Congo's eastern fringes and marching them back out to the sea and Zanzibar across Tanganyika.

However it was not until the latter half of the nineteenth century that the famous explorer, Henry Morton Stanley, mapped out the Congo in more or less the shape we know it today. Stanley did the job for Belgium's rapacious, ambitious King Leopold II. Leopold's imagination was fired by Stanley's earlier travels in the Congo after he discovered Dr. Livingstone. He sent him back, after Stanley's native Britain had spurned the explorer's proffered services, to tie up the territory with a series of treaties with African chiefs. Ostensibly Stanley was acting as agent for the International African Association, of which Leopold was president. But in fact he was Leopold's man, and, after diplomatic dealing at a famous Berlin conference of 1885, Leopold emerged with the Congo Free State, as it was called, as his personal and private possession.

In theory Leopold's mission in the Congo, although he in fact never set foot there himself, was motivated by the highest, civilizing intentions. In practice, he ruled it for twenty-three years as a personal preserve, a sort of royal park, the fruits from which were to fill the royal coffers.

Leopold apportioned large sectors of the Congo to himself personally and to his concessionaries with bland disregard of the Congo's African inhabitants. Then his agents and concessionaries forced Africans under threat of the whip and the gun to gather rubber and ivory for export. From all this Leopold made a fortune.

African troops raised under white officers ensured that the forced laborers produced the quotas set for them. There followed a chapter in the Congo's history which, if the official documents of the day are to be believed, was more gruesome than anything that has occurred since the Congo's recent independence.

The records indicate that mutilation was a common practice for Africans who failed to fill their quotas of rubber or ivory. Usually the punishment was summary amputation of a hand. According to British documents, an African soldier was required to produce a hand for every bullet he expended.

Roger Casement, then a young British consul in Africa, was sent by his government to the Congo to investigate the growing rumors of atrocities. His estimate was that the population had declined by 3,000,000 in ten years alone.

The reports of Casement and others like him touched off an international clamor to end the bloody scandal. Finally Leopold handed over his private African domain to the Belgian government which ruled it as a colony from 1908 onward.

. . .

With this depleted jungle land, the Belgians in their half century of rule thereafter wrought many miracles. Some believe the

Belgian government was determined to write a history of achievement which would wipe out the sordidness and disgrace of Leopold's unhappy venture. Certainly in the economic sphere the Congo bustled with progress which drew praise from the majority of its visitors.

Railroads appeared, and a river transport system, and fine new cities hacked out of the bush. The pattern of agriculture changed. Cash crops like coffee and cotton began to appear on the docks for export. Thousands of acres were cleared for palm oil plantations, with Unilever playing a major role in production for its margarine and soap factories.

But in minerals, not agriculture, the Belgians discovered the catalyst for the Congo's development, and wealth such as Leopold could hardly have dreamed of. There were rich copper finds in the province of Katanga, a diamond strike in Kasai province and discoveries of various other minerals.

To exploit the new riches, the Belgians built a pyramid of interlocking monopolies. At the top sat the Belgian state and big business in cheery partnership. Giant of the group was the huge copper-mining company, Union Minière du Haut Katanga. Union Minière grew to be the third largest copper company in the world, lesser only than Anaconda and Kennecott.

Union Minière was the goose that laid the golden, or at least the copper, egg. Yet besides copper in Katanga, it produced cobalt, tin, zinc, coal, radium and other minerals in a fabulously profitable series of mining operations. From Union Minière's Shinkolobwe mine came the uranium for the United States's atomic bombs in World War II.

For the Belgian government, Union Minière was a twofold money spinner. Not only did the government collect taxes on the company's profits, but it also collected dividends as a shareholder. Through holdings in interlocking groups, such as the Comité Special du Katanga and the mammoth Belgian financial concern known as the Société Générale, the Belgian government was an important part-owner of Union Minière. Other shares were held by various financial groups including the British Tanganyika Concessions Company and even the Rockefeller family.

From all this the Belgians ploughed back a percentage of the profits to fund considerable development in the Congo. Union Minière profits were so immense that taxes on them provided between a third and a half of the Congo's whole budget. Thus in a way Union Minière paid for many of the power stations and hospitals and schools and so forth which the Belgians displayed to visitors.

The Belgians never encouraged permanent settlement by whites in the Congo and at most the number of Belgians living there totaled about 90,000. Of these, Brussels has itself put the figure of "real" settlers at between 6,000 and 7,000. Of the remainder, some 6,000 were missionaries, about 10,000 government servants, and 15,000 technicians, together with their wives and families.

Officials and businessmen to whom one talked seemed to have but one aim. Salaries and allowances in the Congo were high and they sought to accumulate enough capital to retire at an early age to some more attractive clime.

The Congo's climate is trying, but during their residence there the whites nevertheless carved out a pleasant little niche for themselves. Indeed a capital like Leopoldville, exuding a rare air of continental charm, was one of the more attractive cities on the beat of any African traveler.

It was set on the bank of the Congo River and strung out along a magnificent, seven-mile-long dual carriageway bordered by blocks of $300-a-month luxury apartments. Similarly Elisabethville, capital of Katanga province at the other end of the country, was a city of broad boulevards and air-conditioned stores, and the finest theater in Africa, so equipped that the actors could play either to an indoor audience in sumptuous surroundings, or to an outdoor one across a series of pretty, cooling fountains.

The stores in these cities were chic and expensive with the latest gowns and perfumes from Paris and Brussels. In the shops you could buy the latest dance records. Once there was a big run on a little piece of Americana called "Bong, Bongo, Bongo, I Don't Wanna Leave the Congo." There were antiques from Japan, and chocolates from Switzerland, and shiny new automobiles from the United States. Magazines and the latest newspapers were flown in from abroad. The bookstores stocked everything from the latest Graham Greene to Albert Camus, and of course, *Hop-*

along Cassidy et son jeune ami, and *Davy Crockett, l'Invincible,* and the inevitable.

The verandas were trimmed with gay blooms. In the sidewalk cafés under brightly striped awnings and umbrellas African waiters would twirl expertly between the tables as they brought the well-dressed diners fish flown in the same day from Brussels, and butter shipped in from New Zealand. There was every delicacy one could reasonably demand here in the heart of Africa.

With Brigitte Bardot at the movies and Blondie and Dagwood chattering away in French in the local comic strip, it all seemed a gay little life to the Belgians, which might go on forever.

The gap between this white way of life and that of the African was of course immense. White wages were many times higher than those of nonwhites, and even the *évolués,* or "evolved" Africans, could not afford to live as whites. Urbanized Africans had their own African suburbs and quarters in the big cities to which they were confined by curfew at night. Technically there was no color bar but in practice one never saw a Congolese in a white restaurant or hotel, for example, and it is doubtful whether many Congolese could have afforded to visit them in any case. The whites and the Congolese thus lived in their separate worlds.

And yet, against a purely African background, and compared to Africans in other states, the Belgians had given the Congolese some of the most impressive material benefits in the continent.

There were pensions, and minimum wage scales, and industrial laws compelling employers to provide housing and a minimum number of calories per day and prenatal care. Any preindependence visitor to Leopoldville would be trundled around on a formidable tour of clinics and schools and estates with some of the most pleasant houses and blocks of apartments for Africans in the whole continent. The Belgians had cracked the migrant labor system in the Congo and allowed thousands of Africans to settle their families in the city, buy their own houses and even own land freehold. Social barriers might remain, but they had dropped the industrial color bar in many categories and there in the smelters of Katanga were Africans operating cranes and automatic ladles with thousands of dollars worth of molten copper at stake, and working at benches alongside Belgian artisans and doing numbers of skilled jobs.

Perhaps most impressive of all, the Belgians put something like 1,500,000 Congolese children into schools. This, they said, was 11 per cent of the entire population, a percentage rate excelled in Africa only by Ghana.

All this was frankly admitted to be within a tight framework of Belgian paternalism, a sort of Papa-knows-best policy under which the Congolese got jam for tea if they were good and did not answer back.

There was no secrecy or embarrassment about the object. This was to buy off political discontent and frustration with economic benefits and material well being. "Ah, monsieur," one Belgian official told me, "give them a bicycle and bread in their bellies and there will be no trouble with the politics."

Officially the Belgians held out no prospect of African political activity on the national level, nor of self-determination. Privately of course individual Belgians would talk, even as late as 1958, of maybe having to get out in twenty-five years' time, but nothing was planned on paper that an African could see. There was no Congo parliament. The country was run from Brussels through a Belgian governor-general in Leopoldville. And if the Congolese had no vote, well, neither did white Belgians. What could be fairer than that, the Belgians asked?

Thus they made no preparations, trained no Africans for responsibility. African political activity was swiftly stamped upon. Agitators were whisked away to jails in the bush. A limited form of local government was introduced in 1957, but until two months before independence in 1960 there had never been an election in the Congo for candidates for national office. Political parties had been nonexistent until 1958.

Even outside the political sphere, the Belgians made few plans for the advancement of Africans to positions of authority. Some 1,500,000 children in schools, yes. But these were primary-school children. How many in secondary schools? Between 13,000 and 17,000, some 3,000 of them white. How many in the two universities the Belgians had just begun? About 800, half of them white. Thus at independence the Congo had not a single African doctor, not a single African army officer. How many university graduates were there in the whole country out of a population of 13,000,000? The United Nations says seventeen, the Belgian government says thirty. How many Africans had been advanced into senior administrative posts? Just one.

Until the late 1950's, Belgium's colonial policy of bread-but-no-politics had seemed to be working well. Even high officials in the British colonial service pondered now and then whether the Belgians had not found the key to successful colonial policy. The Congo seemed so peaceful and prosperous. Even the Belgians' own Congo Information Bureau, Inforcongo, allowed itself a sly dig at the other troubled colonial powers: "The Congo is preoccupied above all with practical ends, and is suspicious of the abstract ideologies which elsewhere in Africa have produced disastrous results." Then, added Inforcongo smugly: "Economic progress is the watchword which has given the Congo its remarkable development, and brought the natives an economic freedom in the form of bicycles, food, medicine and housing which no amount of political liberty could have done."

It was a theory, as we know today, which backfired with tragic explosiveness. Throughout Africa, change was in the air. The broad Congo River could not halt the spread of new ideas. In 1956 a group of Congolese évolués startled the Belgians by issuing, in the journal Conscience Africaine, a manifesto virtually demanding self-rule within thirty years. But this was mild indeed compared with the pace soon to develop.

In 1958 came General de Gaulle's new deal for French Africa. The General talked of political self-rule in the capital of French Equatorial Africa, Brazzaville, just across the river from the Congo. Some of these "French" Africans for whom a new horizon now had opened were tribal brothers of "Belgian" Africans. They belonged to the same tribes, spread across both banks of the Congo River. Yet in French Africa they were promised rapid political strides, while in Belgian Africa, for all the schools and clinics, there was no prospect of politics at the national level.

Two fledgling political parties had by this time emerged in the Belgian Congo. One was the Abako, the Association des Bakongo, primarily a tribal party centered on the Bakongo tribe in Leopoldville province. This had graduated from a cultural organization to a political party under the hand of Joseph Kasavubu. Kasavubu, grandson of a Chinese coolie who worked on construction of the first Congo railway and who subsequently married a woman of the Bakongo tribe, was a clerk in government service who had become burgomaster of the African commune of Dendale, in Leopoldville. He had separatist leanings, even dreaming, say some, of the revival of the old Bakongo kingdom at the mouth of the Congo stretching across Portuguese, Belgian and French territory.

By contrast, the second party, the Mouvement National Congolais (MNC), campaigned on a broad front, aiming for national support. The MNC opposed the Abako's drift toward regional separatism. It demanded strong central government in an independent Congo. Its leader was a volatile former post office clerk with a capacity for spellbinding oratory, Patrice Lumumba. After a two-year jail sentence for embezzling post office funds in the town of Stanleyville, Lumumba became director of a brewery in Leopoldville and then, when political parties were authorized in 1958, a full-time politician.

At the end of 1958, Mr. Lumumba traveled to the All-African Peoples Conference in Accra, there to become inspired by the dynamic nationalism of Ghana's Kwame Nkrumah.

Meanwhile, in January, 1959, the Congo's long calm exploded with vicious riots in the capital of Leopoldville. The Abako was proscribed, its leaders arrested, and Mr. Kasavubu and his lieutenants flown out in secrecy to Belgium.

The Belgians reacted swiftly. King Baudouin of Belgium made his famous speech of concession, promising independence "without harmful procrastination but also without thoughtless haste." The Belgians claimed that they had been on the verge of announcing reforms when violence broke out, although inevitably it appeared as though violence had forced their hand.

Now the Congo entered months of uncertainty. Mr. Lumumba charged that the Belgians were negotiating secretly with Mr. Kasavubu in Brussels while "moderate" parties like his own MNC, uninvolved in violence, were being disregarded. With Mr. Kasavubu's return, enhanced in reputation by his arrest and deportation, there followed an intense duel between the two for political support among the Congolese people. Each was forced to pile on the pressure, the demands and the promises in an effort to outdo the other.

Early in 1960 the Belgians at a round-table conference with Congolese leaders in Brussels agreed to independence for the Congo on June 30 of that year. Independence would be preceded by the Congo's first national elections to elect the first members of its first parliament. Patrice Lumumba, jailed for incitement after more riots in the Congo, was released and flown to Brussels to take part in the conference.

Up to little more than a year previously, politics and political parties had been banned in the Congo. Now this vast country eighty times the size of Belgium itself was to have democratic elections and independence. Belgian colonial policy had undergone a complete turnabout. There are indications that even some Congolese were surprised, despite their demands for immediate independence which were the routine gambit of the African nationalist. Only a short while before, some had told me privately and gleefully that the Belgians were on the run and that the Congo now might get independence within five years.

In any event, the preindependence election campaign was one of confusion. Political parties mushroomed and candidates who had never before been permitted experience in politics campaigned among a politically unsophisticated electorate. The promises became more outrageous. Whatever the extent of sensationalism and distorted reports, there is evidence enough that some contestants led Africans to believe that white houses, white cars and white women would be theirs come independence. As further complication, the campaign took place against a backdrop of mounting tribal war and intertribal violence in some areas.

Mr. Lumumba's MNC emerged from the election with the largest number of seats won by any single party. In the key 137-seat Chamber of Representatives it had won between 33 and 36 seats, the exact number still confused by claims and counterclaims of electoral abuse. The Abako won 12 seats, all of them in Leopoldville province.

Lumumba had not enough seats to form a majority, but, as the leader of the largest party, the Belgians invited him to form a government. He failed and Mr. Kasavubu had a try, only to fail too. Finally Mr. Lumumba, with a rickety coalition including twenty-two ministers and fourteen state secretaries drawn from every parliamentary party except one, formed a government in a compromise deal with Mr. Kasavubu. Mr. Lumumba became prime minister and Mr. Kasavubu assumed the figurehead position of president, and head of state.

With the last creaky plate bolted on barely in time, the new independent state of the Congo was poised at the head of the slipway, ready for launching.

CHAPTER IX

Congo: A Nation Adrift

WITHIN A FEW WEEKS, the brand-new Congolese ship of state had become a waterlogged hulk, yawing helplessly this way and that, and a menace on the high seas of international diplomacy. Its mutinous crew and several captains fought among themselves over the course to take. Each day, the barnacles grew a little larger and the engines rusted a little more.

What went wrong?

Now that their colonial policy, which had seemed to be faring so well, has failed, the Belgians are criticized on two main counts: 1) that they withheld from Africans any training for government and political responsibility, and 2) that they compounded this mistake by bestowing independence upon Africans whom they had not prepared for it.

The Belgian answer is that these were errors of judgment and timing which anyone might have made. Could anyone, they ask, have foreseen five years ago the tremendous pace of events to come in Africa? Even admitting Belgian failure to gauge the pace and prepare Africans, can the world not appreciate the dilemma which faced us? Either, they say, we had to accede to demands for independence, or we had to attempt to retain the Congo as a colony—probably at the cost of a long, Algerian-type war which little Belgium could never sustain or win.

It is all too easy to make the Belgians the scapegoats for everything that happened in the Congo. One can understand their bitterness over the criticism, and their confusion over the shame the Congo has brought their country. There can be nothing but deep sympathy for the suffering of individual Belgian refugees from the Congo, bearing their tragedy of raped women, humiliated missionaries and all the rest.

Yet some of the most damning charges leveled against the Belgians are not for their failure to assess the trend before the Congo's independence, but for the meddlesome actions of some of their countrymen in the Congo after independence. The sad fact is that the Belgians are not emerging from all this with that proud and unsullied record of colonial achievement for which some of them had perhaps hoped.

It is evident that there were Belgians who regarded the Congo's sovereignty only as a technicality, and that they hoped to continue their dominant role thereafter. It was only with reluctance that some abandoned the idea of a Belgo-Congolese community, in which Belgium's king would be king of the Congo too. Even after they abandoned the idea it is difficult to avoid the suspicion that some Belgian circles believed they could somehow mastermind events in the Congo after independence.

This was perhaps not official government policy, although the Belgian government was itself split into various factions and wings holding divergent views on Congo policy. But there were many groups with interests in the Congo from the government to the mining companies and the big business combines. In the Congo itself there were individual officials who did not always follow the Brussels line, traders who never supported early independence for the Congo, and later the army officers ejected from their jobs, but tempted to stay and sell their services to one Congolese faction or another. There can be no doubt of the postindependence dabbling and politicking in Congo affairs by at least individuals from some of these groups.

In the financial sphere, Congo assets and reserves were transferred to Brussels and at independence the Congo found itself in debt and involved in credit arrangements with Belgium which, as one British observer put it, "tie the Congo hand and foot."

After independence the United Nations complained repeatedly that Belgians in the Congo were working against the UN and that Belgian officers were directing separatist Congolese forces, particularly in Katanga province, which had been responsible for violence.

Among foreign diplomats and officials in Leopoldville there was bitter denunciation in private talk of Belgian "foot-dragging" in relinquishing control. These complaints came from some diplomats who had no particular ax to grind against Belgium in normal circumstances.

After independence Belgium steadfastly proclaimed its right to maintain technicians in the Congo, not as a "voluntary bilateral program" but as a "prerequesite of the sovereignty of the Congo" tied up in the preindependence Treaty of Friendship between the two countries.

Of course the Congolese would badly have needed assistance from somewhere after independence. The Belgians, provided they desisted from political meddling and became the loyal employees of a sovereign African government like Britons in Ghana, were, and still are, in many respects the most logical people to help. They know the country, the people, the language. Nor is there any reason why Belgian commerce and industry such as mining should not continue to contribute to the Congo's economy.

But despite the official decision to give the Congo independence, there remained among some Belgians this niggling temptation to keep a finger in the Congo's governmental pie. Probably this would have led to trouble anyway. But a tussle for real power need not necessarily have led to the chaos and anarchy, which in fact transpired in the Congo after independence.

For the cause of this we must look to the Force Publique, the Congo's army. This army is worth more than a passing glimpse, for it is at the root of many Congo problems. At independence, the force numbered some 25,000. Of these, 24,000 were Congolese troops and noncommissioned officers. Of the 1,000 officers, every one was a white Belgian. Military men say this was a well-drilled and competent force, issued with excellent equipment and small arms. Its oldest rifles were made in 1952.

Yet within a week of independence the army was in revolt, committing atrocities and rape. Principal initial target of the soldiers seemed to be their white officers and the unfortunate wives and families of these officers. However, there were assaults on other whites such as missionaries and nuns, as well as some African civilians. These were days of horror. What is not generally known, however, is that the criminals were confined almost exclusively to the soldiery, and that many African civilians in Leopoldville, for example, were just as terrified of the troops as were whites.

The army revolt set off a chain reaction of events with sweeping implications for the Congo.

As a result of the army's rampage, Belgium flew in paratroopers to seize the Leopoldville airport and protect Belgian nationals. As a consequence of this action, the Lumumba government appealed to the United Nations for help and the first troops of the UN's Congo army came winging into the Congo.

The "reoccupation" of the independent Congo by Belgian troops, coupled with other events, such as the secession of Katanga province containing most of Belgium's mining interests, convinced Mr. Lumumba, mistakenly or not, that the Congo's independence was already threatened.

He appealed to Moscow for help, and Mr. Khrushchev cabled that the Soviet Union would "not shrink from resolute measures to curb aggression" in the Congo. Now the Cold War had reared its head in the Congo, threatening even to become a hot one.

An immediate consequence of the revolt was the panicstricken flight from the Congo of many Belgians who had remained after independence. As the story of the mutiny swept the country, Belgians left their homes and jobs and fled across the border to Northern Rhodesia, or to Congo airports for planes out, or crammed ferries across the Congo River to Brazzaville. Automobiles worth $3,000 were offered for a few hundred dollars, but there were not many purchasers. Hundreds of abandoned cars clogged the car park of Leopoldville airport.

Doctors left their hospitals and clinics, Belgian meteorologists and airport controllers and communications experts walked out of their offices, magistrates fled leaving cases unfinished and defendants both innocent and guilty in jail. Hygiene collapsed, the port of Matadi became clogged, the administration ground to a standstill.

Such was the tragic harvest of the army's revolt.

What caused the mutiny? It has been suggested that the soldiers were fed up, that they were ill-paid, that they had been on continuous heavy duty for several months before independence and that they saw few fruits of self-rule for themselves. There is a school of thought which maintains that the Belgians trained the soldiers to be vicious animals and that at the first opportunity the animals turned on their masters.

One of the most reasonable explanations I have heard is that frustrated Congolese noncommissioned officers encouraged the mutiny in the hope it would bring them promotion. Although independence had come to their country, their white officers were remaining. They saw little prospect of replacing them for at least some years. So they assisted the mutiny to speed the process.

If this is true, the mutiny was a particularly unhappy dividend of the Belgians' failure to advance Congolese into positions of authority. It is fascinating to speculate on the course of events had the army not rebelled; the Belgian paratroopers might not have come, nor the troops of the UN nor the bluster from Moscow. Belgian personnel probably would not have fled and the administration might not have collapsed. It is tragically ironic that Congolese troops under white officers should be at the heart of the Congo's twentieth-century disaster as were Congolese troops under white officers at the center of crisis over King Leopold's reign.

In an attempt to calm the rioting troops, Prime Minister Lumumba agreed to sack the army's white officers and replace them with Congolese. He promised pay increases and a one-rank promotion for every soldier in the ranks. This, as someone drily remarked, made the Congolese army the only one in the world without any privates, for they all became lance corporals overnight.

Eventually the troops stopped their immediate rampage, but with the collapse of command the damage was done. A Congolese sergeant major became commanding general. Congolese who had been lance corporals and sergeants a few days before now were lieutenants and captains in charge of the same men they had known in the ranks. Often they commanded scant respect.

Discipline degenerated and the army became a disorganized rabble of uncertain loyalties. In crumpled uniforms, small bands of soldiers armed with loaded tommy guns and rifles would slouch through the streets of Leopoldville hunting they knew not quite what. This time it would be "Russian spies," the next time "Belgian paratroopers." Once they arrested as a Belgian paratrooper an indignant, coal-black Liberian colonel with the UN forces. Sometimes they would seize a UN official, sometimes a correspondent or a press photographer. There was more than one incident when a wailing photographer became the subject of a tug-of-war between Congolese troops who had captured his head and arms, and his newspaper colleagues who held onto his legs and refused to let him go.

Sometimes the troops would conduct sweeps and throw up roadblocks without the knowledge or authorization of their new officers. Ofter the danger lay in misunderstanding or the sheer bumblingness of it all. When I flew into Leopoldville after independence, the white man ahead of me passed the Congolese immigration officer without trouble, but something about his papers disturbed a Congolese sergeant on airport duty. In one of those sudden, incomprehensible little flare-ups of anger, both the white man *and* the Congolese immigration officer found themselves at the business end of the sergeant's tommy gun.

Once a group of Congolese troops on some quite peaceful mission to the American embassy put embassy officials into a lather of perspiration. As the troops stood talking to Ambassador Clare Timberlake, one swung his tommy gun absently to and fro along the line of the ambassador's stomach.

On another occasion a Congolese cabinet minister paid a formal call on the embassy followed by his bodyguard pointing a tommy gun innocently, but dangerously, at his back. The safety catch, an embassy official noted with horror, was in the "off" position. Said the shaken official later: "Just imagine if the guard had tripped and shot a Congolese cabinet minister in the American embassy."

.   .   .

Of the daily chronicle of events in the Congo in these first months of independence the reader will be aware, for the newspapers and the television networks broadcast it to the ends of the earth.

The UN's technicians got essential services under way, but the political crisis worsened. The shaky compromise between Prime Minister Lumumba and President Kasavubu burst asunder under the strain. The president announced he had fired the prime minister and the prime minister announced he had deposed the president. Each claimed to be in charge. Each retired into his villa behind a protective cordon of Ghanaian troops of the UN force, British-trained, and stamping and snapping as smartly even in the tropical sun as guards outside London's Buckingham Palace.

At the other end of the Congo, Moise Tshombe, pro-Belgian leader of the Conakat party in Katanga province, had emerged as "president" of an "independent" Katanga, advised by Belgians, working in close alliance with Belgian mining interests, and diverting the taxes from the mines which used to go to the Congo's central treasury to Katanga's own treasury. Mr. Tshombe admitted UN troops to Katanga only with reluctance, and with UN Secretary General Dag Hammarskjöld himself at their head.

Both Mr. Kasavubu and Mr. Tshombe charged Mr. Lumumba with opening the door to communism in the Congo. Few sensible people suggested that Mr. Lumumba was himself a Communist. Indeed, it is not generally known that before Mr. Lumumba appealed to the United Nations, and then the Soviets, for help, his government at a cabinet meeting under the chairmanship of deputy premier Antoine Gizenga had appealed to the United States for troops. Properly, the meeting was given the American reply that the United States must work through the United Nations.

However, there were in Mr. Lumumba's entourage and cabinet individuals with Communist leanings. He had apparently sanctioned a flow of Communist technicians to the Congo. Some four hundred from the Soviet Union and eighty from Czechoslovakia had reportedly entered the Congo. Some came with eighty trucks given by the Soviet Union to the Congo, while sixteen Soviet Ilyushins, one a personal gift to Mr. Lumumba and fifteen on loan, had been flown in with crews of eight instead of the normal four men.

To the Communists, Mr. Lumumba might have seemed the most

promising of the Congo's leaders for their own ends. To the West
he had appeared irresponsible and unpredictable in earlier actions. He seemed vastly less experienced than African leaders like
Ghana's Kwame Nkrumah, for example. Maybe he himself did not
plan to make the Congo a sphere of Communist influence, but the
Communists apparently did, and was Lumumba the man to resist
them? So pondered the West. Yet to many African states, Lumumba appeared a man cast in the true African nationalist mold,
waging a desperate battle for the Congo's independence and
unity against colonialism and its stooges such as Mr. Tshombe.

Then with the Congo's political situation in suspense, a new
development occurred. This was the bloodless military coup of a
young Congolese army officer, Joseph Mobutu.

I had been in the United States only three days on vacation
from Africa when my newspaper recalled me from Florida to fly
to the Congo. After several days of frustrating negotiation over
visas in New York, and a night flight across the Atlantic and another down from Europe, I arrived weary in Leopoldville.

After a quick survey, I filed, to catch my paper's deadline, a
first-impression story of a capital which was taking its anarchy
quietly. Mr. Lumumba was safely in his villa at one end of town,
Mr. Kasavubu in his at the other. On the road in from the airport,
smiling Congolese were pushing clear of a railway line a stalled
truck with a Belgian and his family in it. Congolese were even
watering the municipal flowerbeds. The UN was on guard, the
city drowsed. After my dispatch was away, I dropped gratefully
into bed for a few hours sleep.

That was at 4:00 P.M. At 8:00 P.M. I awoke and made my way
to the hotel foyer. It was crammed with shouting Congolese soldiers waving machine guns. They spilled out onto the sidewalk,
intermingled with crowds of spectators and the three hundred
correspondents covering the Congo story. The television flood-
lamps were set up, the cameras were ready, the hotel was in confusion. "What happened?" I asked a British correspondent.
"Haven't you heard, old boy? There's been a revolution," he
replied.

During my siesta the young Colonel Mobutu had indeed seized

command of the army, had "frozen" parliament and was now on his way to tell us his plans. Such was Leopoldville for a newspaperman, and soon it was barely safe to sleep at all for the capital popped with new developments at any hour of night and day.

Far from simplifying matters, Colonel Mobutu's coup confused them. His plan was to neutralize both the Lumumba and Kasavubu camps for several months, while the country would be run by a "College" of "High Commissioners," young Congolese students. But it in fact made no difference either to Mr. Lumumba or Mr. Kasavubu and the country continued with three or four rival governments, while outlying areas declared their independence from time to time to confuse the issue further.

With parliament neutralized, the press conference now became the forum for political debate and maneuver. Newsmen were summoned to a string of conferences at all hours of night and day for some new declaration. Once there were five separate press conferences running simultaneously in different parts of the city.

Mr. Lumumba's conferences were always the most sensational. Often he would appear an hour late, to the irritation of the busy reporters. Then he would announce a special meeting of parliament at four o'clock that afternoon, with all newsmen and diplomats invited. We would roar off to parliament to find only a wizened caretaker, complaining: "Parliament's closed. Come back in three months." Or perhaps Mr. Lumumba would announce a reconciliation with Mr. Kasavubu and wave impressive, signed documents to prove it. But when you rang up Mr. Kasavubu he would deny the existence of any such document. The UN man whom Mr. Lumumba had said had been a witness would deny ever having been there. Yet one could not discount Mr. Lumumba, for while Mr. Kasavubu sat in his villa with a kind of Oriental impassivity, Mr. Lumumba was volatile, dynamic, always on the bounce with some new scheme which might be pure fantasy, but which might just be the breakthrough which nobody dare ignore.

Leopoldville was a city of constant rumor, intrigue, plot and counterplot. Perhaps a courier would appear breathlessly at breakfast to shout: "Pro-Lumumba troops have sailed down the Congo from Stanleyville. They're disembarking now, and about to storm Leopoldville." We would race down to the riverside to discover a boatload of green army recruits being shipped in for depot training.

Just after midnight one night, an explosion shook the capital. We rushed to our hotel door. "It came from there," exclaimed the doorman, pointing in the direction of Mr. Lumumba's house two miles away. Carloads of newsmen sped to Mr. Lumumba's house, standing peaceful and undisturbed. "It came from there," said one of the guards, pointing to the military camp and Colonel Mobutu's house. But there too all was quiet. "Perhaps it was Kasavubu's house," suggested another soldier. But it was quiet there as well. Puzzled, we motored back to our hotel. "Heard about the explosion?" asked a British correspondent, lounging in a chair. "Somebody chucked a bomb at the *Echo* office." The *Echo* was a newspaper, just fifty yards around the corner from our hotel.

Center of frustration for many correspondents was the cable office. Sometimes a reporter would spend eight or nine hours of a day engaged in the physical task of getting his dispatch away. Congolese teleprinter and radio operators worked the system under UN technicians but it was constantly bedeviled by failure and collapse. One of the reasons it had proved so difficult to operate, one Congolese told me, was because someone, during the chaos of the Belgians' departure, had carefully unscrewed and taken with them all the little brass tags on the equipment which indicated the purpose and function of the various plugs and meters and switches and fuses.

Sometimes Congolese troops would close down the cable office and wave newsmen away with their guns, effectively cutting off the Congo from the outside world. This they did the night of Colonel Mobutu's coup. Three enterprising correspondents took a dugout canoe across the Congo to Brazzaville, no mean feat across this crocodile-infested, fast-flowing river, just above the rapids, at dead of night. But sad to say, the Brazzaville cable office was closed too.

And so the story drifted on. There was a dramatic day, of course, when Colonel Mobutu's men ousted the Soviet and Czechoslovakian diplomats. Few people had believed he would enforce his forty-eight-hour ultimatum to them to leave the Congo, after he allegedly had discovered seven Soviet officers in civilian clothes within Leopoldville's principal Congolese army camp.

But at dawn on the appointed day his troops ringed the embassies, the smoke from burned papers poured from the Soviet embassy garden and behind the drawn curtains the diplomats packed their trunks and crates. Eventually the flag of the Soviet Union was hauled down from the flagpost outside and the convoy of Communists drove off to the airport. There they packed the Ilyushins they had loaned to the Congo and the heavily laden aircraft trundled off into the tropical air.

During all this time, the capital of Leopoldville presented a deceptive air. Along the principal two hundred yards of the main Boulevard Albert, business seemed to be as usual. There were whites dining at the sidewalk cafés, and the shops were open. Even the African curio sellers were back on the Place Braconnier offering their carved animals and bogus ivory figures to UN men off duty.

But all this was like a theatrical set with an impressive front and nothing behind it. If you stepped beyond this artificial little center of activity past the UN guards with their bayonets glinting in the moonlight there was nothing but backstage emptiness.

Shops were to let, apartments and houses empty. Garbage lay uncollected and, with the beginning of the tropical rains, the tropical growth began to creep back over the gardens.

Of course, the 500 civilian officials of the UN and the more than three hundred newsmen in the capital made business brisk for the remaining restaurants and the three main hotels. Once, so the story goes, the hotels were so crowded that an American photographer had to sleep in a broom closet. Yet all this gave employment to only a handful of taxi drivers, waiters and domestic servants. Leopoldville existed on an artificial little boomlet.

The majority of the city's Africans were unemployed. All but essential services had collapsed. Dr. Sture Linner, Swedish chief of the UN's civilian operations, warned of the "grand panorama of disaster" which loomed unless the economy started rolling again soon. Income which used to come to the Congo from taxes on the big Katanga mining companies now was being diverted to the treasury of that province.

With rival factions each claiming to be the legitimate government of the Congo, yet none of them with the real strength to rule, the political crisis dragged on from week to week.

CHAPTER X

Congo: Salvaging the Wreck

IN THE EARLY months of 1961, the murder of Patrice Lumumba jolted the world. Besides its impact within the Congo, it set off angry riots in capitals across the globe. Protesting crowds, charging Belgium's complicity in the slaying, attacked and wrecked Belgian embassies. In some instances there were demonstrations outside American missions as well.

Some weeks earlier, Mr. Lumumba had fled his villa and the protection of his UN guards in Leopoldville. His archrival, President Kasavubu, had been recognized as the Congo's representative at the UN in a 53–24 General Assembly vote which overrode the protests of pro-Lumumba African and Asian nations.

Mr. Lumumba made for Stanleyville, his own political stronghold in the eastern Congo. He intended joining his deputy-premier, Antoine Gizenga, and other lieutenants who had already set up base there. Almost certainly, he planned to preside over a government there in opposition to Kasavubu's.

But troops of Colonel Mobutu captured him en route. Mobutu's earlier attempts to arrest Lumumba in Leopoldville had been foiled by the UN. Now, however, Mobutu's men returned Lumumba to the capital and after public humiliation and roughing up he was transferred to imprisonment in the Thysville army camp, south of Leopoldville.

There he stayed for some weeks, but even in prison his fortunes seemed to prosper. His cohorts in Stanleyville seemed to be extending their influence, mobilizing Congolese troops loyal to Lumumba and gaining ground until they could claim about one-third of the Congo under their control. In Thysville camp, the Lumumba personality began to convert even some of the troops guarding him. Finally both Colonel Mobutu and President Kasavubu sped one day on an emergency mission to the Thysville camp. The full story is not known, but it is suggested that some troops were on the verge of new mutiny and Mr. Lumumba was within reach of his freedom. It is also suggested that he turned down a Kasavubu-Mobutu offer of freedom in return for an undertaking to work peacefully in a new government to be headed by Kasavubu's nominee, former journalist Joseph Ileo.

Within a few days, Lumumba was flown secretly out and across the Congo to the province of Katanga controlled by another of his bitter enemies, Moise Tshombe, in close association with the Belgians. At Elisabethville airport, Mr. Lumumba underwent a savage beating by Tshombe's gendarmes.

Then, according to the Tshombe administration's story, he was transferred to a farmhouse prison. The Katanga provincial government persistently refused international requests for a Red Cross team to examine him and the two aides imprisoned with him. Finally, goes the official Katanga story, the three escaped from their jail, made some distance in a car which was conveniently to hand, and then were "massacred by the inhabitants of a small village."

The Katanga administration refused to name the village, refused to produce the bodies, refused to say where Lumumba was buried. The Belgian doctor who signed the death warrants refused to give the cause of death, or the date.

The world expressed open skepticism of the story. It suspected instead that the Tshombe regime, wary like the Kasavubu camp of Lumumba's increasing influence in the Congo, had had him murdered within hours of his arrival in Katanga.

So by violence ended the tempestuous career of Patrice Lumumba. In his short reign as prime minister he had himself condoned brutality and ordered an assault on secessionist factions which the UN termed massacre and genocide. Although he came nearest to any of being a national Congolese leader there were many ordinary Congolese who did not support him. Even among African leaders elsewhere on the continent there were doubts expressed privately of his course, particularly in foreign affairs.

Yet with his death Patrice Lumumba became a martyr of a stature he might never have achieved had he lived. It would be unrealistic to imagine that his name will disappear from Congolese politics and history. For in a way he had become to many non-whites, as one commentator put it, a sort of African David challenging the Goliath of neocolonialism.

Neocolonialism? In African eyes this is the attempt by a colonial power to retain dominating economic and political influence in a former colony after independence. As Africans see it, this is a crime of which Belgium is guilty in the Congo. It is a charge endorsed by the UN.

Belgium is the principal target, but other Western nations are not immune from African attack. Under suspicion from time to time by Africans are Belgium's fellow colonial powers, and those NATO allies who in the past have extended their military ties to political defense of each other. Thus the noncolonial United States has not avoided occasional nonwhite wrath, as the riots outside American embassies after Lumumba's death bear out.

Before Lumumba was flown as a prisoner to Katanga, the United States had undergone a change of presidents. The new administration appeared to take up a more neutral standpoint toward Mr. Lumumba than its predecessor. The Eisenhower administration had supported recognition of Kasavubu and leaned its weight against Lumumba. Undoubtedly this American attitude was partly motivated by Lumumba's apparent encouragement of the Communists. It was an attitude which many nonwhites were to remember at Lumumba's death.

However, the real villains of the piece in African eyes were Belgian manipulators in the Congo and those Congolese leaders dubbed "puppets" by the determined nationalists of Africa outside the Congo's borders. Of these "puppets," the leading one appeared to be Katanga's Moise Tshombe. By declaring Katanga independent, moreover, and resisting pressure to bring it once again under Leopoldville's central rule, Mr. Tshombe had diverted to the treasury of his own province the enormous taxes on Union Minière profits which previously had gone to the Congo as a whole.

Although Belgium at first officially frowned on Katanga's secession, it has since proved a prosperous arrangement for both Mr.

Tshombe and the big Belgian copper mining company, Union Minière. The Katanga mines have kept on operating and the smokestacks have continued puffing. Union Minière's mines lost only four or five days' work in the postindependence turmoil. For all that, the company managed to produce a record tonnage of copper during the Congo's troubled year of independence. Mr. Tshombe's treasury benefited to the extent of some $50,000,000 in taxes. In 1961 Union Minière launched a $20,000,000 investment program in Katanga as an apparent indication of its confidence in the territory's future.

Thus Belgians who departed temporarily until they could see which way the wind was blowing soon came flooding back. Houses and apartments have their old tenants, the night clubs are open and the hotels are so full it is difficult to get a room. Businesses are open again.

Yet suspicion has lingered over the Belgians who officer the Katangan police force, who command the army, who have flown the air force planes and who have been sprinkled as advisers throughout all the government departments. When the UN put pressure upon Belgium to recall these nationals, Mr. Tshombe made them "nationals" of Katanga.

Meanwhile, as a successful businessman before he turned politician, Mr. Tshombe knew the value of the money which came flooding so bountifully into Katanga's treasury and he used it to buy mercenaries and military equipment from abroad to protect his position.

Thus in addition to his Belgians he recruited paratroop officers from Europe and infantry commanders from the Rhodesias and even some white South African jet pilots. These were for French jet planes which he acquired via Belgium. Soldiers of fortune of various nationalities were sprinkled through the army of Congolese troops loyal to himself which he sent into action against dissident elements within his own province and troops of the Lumumba camp threatening from the north.

All this has contributed to Mr. Tshombe's rejection by Africa's dedicated nationalists. However, it is for his suspected involvement in the murder of Patrice Lumumba that they despise him most. Lumumba threatened the security of this private little empire which Tshombe carved out in close association with the Belgians. Lumumba it was who sought to bring Katanga back into the Congo fold as one of the country's original six provinces. Yet Lumumba was murdered in Katanga in highly suspicious circumstances.

Another Congolese leader enjoying prosperity is Albert Kalonji, a former accountant who declared himself president of an independent state. This is the so-called "mining state" of Kasai, or at least that portion of the province which contains the diamonds mined by the Belgian company Forminière.

Finally in the group held suspect by some African nationalists is the Kasavubu-Mobutu faction centered upon Leopoldville. Here too Belgian advisers reappeared and Belgian officers were seen retraining some of Mobutu's troops.

Inevitably, African nationalists have charged Kasavubu and Mobutu with implication in Lumumba's killing. Even if they were not party to a plot, they must have recognized that they were endangering Lumumba's life by delivering him to his enemies, both Congolese and Belgian, in Katanga. Certainly they could have had little confidence in their ability to retrieve him from Tshombe's hands had they wanted to.

Basically the quarrel of Kasavubu, Kalonji and Tshombe with Lumumba was over the type of government their country should have. Lumumba, following the well-trodden path of other African nationalists, demanded highly centralized unitary government to combat just such secessionist trends as have arisen in Katanga and Kasai. His opponents, fearing to give national power to a man they saw as a ruthless demagogue, sought a looser, federal form of government giving them authority within their own regions.

The Belgians had encouraged neither political experience nor national unity or consciousness. Many of the Congo's hastily developed politicians met fellow politicians from other parts of the country for the first time only a few months before independence. Against the over-all background of tribal affinities it perhaps was overoptimistic to expect unitary government to emerge and survive. Even Nigeria, with much greater preparation for self-government, resorted to federal government to resolve antagonism between various regions.

In practice, the Congo has drifted toward a kind of federal system if only because interregional jealousies and hostility have made strong central government impossible. No leader strong enough to unite the whole Congo behind him has emerged. Mr. Gizenga, Mr. Lumumba's deputy prime minister, claimed that with the latter's death he had become rightful premier of the whole Congo, and he secured recognition by various Communist and African states. Congolese leaders meeting without Mr. Gizenga have tried to draft a federal constitution, but at one such conference Mr. Tshombe himself was arrested and made prisoner by the Kasavubu camp.

Crystal gazing is a hazardous occupation in this tangled land and few can forecast the outcome. However, one thing upon which one can speculate with certainty is that the UN, provided it is permitted to remain, has a job on its hands for long years to come. Top UN men in the Congo do not blink an eyelid when a span such as twenty to twenty-five years is mentioned.

Initially the military aspect of the UN's mission in the Congo has been to the fore. But the great gaunt problem looming beyond that is one of economic reconstruction. The Belgians before independence framed five-year plans for the Congo's development but all those have disappeared in the upheaval. First the UN has an immense task of rehabilitation, of reinstituting medical services, reclaiming run-down farms, re-establishing a legal system and a government administration. Then when it has got the Congo back to where it was before anarchy replaced order, it can plan new development and the training of Congolese for the jobs the Belgians never taught them.

For the UN, its Congo assignment has tested the international organization sorely. The Soviets have thundered abuse at it, using the Congo operation as a bludgeon for an attack upon Secretary General Dag Hammarskjöld. One Congolese faction after another has reviled it, although it was at the request of the Congolese that the UN first entered the Congo. The Belgians have openly flaunted it. Various nonwhite member nations have sniped at it, some withdrawing their contingents from the UN military force in the Congo.

It is easy to say the UN failed in the Congo. As the crisis and the political stalemate dragged on, many ordinary citizens in countries outside the Congo became discouraged and asked why the UN had not achieved some settlement.

Yet the UN's mission in the Congo as assigned by its international employers was not to govern. Perhaps its task would have been simpler if it could have taken over the Congo from the first as a trust territory, ruling it virtually as a UN colony. But there could be no question of that. The Congo was an independent sovereign state. The UN was called in at the request of the Congolese to help restore order. Its mission as it interpreted it was to work with whatever turned out to be the legitimate government of the Congo. Only the Congolese themselves could decide which that would be. Thus when the UN sought to be nonpartisan it was called "ineffective," yet when it attempted effective action it was labeled "partisan." It was an unenviable dilemma.

Where the UN did seem least effective, at least in the early stages, was in the military rather than the political sphere. When UN troops first landed in the Congo the UN command passed up the opportunity to disarm the officerless rabble which the Force Publique, later renamed the Congolese National Army, had become. If they were to be disarmed, that was the time to do it, but the UN rejected the chance and thereafter reaped a bitter harvest from that decision, for these disorderly troops were at the core of many troubles later on.

Of course, it was not until later that the Security Council gave the UN troops "teeth" in the shape of permission to use force where necessary. Even so the troops seemed to fall short on routine security duties and there were many instances where UN troops stood by while individuals were beaten up. Most notorious was the beating of Mr. Lumumba upon his arrival as a prisoner at Elisabethville airport, which onlooking UN troops did nothing to stop.

On the other hand, one cannot underestimate the difficulties confronting the command of an uncoordinated force of some 20,000 troops from thirty countries, each with its own language, customs, equipment and training. Further the UN force in its early days was strung out on guard duty at widely separated points so that the command rarely had a sizable body of troops at any one point.

Bureaucracy in any form is rarely efficient and when it becomes internationalized, as in the UN, there are tales enough of ineptitude and wastage and so on. And so there were in the Congo. At the ordinary newspaperman's level, anyone who became entangled in the prevarications of the UN public relations setup, or who sweated through yet another failure of the UN-supervised cable system, can testify to that.

Yet if anything did work after the Belgian exodus, it was generally the UN working it. Somehow they kept the port open and the water flowing in the hotel rooms and the electricity going.

Most importantly, whatever its ponderousness and failings and fumblings, it was the availability of the UN which held at bay the threat of great power war over the Congo. Without the UN, Soviet and American troops even if not at war could just conceivably have been practicing Cold War maneuvers in the hot Congo jungles. Pause for a moment and let the cold shivers run up and down your spine when you think of a world without the United Nations. The UN may have been an ill-fitting, leaky sort of bung to thrust into the hole in the sinking Congo ship, but at least, through its being there, the ship is still afloat.

CHAPTER XI

Portuguese Africa: End of a Siesta

PORTUGAL'S COLONIES are the Rip van Winkle lands of Africa.
For long years they have slumbered on both economically and
politically while the rest of Africa changed about them.

Elsewhere, the tide of change has gone surging across West
Africa, swamped the Congo, swirled up into East Africa, and sent
its long fingers probing down even into the white strongholds of
Southern Rhodesia and South Africa. Somehow, Portugal's African empire slept on undisturbed.

But now the long Portuguese siesta has been brought to an
abrupt end and the Portuguese have awakened to find the tide of
African nationalism lapping at their feet.

So well have the Portuguese colonies remained hidden until
recently that some readers may be surprised to learn that Portugal
has any stake in Africa at all. Yet Portugal is the owner of an
African empire about a quarter of the size of the United States,
which has made it a major colonial power.

There are the Cape Verde Islands, and São Tomé in the Atlantic
Ocean off the African mainland, and there is a little pocket of
Portuguese influence, Portuguese Guinea, sandwiched between
Senegal and former French Guinea in West Africa.

But the colonies that count are two big territories on either
coast of Central Africa, separated by the Rhodesias. On the west
coast there is Angola, and on the east Mozambique.

Of the two, perhaps Mozambique is the slightly better known.
Cruise liners, plying between Europe and Africa via Africa's east
coast, make Mozambique ports a routine call, and once they have
dropped their gangways hundreds of tourists squeal excitedly

ashore to buy Mozambique straw hats and baskets, and carved wooden crocodiles, and other tourist bric-a-brac.

The two principal coastal cities of Beira and Lourenço Marques also support a tourist trade from the landlocked Rhodesias, and even from the South African city of Johannesburg, 400 miles away from the nearest sea in the hot interior. Many Johannesburgers think little of an 800-mile round trip on a long week end for a day or two at the ocean's edge.

To the seasoned traveler, Mozambique might seem rather a tame little spot, unremarkable except for some first-class seafood restaurants where the Portuguese prawns come as free and plentiful as potato chips.

But there is something of a Latin flavor about the pastel-painted villas, and the night clubs pounding out rhumbas and sambas above the curving beaches, and the beachfront hotels with their swimming pools. For younger South Africans and Rhodesians who perhaps have never set foot in Europe this may be their first daring sip of the Continental way of life, tinged with all the innocuous naughtiness of a day trip across the English Channel to France for British trippers in the thirties.

There is also a week-end traffic across the border of tourists coming to watch Portuguese bullfights staged in Mozambique. Happy to report, the bulls do not meet the same gory death as in Spanish bullfighting.

But aside from the tourist trade, Mozambique sees few visitors and its population of 5,500,000 Africans and only 50,000 Portuguese remains relatively undisturbed by the outside world.

Angola, across the continent on the western coastline, is even more remote. There is the British-owned Benguela Railway, whose engines clatter over the 800-mile track between the Congo border and the terminus and port of Lobito on the Angolan coast. But this is used mainly to haul copper and other exports from Katanga. There is little or no tourist trade and even by Portuguese standards Angola has remained the Cinderella sister, with the capital and port of Luanda its principal showplace.

However, it was Angola which hit the headlines in 1961 and stripped much of the obscurity from Portuguese colonialism in Africa.

The cruise of the *Santa Maria,* the Portuguese liner hijacked
by Captain Henrique Galvao as a dramatic gesture of opposition
to the Salazar regime in Portugal, might alone have been sufficient
to direct a spotlight of attention on Portuguese Africa.

Of course the object of Captain Galvao and his mentor, General
Humberto Delgado, was to embarrass the metropolitan government of Portugal itself. But at one stage Captain Galvao indicated
his intention of sailing the liner to Angola. It seems evident that
both he and General Delgado, perhaps remembering that the
Spanish Civil War began in Morocco, believed there were substantial forces of opposition to the Salazar regime among both
Angola's 170,000 Portuguese citizens and its 4,000,000 to 5,000,000
Africans.

It was in Angola in previous years that Captain Galvao had
first roused the ire of the Salazar government. He was a high
official in the colonial service and after World War II submitted
a grim report on forced labor in Angola. Nothing was done, but
Captain Galvao continued his campaign as a deputy from Angola
in the Portuguese parliament. Later he was arrested and jailed
for three years as a political prisoner. Sentenced to another sixteen years for his continuing opposition, he escaped to Argentina,
moving later to Brazil and Venezuela.

As we know, the *Santa Maria* did not sail to Angola. But events
there since have left the Portuguese in little doubt of the existence
of a militant opposition to their colonial rule.

In 1961, African rioting broke out in the Angola capital of
Luanda and violence soon spread throughout the country.

The Portuguese imposed an even more rigid censorship than
usually exists in their territories. There was a clamp-down on news
dispatches, which had to be translated into Portuguese and then
argued out with the censors and changed to their satisfaction
before they could be cabled. Correspondents telephoning their
stories out were cut off in the middle of their calls. Press photographers' films were confiscated and news and television movies
stolen or destroyed during transmission.

None of this could hide the fact that the Portuguese were in
serious trouble in Angola. Soon it became clear that far from dealing with scattered rebellious incidents, the Portuguese were em-

broiled in a full-scale, Algerian-type colonial war. They flew in paratroops from Lisbon and troopships shuttled regiments of infantrymen into the territory. These, with the Portuguese air force, went into action on a massive scale against African rebel groups roaming northern Angola.

Portugal charged the Africans were being armed and assisted by foreign powers and were operating from the Congo, across Angola's northern border. Within a few months the fatality figures had run into many thousands, the majority being Africans killed by the Portuguese, but including a large number of Portuguese settlers wiped out by Africans. Each side accused the other of a list of grim atrocities.

Long before violence erupted, reports of opposition had dribbled out of Angola. There were secret trials before military tribunals, and political jailings of clandestine opposition leaders, some of whom were flown to Portugal for imprisonment. The opposition included Africans and Portuguese disillusioned with Salazar rule.

Now the UN is asking embarrassing questions about Portuguese colonialism in Africa, and meanwhile Angolan exiles and nationalist organizations in various capitals are steadily building their case.

The União das Populaçãoes de Angola (UPA) operates from headquarters in the Congo capital of Leopoldville, issuing pamphlets demanding immediate independence for Angola. A coordinating group called the Frente Revolucionaria para a Independência Nacional das Colónias Portuguesas (FRIAN) is based upon the Guinea capital of Conakry. There is an exiled freedom movement for Portuguese Guinea. Mozambique Africans working in Tanganyika and Kenya have pledged themselves to overthrowal of Portuguese rule in Mozambique.

These groups are increasingly active. Their delegates attend pan-African freedom conferences. They lobby at the United Nations. They publish pamphlets and newspapers. Their object is to whip up action against Portuguese colonial rule, both inside the Portuguese colonies and in the world outside.

The Portuguese were the first of the colonists into sub-Saharan Africa. They have been the last to feel the buffetings of African nationalism. Now they are face to face with it as their quiescent colonies stir.

.   .   .

Ignorance and isolation are the factors which have till now helped to insulate Portugal's colonies from the mainstream of African change. The Portuguese recognize this. Some of them are rather proud of it. They have enshrined these factors in their colonial policy and they believe in giving their Africans civilization in minute potions at a time.

The Portuguese want no truck with the encouragement of an African intellectual elite for responsibility and political power. They themselves have no intention of abandoning power or rule from Lisbon. The African territories are not officially colonies at all, but overseas "provinces" of Portugal for which there is officially no question of independence.

The Portuguese goal, say colonial officials, is to raise the Africans gradually and en masse. One of them told me: "We do not believe in encouraging Africans individually to reach great heights. They only become 'displaced persons' of no use to their own people or to us. These Africans are still children and we must adapt them to civilization very slowly. Otherwise they become gorged."

However, this gradual advancement of Africans is painfully slow. Of the 10,000,000-odd Africans in Angola and Mozambique, only about 3 per cent are literate.

The Belgians in the Congo also tried to stifle political foment among their African colonial subjects. Their policy attempted to buy off political frustration with economic blandishments, pension schemes, impressive social services and so forth.

This alternative is not available to the Portuguese. Their colonies are poor. Of course by its own standards Portugal has launched colonial development schemes in the past decade which are impressive and an advance on previous years. The colonial budgets have taken a sharp upward swing. Programs are on hand for improved railways, port facilities, communications, power and water supplies and irrigation systems. A flow of Portuguese settlers has gone to Angola and there has been a strike of oil there.

Yet all this must be viewed against the background of Portugal's own economy. Portugal is one of the poorest countries in Western Europe and perhaps the most backward. From Lisbon, Portuguese colonial development looks good and is beginning to pay off. Yet measured against progress in other African states and colonies, development in Angola and Mozambique still lags way behind.

Thus partly out of economic necessity, and partly out of Portuguese conviction that African advancement spells trouble, the Portuguese colonies remain the most underdeveloped in Africa.

Whenever this policy of conservative gradualism fails, and frustration rears its head nonetheless, it is beaten down with all the apparatus and paraphernalia of the Portuguese secret police with their midnight knocks and toughness and censorship and secret trials and political jailings and deportations. To make the point clear that they are standing for no independence movements or other freedom nonsense, the Portuguese in recent years have staged obtrusive military exercises and displays of napalm bombing by their air force in front of the largest African crowds they could assemble.

While nobody, black or white, is permitted to challenge Salazar rule, the Portuguese nevertheless argue that there are opportunities for Africans in the economic and social spheres. As justification they point to their *assimilado* system under which Africans who meet certain stringent requirements may graduate as "assimilated" Africans and claim equality before the law with Portuguese.

The system does indeed exist and there is a curious type of double talk about Portuguese African policies which appear on paper as a contradictory blend of liberalism and suppression.

The Portuguese are proud of the fact that there is no official color bar in their territories, for example. There is no particular stigma to miscegenation. The road to assimilation is open to the African.

Yet on the other hand the number of Africans who have actually become *assimilados* is negligible. The figure is probably not more than 60,000 out of the joint African population in Angola and Mozambique of around 10,000,000.

It may be nothing like as high as that. In the 1950 census

assimilados in Angola were listed as 30,039, and in Mozambique as only 4,353 and, although officials have tried to boost the latter figure since then, it is believed that the number of Africans newly assimilated is not great.

Meanwhile, if there is no official color bar there is a rigid culture bar which often seems to have the same effect. There is a clear-cut division between *indígenas,* who are Africans classified as uncivilized, and *nao-indígenas,* who are Portuguese, *assimilados* and mulattoes. The *nao-indígenas* are grouped on the upper, privileged side of the culture bar and the *indígenas* are relegated to the lower side. There are separate laws for each group and, clearly, the *nao-indígenas* get the plums. Many observers have difficulty in discovering where cultural inequality ends and racial equality begins.

It is the *indígenas* who supply the forced labor in Portuguese Africa. This is the most controversial of all aspects of Portuguese policy. Till a century ago, slavers operated on a massive scale along the coast of West and Central Africa. Millions of slaves were transported from the territories of Angola and the Congo to Brazil. Slavery is now outlawed and the slave ships no longer weigh anchor with their cargo loads of wailing Africans for foreign shores. Yet there is undisputable evidence that forced labor still exists in Portuguese Africa, where Africans are recruited in substantial numbers for compulsory work for both the government and private employers.

Thousands of Africans flee Portuguese territory rather than work under the conditions of contract, or forced, labor, and this illegal emigration is a serious drain on the population. Even Captain Galvao touched upon it in his report on Angola labor which was suppressed in 1947 by the Salazar regime.

Captain Galvao estimated that Angola, Mozambique and Portuguese Guinea had lost some 1,000,000 Africans in the previous ten years by clandestine emigration.

To cover labor shortages there had been recourse to reprehensible violence—"only the dead are really exempt from compulsory labor," Captain Galvao reported. He attacked employers for the "indifference to the physical and moral health of their laborers" and spoke of the surviving influence of "the exterminating spirit" still rooted in the last century. Some employers, charged Captain Galvao, had "lost" 35 per cent of their laborers but had never been prevented from obtaining fresh "supplies."

Meanwhile, between 80,000 and 100,000 Africans are siphoned away from Mozambique's labor force each year for employment in the Transvaal gold mines. These Mozambique Africans are the backbone of the South African mine labor and their recruitment for yearly contracts dates back to a deal under which Mozambique permitted the mines to take the labor in return for a guarantee by South Africa that it would direct a fixed percentage of revenue-earning rail traffic to the Mozambique port of Lourenço Marques rather than South African ports.

However Portugal may wriggle in the face of international criticism, and even pay lip service to certain international treaties concerning protection of labor, and draw up conditions for employment of Africans in its own colonies, there is evidence enough that many thousands of Africans are still forced laborers in the forcible employment either of the state or private companies. Government-licensed agents recruit the "contract" laborers and there are widespread allegations of abuse and cruelty to both women and child laborers as well as the men who are forced to work, despite all the paper work and legalities, which count for nothing when they are rounded up.

For contraventions of Portugal's unique code of colonial rule there are various punishments. Political infringements may send the unfortunate transgressor to exile on the island of São Tomé, or to desert regions within Angola itself. For lesser crimes, which need only be brought to the notice of a colonial administrator and not necessarily taken to court, there is the palmatoria. This looks like a wooden table tennis bat but in its surface are punched four or five holes. African offenders are struck sharply with it on their extended palms. The holes suck up their flesh into angry blisters. It is a punishment which by all accounts makes the African offenders scream with pain after the first four or five blows.

And so the Portuguese have pursued their rule over the years in these remote and rarely visited colonies. The pressure upon them is mounting in a world which is becoming increasingly interested in the last strongholds of colonialism, and less and less able to tolerate such practices as it scents in Angola and Mozambique. In and around the colonies themselves, opposition is clearly gaining strength.

Despite all of Portugal's colonial strategy, and all the isolation and backwardness of its colonies, the ideas and stimulus of a changing Africa have come seeping in among its colonial peoples.

The Portuguese are wide awake to the threat now. But there is no hint of official change or reform. The Portuguese answer has been to speed in the troops and planes to beat down trouble when it erupts. There is no suggestion of negotiation or concessions to head it off.

Can the Portuguese hold on? Or will their proud, poor empire dwindle as have their past glories? Stubborn Portuguese nationalism is face to face with frustrated African nationalism, perhaps aided by Portuguese dissidents and even the influence of foreign powers. This is an explosive situation and could bring Congo-like chaos to a country where Africans have similarly been withheld from political experience and administrative responsibility.

Portuguese seamen and navigators were the first to map out much of Africa and to gain a foothold on the continent and colonize a great portion of it. Now their countrymen have battened down the hatches and are determined to ride out the colonial storm they see approaching. For many observers, it is difficult to avoid the impression that they are heading for the heart of the hurricane.

CHAPTER XII

Land of Rhodes

DEEP IN THE tawny heart of Africa lies one of the world's great wonders.

You can hear the thunder seven miles away. You can see the towers of spray for twenty-five miles. They call it Mosi-oa-Tunya, the "Smoke That Thunders." It is Africa's fabulous Victoria Falls.

For miles above, the broad green Zambesi River heaves green and lazily. A sunbathing crocodile slinks silently into the water at your approach. A hippopotamus goes down with a complaining splutter of bubbles. A batch of bearded baboons, like wizened old gentlemen in a park, stop their morning gossip to watch you safely by. Africa is about its business.

But then at the brink of the falls, as though whipped by a monstrous mixer, the river becomes a churning, leaping avalanche of dazzling whiteness which thrusts out and down into a mile-wide gash across the red dust of Rhodesia at 75,000,000 gallons a minute.

It spills massively 350 feet, twice the height of Niagara, to the chasm's bottom. This is a fissure in the flat terrain. The gorge zigzags and widens, carrying off the frothing flow until miles lower the Zambesi regains its old pace.

Hundreds of gallons of water funnel back up the face of the gorge, however, in great banks of spray from the bottom to the brink and then higher again. In April the river level is fifty feet higher than in the hottest and driest month of November and then the spray sometimes obscures the view from the opposite bank altogether.

But when it does it provides an alternative spectacle. For the spray that falls again like heavy rain nourishes an Eden in the heart of the parched Rhodesian scrub. On the bank across from the falls is Africa's most famous rain forest, a rain forest made by spray.

There is lush tropical growth. There are great banks of blazing wild flowers. Creepers festoon the trees, which arch up and over into leafy rooftops on which the spray drums continually. The ground is soggy, the bushes dripping and you slosh through great pools in the path. Everything glistens. The falls roar constantly, and occasionally you get a glimpse of the thundering torrents through leafy openings.

Usual garb for a forest walk is a raincoat, hat and boots, but everyone gets drenched by the "rain" nonetheless.

It is more than a hundred years ago that David Livingstone crawled through the spray to the edge to discover the falls. There is a statue of him there, peering out from under his explorer's cap, and the nearest little town a few miles away is named Livingstone after him, as he named the falls after Queen Victoria.

But, although there is a good hotel near the falls, it is all relatively free of commercialism, and Africa is all around you. Once when we were strolling through Livingstone we saw a dead lion on a veranda. Hounded by drought and hunger it had stalked into the town and been shot.

The Zambesi itself is full of crocodiles and notices along the bank warn starkly: SWIMMING IS SUICIDAL. On the path from the hotel to the falls there is another sign: ALL WILD ANIMALS ARE DANGEROUS, and once when we were there an armed game warden urged us to go cautiously through the rain forest as a bad-tempered elephant was thrashing somewhere near by. Charter a little plane from the dirt airstrip near by and within a radius of half an hour's flying time you will see all the game you have dreamed of, with great herds of buck galloping in their hundreds from the sound and shadow of the aircraft, and elephants cutting wide destructive swaths through the forests.

Spray from the falls flings multicolored rainbows across the gorge by day and a striking spectacle is the lunar bow at night. However, this excursion through the forest in the African darkness is not one for those who fear things that go "Woomp!" in the night, for you may not be sharing the sight alone.

One early traveler, James Chapman, noting the spoor of rhino and elephants and buffalo on the edge of the gorge noted thus: "It makes one's hair stand on end to see the numerous indications of their midnight rambles on the very edge of eternity. Here they come at the dead, dark midnight hours to drink the spray and wallow in the mire; and on my asking a native how it was they were not afraid, he asked me in return: 'Didn't they grow up together?'"

. . .

More than two hundred miles down river from the Victoria Falls there is another, newer wonder. This is the great Kariba Dam. Here the Zambesi is once again convulsed, but this time by man, and sent frothing through hydroelectric turbines.

The dam is a massive arc of concrete, wedged into a narrow gorge through which the Zambesi roars on its long journey across Rhodesia and Mozambique to the Indian Ocean. Besides making electric power for Central Africa, the dam backs up the Zambesi into the biggest man-made lake in the world, 175 miles long, and in parts 40 miles wide. The lake has transformed the map of Rhodesia. It has given birth to a commercial fishing industry, among other things, and perhaps in time as it develops into a resort area, motorists may drive to Kariba, put their cars on a lake steamer and sail up the length of the lake to within reach of the Victoria Falls.

Before work started on the dam, Kariba was a desolate spot in one of the wildest parts of Africa. When the first engineers moved in there were no roads, no power, no living quarters, even no water fit for immediate drinking. There were wild animals on the site and, though these soon left, one curious hippo persistently paddled back upstream to constitute a sort of one-man sidewalk watcher's club.

When I first visited Kariba, the routine was to bounce down in a plane crammed with cargo on a dirt landing strip. That strip is 200 feet under the lake now, but even the new airfield has a lion's pug mark for a souvenir in the tar.

Some 10,000 men built the dam, 8,000 of them African laborers, and the rest men of many nationalities, but mainly Italians specializing in the concrete work. A consortium of British and French engineering firms supervised the construction in a climate soaring to 120 degrees. But as the wife of one of the leading French engineers, resident on the site, told me philosophically: "My 'usband, 'e does not notice the 'eat. 'e notices nothing. 'e is in love with that dam."

Of course, there were problems. There was the controversial removal of 50,000 Batonka tribesmen from their lands which were to be flooded by the new Kariba lake. Then during construction, the Zambesi hurled down floods which it had been estimated could come with such ferocity only once in every 10,000 years. When the lake began to fill, hundreds of wild animals were trapped on slowly submerging islands. Many were drowned but many more rescued in "Operation Noah," an operation conducted by game rangers who either trapped the animals, then freed them on shore or persuaded them to swim for it themselves.

But eventually the dam, one of the biggest projects the International Bank had ever helped finance, rose to its finished height of 420 feet, and a length along its crest of 1,900 feet. In its initial stage it cost $224,000,000 and when its capacity for hydroelectric generation is enlarged to its utmost the bill will top $316,000,000.

There it stands today, "the greatest piece of masonry in Africa since the days of the Pharaohs and the pyramids," as one reporter put it.

The Kariba scheme was part and parcel of the first flush of international enthusiasm for a big new nation in Central Africa born in 1953. This was the Federation of Rhodesia and Nyasaland which drew together three separate countries to make one new one, about a sixth the size of the United States.

From the beginning this enthusiasm was not shared by the African inhabitants of the territories, but there will be more of that later. Meanwhile, their fears were overridden by white arguments, mainly economic, in favor of federation.

The three countries involved were Northern Rhodesia and Southern Rhodesia, separated by the Zambesi River, and Nyasaland, dangling like an elephant's trunk from the eastern face of

Northern Rhodesia. They brought together an over-all population today numbering some 8,000,000 Africans and 300,000 whites. The Africans are spread about equally between the three countries, but 70 per cent of the whites are centered in Southern Rhodesia.

The principal argument for federation was that one strong nation in Central Africa would prosper much more swiftly than three separate, weak ones. Northern Rhodesia had rich copper mines and the revenue from these would complement the threadbare farming economy of Southern Rhodesia. Meanwhile, Nyasaland, with little development of its own, was a reservoir of black African labor for the two other territories. The needs and assets of the three interlocked neatly, went the argument, and united they would attract foreign investment and generate progress bringing benefits to both Africans and whites.

The countries thus meshed were very different in character.

Nyasaland and Northern Rhodesia were British "protectorates," territories protected by Britain in accordance with treaties signed by African chiefs. In practice they were governed by the British Colonial Office in London through British governors and officials on the spot.

Southern Rhodesia was a British colony, but one which had been self-governing, and thus under the control of its local white settlers, for years.

Of the three Nyasaland was, and still is, the most painfully underdeveloped. It is a charming but remote little land, strung for some five hundred miles along the side of Lake Nyasa, down which it seems Katherine Hepburn and Humphrey Bogart might come pounding any minute in the *African Queen.* Lake steamers are an obvious form of transport. There is only one little railway line running south across Mozambique to the port of Beira, and apart from a hundred miles of tar, all the roads are dirt.

Scots missionaries played a large part in opening up Nyasaland to outside ideas. Indeed it was the great David Livingstone himself who discovered Lake Nyasa in 1859 and summoned his fellow missionaries to work there.

But in terms of material wealth Nyasaland has not made great strides, although it is the most densely populated territory per acre of the three Federation countries. Federation has brought some development capital its way, but for all that the official capital of Zomba and the biggest town of Blantyre are sleepy little spots. Tea and tobacco are the principal exports, but they bring in little more than $20,000,000 a year between them. So thousands of Nyasas trek to the Rhodesias and the mines of South Africa for work, and one finds them all across southern Africa, gossiping of their families and friends back in their little lakeland home.

Northern Rhodesia is by contrast a broad, flat, open land stretching from the Zambesi up along common borders with Angola and the Congo to Tanganyika. Across this dusty nothingness runs the Great North Road which begins in Cape Town and ends at Nairobi. Or if you are particularly venturesome and have the equipment to cross the desert Sudan, you can grind right on to Cairo.

From an African hamlet with the delightful name of Kapiri M'Poshi the route shears off across the 500 miles of Northern Rhodesia to the Tanganyika border with never a garage or mechanic in sight.

Once when we stayed the night at a spot called Isoka we got a dramatic insight into the sheer physical hardship of existence in such out-of-the-way places. Isoka is one of those dots on the map which turns out to be a two-man village inhabited by a district officer and a veterinary official when you get there. Our shelter was one of the humble little rest houses provided by the government for travelers in a region where hotels are few and far between.

We unrolled our sleeping bags and ate our corned beef, which we had brought with us, by the light of candles stuck in bottles. Then, as is my custom, I cleaned my teeth under running water from the communal tap in the communal bathroom. In the middle of the operation I became conscious of the wizened little African caretaker, observing me sadly through the open door. Was there something he wanted? I asked. No, master, there was nothing really. It was just that, well, he hardly liked to mention it, but it would help if I could stop the water running and perhaps use a mugful to clean my teeth. For though the water ran so smoothly from an iron tank through the tap, this bent little man had personally to draw every drop of that water from a well near by and then transfer it by bucket to the tank.

However, it would be a mistake to think that Northern Rhodesia is poverty-stricken, for all its aridness and barrenness. If, instead of forking off at Kapiri M'Poshi to Tanganyika, you continue your journey northward you come to the Copperbelt and the source of Northern Rhodesia's considerable wealth.

Here is the string of mining towns such as Kitwe and Chingola and Mufulira, whose copper is the principal economic prop not only of Northern Rhodesia but of the whole Federation of three countries. These mining towns are just across the Congo border from the copper mines of Katanga, and in fact the copper is all part of the same deposit. Whereas the Katanga mines are opencast, however, and the copper is scooped out with ease, the Belgians drew the border, to the everlasting suspicion of many Rhodesians, just where the surface deposits end. As soon as it enters Rhodesia the seam dips sharply down under the surface and the Rhodesian mining companies have to go down deep for it.

As in the Congo, Northern Rhodesia's copper mines have been responsible for enormous slices of the country's revenue. Despite the deep-mining, the companies were producing $320,-000,000 worth of copper a year in the Federation's early days, thus providing 60 per cent of the Federation's exports by value, and 40 per cent of the Federation's total revenue by way of various taxes and royalties.

For the white miners, the inducement to live in this relatively remote part of Africa was fabulous in those days. Besides hefty salaries there was a copper bonus which often doubled a man's pay packet. The average wage for a white miner was more than $6,000 a year, when money was worth a lot more than it is today.

When I lived for a while in Rhodesia in 1957 the Copperbelt was roiled by a strike of "rockbreakers," the elite among white miners with key underground jobs. These men were at that time averaging between $800 and $1,100 a month in pay, depending on the quality of ground they were working and the amount of rock they broke. In a bleak month their salaries might drop to

$550, but in a good month they would soar to nearly $2,000 for one month's work. The strike revolved around their demand for a two-hour reduction in their forty-eight-hour working week.

The salary was not all, for there were many fringe benefits for all mine employees. Annual vacation time was liberal, and attractive houses were given many mineworkers at nominal rentals between $15 and $30 a month. There were golf courses and flying clubs and swimming pools and even a yacht club on an artificially made lake.

Visiting journalists wrote stories about white miners waiting for their wives outside the beauty parlors in sleek new Jaguars, and the stories were no exaggeration. If anything, the Jaguar was probably the family second car.

The key white miners numbered some 4,000 compared with about 40,000 African mineworkers employed for the tougher, lower-paid work in the copper mines. Inevitably the disparity between white salaries and African was tremendous. Usually the white average was about ten times higher than the African average. Nevertheless here as in the Congo, copper had brought prosperity to many thousands of these Africans, giving them much higher wages than other labor in the Rhodesias, with excellent housing and other amenities.

Of course all this was in the post-World War II heyday of copper. World prices were high, the copper market boomed and much of the prosperity was passed on in bonuses and special services to mineworkers both white and African.

Today the story is a different one. There is a glut of copper and prices are down. The copper bonuses for mineworkers have evaporated and so has the high old way of living. Copper is not quite the money spinner it once was for the Federation's treasury. Nevertheless copper mining remains the most important industry and the Federation's economy is keyed to it.

Two big companies run the mines. They are the Anglo-American Corporation and the Rhodesian Selection Trust. Despite its misleading name the former company is based in South Africa and there is little American capital in it. It is the latter one which holds most interest for Americans, for a majority of its shares are held by American Metal Climax, Inc.

Of the two companies, Anglo-American is sometimes, and perhaps unjustly, charged with being the more conservative, particularly in the sphere of race relations. It is said that Anglo-American must tread quietly lest it antagonize its key white workers in the mighty South African mines where its main interests lie. Anglo-American officials sometimes grumble privately, however, that Rhodesian Selection Trust only looks more progressive alongside their own company because of its excellent public relations setup. Be that as it may, RST, as it is generally called, does have a story of achievement to sell.

Its chief is an enlightened British industrialist, Sir Ronald Prain, who has pointedly called for reforms and faster African advancement on a number of occasions, including his annual reports to the RST group. Sir Ronald has apparently taken a long clear look at the situation in Northern Rhodesia and arrived at a conclusion which although inevitable nevertheless seems to have escaped most of the resident whites. This is that Northern Rhodesia in the not-too-distant future will be under African rule. It is difficult to see how it could be otherwise when Africans outnumber whites by more than thirty to one in the territory.

It is in this country that RST hopes to mine copper for many years to come. Under Sir Ronald's hand the company has gone out of its way to indicate its understanding of African ambitions.

RST has played an important role in the advancement of Africans into jobs previously the exclusive preserve of whites. It has made substantial grants for an educational program for African children in Northern Rhodesia. It has launched an agricultural research program for the country on the Kafue Flats which might make this area the "granary of Central Africa." With other projects and loans and subsidies, some of them in conjunction with Anglo-American and other big companies, it has set about proving its good citizenship of the country.

The third of the territories which make up the Federation is Southern Rhodesia. This, although the whites number only some 10 per cent of the over-all population, is clearly white settler country. Whites own half the land, most of it the best land, laid out as tobacco plantations or fenced off into big cattle ranches, and it is they who control the economy and the government.

Southern Rhodesia takes its name from Cecil John Rhodes, the Englishman who made his fortune in Africa, and sought to win so much of the continent for the British Empire. Rhodes formed the British South Africa Company, incorporated by royal charter, to exploit the Rhodesias as they are known today, but which at that time was a relatively unknown territory vaguely termed "Zambesia."

Rhodes's men, a column of armed Pioneers from South Africa, marched up to occupy the country and it is a striking commentary on the briefness of white settlement in the area that they did it little more than seventy years ago.

Although white traders and missionaries and prospectors had penetrated the country north of the Limpopo River earlier, white settlement dates from as recently as 1890 when Rhodes's men hoisted the British union jack on the spot where the capital of Salisbury now stands.

In the years since, the flow of settlers and of many ideas from the south has continued strongly. Most of the Copperbelt's white miners are South Africans, and there has been major settlement in Southern Rhodesia by white South Africans. Many of them, though perhaps now Rhodesian nationals, hold key posts. Even the Federation's new high commissioner to London in 1961, occupying the Federation's top diplomatic job, is a South African born and bred, a former member of the South African parliament, who lived most of his life in South Africa, settling in Southern Rhodesia only in the mid 1950's.

The earliest inhabitants of Southern Rhodesia are shrouded in mystery and are likely to remain so until archaeologists solve the puzzle of stone ruins set in an amphitheater of granite-domed hills near the town of Fort Victoria. This is the site of the Zimbabwe ruins, a fortified Acropolis and the remnants of a walled town built of stone with considerable skill. There are the outlines of what is thought to have been a temple, and the first white arrivals discovered gold ornaments and crucibles indicating the mystery men who lived there smelted gold.

Some romantics believe that Zimbabwe dates from Biblical times, was perhaps even the site of King Solomon's mines. A few years ago, scientists believed they had established the age of Zimbabwe when they discovered pieces of wood in a drain in the elliptical temple.

The wood went off to Chicago and London for examination and scientists, using Geiger counters to measure the radioactivity of the carbon content, calculated its age at between 1,200 and 1,300 years.

But the controversy still rages over whether Zimbabwe was actually built at that time. A South African timber expert, for example, advanced the view that the wood was from the tambootie tree which decays very slowly once cut. Upon felling, the tambootie tree releases an unpleasant caustic latex and, to avoid it, Africans who use the wood for building often select tambootie trees which have been dead for centuries rather than chop down new ones. Thus, goes the theory, the wood in question might have been used for building Zimbabwe much more recently than 1,200 years ago.

Sadly, the mystery of Zimbabwe has become a political issue now. For black Africans it is an attractive theory than an African civilization of considerable ability and sophistication existed here some centuries ago. Many whites dismiss the suggestion on grounds black Africans are incapable of having constructed anything so complex and skilled.

However, when Rhodes's column marched into what is now Southern Rhodesia, it was held by an African tribe, the Matabele. Like the white newcomers these tribesmen had also emigrated from South Africa, though about fifty years before. They were an offshoot of the Zulu tribe and had conquered and settled in their present lands, claiming suzerainty over a neighboring tribe, the Mashona.

Before the white pioneers marched in, Rhodes's emissaries had negotiated a treaty with the Matabele king, Lobengula, for mineral rights on his land.

For this enormous concession, Lobengula got a pension of $280 a month, 1,000 Martini-Henry rifles, and a promise, never fulfilled, of a river steamer for kingly cruising on the Zambesi. But from the beginning it seems evident that Rhodes envisaged conquest and settlement of the land by the Pioneers of his British South Africa Company.

Three years after they raised the British flag at Salisbury, the settlers crushed the Matabele by force of arms in the Matabele War, which some historians believe to be a shabby chapter in imperial history. One reason stated by the settlers for the war was their interest in protecting the Mashona from the Matabele. Yet in another three years both the Mashona and the Matabele rose in rebellion against the whites, were subdued and have remained subject to white rule since, first under the private rule of the British South Africa Company, and later in a British colony under local white government.

Rhodes himself negotiated the end of that rebellion with African chiefs at a remote spot in the Matopos Hills. It is not far from what is today the attractive city of Bulawayo. He chose to be buried there in the land to which he gave his name. His remains lie beneath a simple slab in the rock in this bare, grand, brooding place set in hills of granite.

During the early years of white settlement, Southern Rhodesia was a harsh, poor country with the air of the frontier about it. For long it could not afford tarred roads over its considerable distances. Thus the government laid two strips of tar, each about eighteen inches wide, along the dirt tracks. The technique for a motorist was to drive perched upon them until he met a car coming in the opposite direction. Then he swung off to leave two wheels on one strip of tar and two wheels in the dirt.

The other driver similarly swung off on his side, to leave two wheels on his strip of tar and two wheels in the dirt. The cars passed in a flurry of dust and afterwards you swung back onto the two strips. It was an exciting business, especially after the seasonal rains had washed away the dirt around the strips, leaving them several inches above ground level.

With Federation came boom time, however, and nowhere symbolized the boom better than Salisbury, previously capital of Southern Rhodesia and now chosen as the Federal capital as well.

Salisbury became the fastest-growing city in Africa. Tall new buildings climbed skyward and the city shuddered with the racket of the demolition men tearing down old buildings to make room for modern ones. Come back to Salisbury after an absence of six months during these busy days and old landmarks had gone in the meantime, business acquaintances moved to newer, bigger offices, and the city changed much of its face.

The streets were full of foreigners, Swiss financiers and Americans selling machinery, and Italian concrete specialists and German engineers, and Cockneys and Welshmen and other Britons swelling the new flood of immigrants.

Investors were confident, foreign countries set up missions with information services and agricultural attachés and all the regalia of international diplomacy. The new Federation seemed to be heading for a bright future and progress at least in the economic sphere which would bring material benefits to whites and Africans alike.

Yet in the last few years confidence and enthusiasm has ebbed. The investors are having second thoughts. The Federation seems a little shaky now.

All this stems from a political crisis which the Federation is undergoing and which may reshape its whole future. It may reshape it, moreover, back into the three separate countries from which it originally grew.

The Federation was an experiment and the experiment is in trouble. In the early stages, there were plans for a fine new Federal parliament to be built to imposing design on a hill outside Salisbury. It would have replaced the present small parliamentary chamber which the country's legislators use in the center of Salisbury. Perhaps ominously, nobody has bothered to pursue that plan. In a way this underlines that atmosphere of impermanence and uncertainty which pervades the Federation today.

CHAPTER XIII

Rhodesia-Nyasaland: State of Flux

WHEN BRITAIN launched the Federation of Rhodesia and Nyasaland in 1953, it intended it to become a sort of experimental space station between the world of black nationalism on the one hand and the world of white nationalism on the other.

To the north of the Federation lay the African states where all-black rule was looming. To the south lay South Africa with its dangerous policy of white supremacy.

Britain hoped the Federation could orbit in a middle course between these two extremities. Racial partnership was the ideal, under which whites and nonwhites would live in amity and equality.

It was an exciting and challenging project. But now after all, it looks to many observers as though Britain was shooting for the moon. Unless there is a dramatic change in direction, the Federation seems way off course.

In all the initial eagerness to get Federation under way, and the enthusiasm for economic advantages stemming from fusion, "partnership" was left as a slogan and never properly defined.

To some observers at the time it seemed to mean ultimately, if not right away, an equal say for whites and Africans in government, and free mixing of the races at all levels from politics and business to social life. Over the years, mutual trust and confidence would grow and eventually there would be fear of racial discrimination neither against the black majority nor the white minority.

To many it seemed that Britain could hardly settle for less

with honor, for it was committing two overwhelmingly African states, Northern Rhodesia and Nyasaland, to the Federation, while still charged with the responsibility of "protecting" their African peoples.

Africans in Nyasaland and Northern Rhodesia never shared this optimistic view of partnership, however. They were suspicious from the beginning. Before the Federation became fact, they opposed it steadfastly. After its creation, their opposition smoldered on.

Why should this be when, as one American diplomat put it, the economic argument for Federation is "unassailable"? Africans are not unaware of economic considerations. In other circumstances, even the Africans of Nyasaland and Northern Rhodesia are not particularly opposed to the idea of a federation to strengthen their economies. They might yet enter a new East African federation which is planned under African rule. But this would be an *African* federation. Their stubborn opposition to the present Rhodesian Federation stems from the fact that it is federation under *white* rule.

In African eyes, partnership is a deceptive slogan, covering up the fact of continued white domination in the Federation.

To the Africans of Nyasaland and Northern Rhodesia in particular, federation seems to have been a setback. They argue that had they not been linked to Southern Rhodesia with all its white pressures, Nyasaland and Northern Rhodesia would by now have been self-governing states under African rule and well on the way to independence. Instead, they are confronted by white settler rule of the Federation, which to them has all the overtones of white supremacy in South Africa which the Federation was supposed to sidestep.

In some eight years under federation, many Africans say they have seen nothing which lessens their suspicions that the whites plan to rule forever. They dismiss as insignificant and unimpressive the record of African advancement under federation.

Justified or not, it is this African suspicion and opposition which looms as the Federation's principal stumbling block. Without African cooperation it is difficult to see how the Federation can survive, unless it be held together by the bayonet and machine gun. Neither Britain nor the rest of the world seem likely to tolerate that sort of federation in these days of Afro-Asian ascendancy.

The Federation's whites, meanwhile, maintain that government of the Federation must be retained in "civilized hands," and that for the foreseeable future these will be white hands. While Africans say the pace of African political advance is ludicrously slow, most white say it is hair-raisingly fast.

Bogey on the scene, in white-settler eyes, is the British government. The settlers object to Britain's continuing responsibility for Northern Rhodesia and Nyasaland and British insistence on political advancement for Africans in these territories. The settlers would like "rule from London, thousands of miles away," ended. They want to see the Federation a sovereign independent nation, within the Commonwealth, but with complete control centered in the federal capital of Salisbury and no interference from London.

There is provision for such independence. From the beginning it was intended that the Federation would eventually take its place as a grand new Central African member of the Commonwealth of independent states.

But independence at this stage would mean white government from Salisbury. That is not the racial partnership that Britain had in mind. It would mean the abandonment to white rule of the 5,000,000 Africans in Nyasaland and Northern Rhodesia whom Britain is charged with "protecting." The Africans themselves never tire of reminding Britain of these obligations. Thus Britain has postponed negotiations on independence.

Until they can convince both the Africans and the British government of a genuine movement toward racial partnership, the whites of Rhodesia are stymied in their efforts to make the Federation independent. That is, of course, unless they abandon constitutional methods and declare the Federation independent in a sort of Central African Boston Tea Party.

·   ·   ·

Has "partnership" been a failure? Some people, like Mr. R. S. Garfield Todd, the white prime minister of Southern Rhodesia who was dismissed by his white electorate for his liberalism, say it has not failed; it has just not been pursued.

Many other whites, on the other hand, point to various breaches of the color bar and progressive steps which they say are moving the Federation along the road to partnership.

Some whites admit the obvious: that Southern Rhodesia's race laws have in the past been patterned after many of those in South Africa. Salisbury has for long had just as rigid a color bar as South Africa's Johannesburg. But, say these whites, the Federation is moving steadily away from racial discrimination, while South Africa is driving more and more into the morass of white supremacy.

In fact, there are important differences between the Federation and South Africa. You can sense the change of atmosphere as you cross the border between the two countries. In the Federation Africans are eligible to vote and in the Federal parliament there are a number of black faces among the white ones. There are even some African junior cabinet ministers. This is a striking contrast to the all-white parliament of South Africa.

Meanwhile, there is on a hill overlooking Salisbury an excellent university college where students of all races are learning to live and work and play together.

The police forces in each of the Federation's three territories are of much higher caliber than the police force in South Africa. They are smarter and more responsible. Thus, while there are undoubtedly exceptions, these young Rhodesian policemen, many of them recruited from Britain, do not seem impregnated with that same senseless brutality toward the African which so often characterizes the relations between police and African public in South Africa.

There are other progressive actions and factors one might cite. The color bar has disappeared in some spheres. It has been removed in restaurants and hotel lounges and movie houses in Northern Rhodesia. Nonwhites have moved into jobs previously reserved for whites on the Rhodesian state railways. The Southern Rhodesia government service has been opened to nonwhites who were previously barred.

These are a few random instances of progress. There are other hopeful signs such as the campaign launched by ten Salisbury women for interracial courtesy. Within a short while, the original ten had been joined by 36,000 signed-up campaigners both white and nonwhite to "spread the gospel of courtesy" throughout the Federation.

Yet there are serious debits too.

For example, although the Federal parliament has a thin black line of African members, the parliament of Southern Rhodesia has remained pure white until recently when plans were announced which would give a little less than a quarter of its seats to Africans.

In Southern Rhodesia too the government has taken sweeping internal security powers, banned African political movements and jailed Africans for lengthy periods without trial. One new bill to enlarge police powers of law enforcement was so repressive that it caused the resignation of the Federation's white Chief Justice, Sir Robert Tredgold, who termed it variously "savage," "harshly unjust," "mean" and "evil."

Viewing the barricades of privilege and segregation behind which most whites entrench themselves, Herbert Chitepo, an African lawyer in Salisbury, was prompted to remark bitterly that whites expected to live in Africa "just as though they were in Chelsea or Golder's Green," or some other London suburb. Numbers of Africans have commented that it is strange that white people should come to live in Africa if they do not like Africans, and cannot bear to rub shoulders with them now and again.

It is in the political sphere that Africans see the gravest indictments of partnership as it is interpreted by local whites. In both the Federal and Southern Rhodesian governments, controlled by whites, the voting system is such that Africans are barred from a decisive influence.

The Federation has adopted the dual-roll system of enfranchisement. One roll is for the minority of voters with high qualifications. They elect the majority of members in parliament. The second roll is for the majority of voters with lower qualifications. They elect a minority of members.

The white argument is that this gives Africans on the lower roll vital experience in electoral procedure, while retaining government in the hands of civilized men. In practice it means government is retained in the hands of white men. They dominate the upper roll while Africans are relegated to the lower. It is another of those instances calculated to erode any slight confidence which Africans might have had in partnership. For, in their eyes, this is a very one-sided partnership.

However, perhaps the most disturbing pointer for Africans to white resistance to change came with the toppling of Southern Rhodesian Prime Minister Garfield Todd in 1958. Mr. Todd, a New Zealander by birth, had come to Southern Rhodesia in his twenties as a missionary. For more than a decade he and his wife lived as the only whites among 10,000 Africans. Eventually he came to politics and graduated to the premiership.

Mr. Todd had a passionate belief in the upliftment of Africans by schooling. He had ambitious plans for education in Southern Rhodesia. And as he talked, ably and with enthusiasm, a tall, handsome man with graying hair, it seemed that he had glimpsed the grand horizon of true partnership to which Britain had perhaps looked at the Federation's inception.

When I interviewed him at the end of 1956, Mr. Todd spoke of all his ideas. "The African is advancing tremendously fast," he told me. "Give us another five years and you will not recognize the country."

But Mr. Todd had overlooked the reaction of the white electorate upon which his own political position depended. He did not have five years. In a year he was toppled from office by a revolt in his party. He was going too far too fast on African advancement. Soon after, he and the remnants of his party which had survived the upheaval were obliterated from the political scene by the ballot of white voters in a general election.

Mr. Todd was succeeded as premier by Sir Edgar Whitehead, the Federation's diplomatic representative in Washington. Sir Edgar returned from the United States to Salisbury still marveling over an interview he had had with Mr. John Foster Dulles, then American secretary of state. During the interview, said Sir Edgar, Mr. Dulles had made it obvious in various ways that he did not have the slightest idea where the Federation of Rhodesia and Nyasaland really was situated.

However, the real settler leader in the Federation is not Sir Edgar, but the Federal prime minister, Sir Roy Welensky. Sir Roy is the chief at the over-all federal level of the same United Federal party which Sir Edgar leads at the Southern Rhodesian level.

Sir Roy is the thirteenth child of a Jewish father and an Afrikaner (white South African) mother and in a way he resembles one of the old-time bosses of American backroom politics.

From a desperately poor background, and with the opportunity for little formal schooling, he came up from engine driver and trade union leader, winning the heavyweight boxing championship of Southern Rhodesia on the side, to politics and eventually the Federal premiership.

He is a bulky, ruddy, tufty-browed man who would fit delightfully, one might imagine, into the crimson Father Christmas suit which he used to don at children's parties in his parliamentary constituency at the mining town of Broken Hill in Northern Rhodesia.

Sir Roy succeeded the Federation's first prime minister, Sir Godfrey Huggins, now Lord Malvern, and the contrast was a striking one. Where Huggins was precise and clipped, Welensky is an informal, spade-is-a-spade man. The story goes that at the press conference where Huggins made his farewells, and Welensky his first appearance in his new office, Huggins answered questions impersonally and formally, then made a dignified exit. When Welensky entered soon after, he slung his jacket over the back of his chair to expose a pair of sturdy braces. Then to the pressman who posed the first question, he replied: "Well, Fred . . ."

Sir Roy's problem in politics is that he is confined within the strait jacket of an all-white political party system. On paper he is prime minister of a multiracial federation of 8,000,000 Africans and 300,000 whites. But in practice it is upon the white electorate that he and his party depend, for the African vote is negligible. Thus Sir Roy has his eye constantly on that white ballot box and on the tactics of the opposition Dominion party, a fairly blatantly white-supremacy party.

Sir Roy argues that he dare not go faster than the white electorate in race relations, else he will suffer the same fate as Mr. Todd. The Dominion party is just waiting, he says, to pounce if his own United Federal party acquires a liberal look.

Some observers of the Rhodesian scene believe that burly Sir Roy more than anybody had the best chance of breaking out of that political strait jacket.

Garfield Todd, with his missionary background, was suspect by the white electorate of being too pro-African, although ironically there were many Africans for whom even Mr. Todd's brand of "liberalism" was far from satisfactory.

Sir Roy, however, is a man of the people—or at least the white people, whose votes are vital. On the basis of his speeches and actions it would be difficult to smear him with the brush of liberalism. He alone among white Rhodesian leaders might have had the stature and popularity to swing the white electorate around to more urgent concessions on African advancement and yet keep his political head.

These concessions might have done much to reduce African suspicion of the Federation, and with his bluff good nature and a trade unionist's understanding of the workers' ambitions, Welensky might have swung important segments of African opinion behind a visible policy of partnership.

Instead, Sir Roy, in many eyes, has preached paternalism. He has seemed to ally himself with the "bread-in-their-bellies" school which holds that economic upliftment is the African's principal concern and that politics will sort themselves out somehow afterwards.

As we know, the dividends of paternalism preached by the Belgians in the Congo were tragic. However, it would be unfair and grossly inaccurate to say that Africans in the Federation have been kept as aloof from political experience as the Congolese. Indeed, Sir Roy would argue that the Federation's policy is to give Africans political experience, albeit in small, slow doses, which the Belgians withheld from the Congolese. The question in the Federation is whether these doses are satisfying Africans, and, if they are not, what happens next?

Now, however, Sir Roy's opportunity for a bold lead on partnership has been diminished, perhaps even overtaken altogether, by the explosion of the Congo.

The Congo is the Federation's next-door neighbor. White Rhodesians have seen white Belgian refugees flooding across their border. They have read, in the stories splashed across Rhodesian newspapers, stories of Congolese atrocities against whites. All this has revived their worst fears. They are apparently in truculent and defensive mood, with little enthusiasm for racial experimentation. Sir Roy stands squarely at their head.

. . .

If the Federation has failed to reach the optimistic heights of partnership first envisaged for it, there nevertheless have been concessions, and steps which though cautious must be chalked up as progress against, say, the background of race relations in South Africa.

Perhaps if these had come in the first days of Federation they might have won African support, or at least persuaded some Africans to give federation a chance. But by African standards they have come too small and too late. They have not eliminated either African suspicions or large-scale opposition to the Federation.

However mistaken and misguided this African opposition may be in white eyes, it is there. It is difficult to see how the Federation can become a success while a substantial proportion of the Africans who make up 96 per cent of its population are opposed to its existence.

Who then are the African leaders who perhaps hold the fate of the Federation in their hands?

Foremost in his opposition to Federation is the Nyasaland leader, Dr. Hastings Kamuzu Banda. Dr. Banda is a fiery little man whose rise to leadership of his people has been a unique one, for it took place almost entirely during his absence of more than thirty years from his people and his homeland.

As a boy he left Nyasaland to work on the mines of South Africa as a clerk and interpreter. He saved his money and with much effort finally arrived in the United States. He studied in Ohio and eventually packed his bags once again for Britain, where he ended his twelve long years of work for a medical degree at Edinburgh University.

Thereafter he practiced medicine for many years in a suburb of London, catering mainly to working-class whites, but opening his home to a stream of young African nationalists from Central Africa. Finally he worked for a few years as a doctor in Ghana. Fired by Ghana's example in achieving independence, he returned to Nyasaland in 1958 to be received with near-hysteria by the African thousands and exalted as a messiah come to free them from both colonial rule and ties with the Federation.

In the months thereafter Dr. Banda stamped across Nyasaland with a sputter of tough talk. "To hell with federation!" he cried time and again. And then: "No moderate has ever achieved anything. It takes extremists like Cromwell and Mrs. Pankhurst to gain democracy." Many observers believe Dr. Banda adopted extremism in his oratory as a conscious and important part of his tactics. He showed a preoccupation with imprisonment. "Let us fill the white man's prisons with our millions singing hallelujah," he roared at the enthusiastic crowds.

On several occasions he expressed his own readiness for imprisonment "whether it be a cell in the Seychelles [where Archbishop Makarios of Cyprus was imprisoned] or on St. Helena [where Napoleon was exiled]." To many it seemed he courted jail as had martyrs like Nehru and Nkrumah before him in the belief it would consolidate his already tremendous following.

If this was so he got his wish, for, in an eruption of violence throughout Nyasaland early in 1959, Dr. Banda was arrested and thereafter spent more than a year in prison in Southern Rhodesia while his country labored through a state of emergency.

Inevitably Dr. Banda emerged eventually in an unassailable political position to lead the Malawi Congress Party which had superseded his African National Congress banned during the upheaval. Just as inevitably, he concluded negotiations with the British government thereafter which set Nyasaland on the road to African self-government.

Dr. Banda has not, however, dropped his opposition to federation. He has announced his determination to take Nyasaland out of its present association with white-controlled Southern Rhodesia, despite the economic disadvantages of such a step. Of late, he has talked of Nyasaland's entry into a new, African-run federation of East African states, perhaps with Northern Rhodesia joining as well.

Although there were rumbles from the Welensky government in Salisbury, Britain's new deal giving Africans control of the Nyasaland legislature went unchallenged, for with only 9,000 white residents in the territory compared with more than 2,750,000 Africans, African rule was clearly inevitable.

Even in Southern Rhodesia plans have been announced for constitutional reforms giving Africans some fifteen seats in a legislature of sixty-five members, the rest of them white. This may still seem slender African representation to outsiders for a country where Africans outnumber whites more than twelve to one. But it is a considerable advance over the previous system, which saw not a single black face in the Southern Rhodesian parliament. As an interim measure it was perhaps all that Southern Rhodesia's principal African leader, a burly ex-auctioneer named Joshua Nkomo, could hope for. He leads the National Democratic Party and, although it too campaigns for one man, one vote, Southern Rhodesia has a settled white population of size, and the African party is not in the same strong position as nationalist organizations in the primarily African territories of Nyasaland and Northern Rhodesia.

Minor reforms in Southern Rhodesia and major ones in Nyasaland were changes the Welensky government could stomach. The Southern Rhodesian ones placed the white man in no political peril, and, although black rule loomed in Nyasaland, it could hardly be avoided in a country of 2,750,000 Africans and only 9,000 whites.

But when the British government proposed constitutional reforms for Northern Rhodesia in 1961, Sir Roy exploded. This was his own old political hunting ground, where he had worked as a trade unionist and sat in the local legislature. It was the site of the copper mines so vital to the Federal economy. African government seemed unthinkable to Sir Roy in Northern Rhodesia.

In fact these plans seemed nothing particularly startling. They envisaged a complex voting system which might, or might not, give Africans a majority in the territory's legislature. The two African nationalist leaders from the country, Mr. Harry Nkumbula of the African National Congress and Mr. Kenneth Kaunda of the United National Independence Party, rejected the system as not going far enough. Sir Roy rejected it as going much too far.

He reacted in a flurry of crisis measures. He summoned the Federal parliament in emergency session, called up white territorial troops, imposed currency control to stop panic capital leaving the territory. He made defiant speeches, antagonized the British government which maintained that government in Northern Rhodesia was Britain's own affair, and breathed hardly veiled warnings that the Federation might be compelled to do a Boston Tea Party if Britain did not heed his views and go slower in Northern Rhodesia. It was all good stuff for the white electorate, of course, which rallied behind with roars of approval for this fighting talk.

Time and again, white Rhodesians talk of the follies of rule from London, thousands of miles away. "We on the spot are the people who know how to handle Africans, who have to live with them, who can best gauge the trend," they say. "What do British officials know of the problem?" The British viewpoint, however, is that the white Rhodesians are the last people able to assess the problem objectively, for they are an interested party, and the one which appears to want to withhold power from Africans and retain it in white hands.

At the time of writing it was not clear how this tussle between the white Federal government and Britain would end. However, one white liberal leader in Northern Rhodesia, Sir John Moffat, claimed that whatever happened, Sir Roy had now "completely dished Federation."

However well his defiant stand on continued white rule went down with the white voters, it served only to entrench the suspicions of Sir Roy's intentions which had lingered all along in the minds of Africans.

Of the two Northern Rhodesian nationalist leaders, it is Mr. Kaunda who will likely prove the more defiant, for all his belief in Indian-style nonviolence. His party is a breakaway movement from Mr. Nkumbula's, pursuing a much more vigorous and determined line. The son of an African teacher and priest, Mr. Kaunda himself became a teacher but graduated to politics. He has been jailed twice for his political activities and has been thrust to the top of the African nationalist movement in Northern Rhodesia on grounds Mr. Nkumbula, whom he formerly supported, has become too "soft."

The best story about him concerns the day when he was cycling through the bush and came face to face with a full-grown African lion. He lifted his bicycle above his head and stood stock-still, ready to throw the machine at the beast if it charged. The lion slunk away.

Thus, although he is gentle in speech and sincere in his dedication to nonviolence, he is a man whose determination and courage it would be a mistake to underestimate. Many people believe Kenneth Kaunda is destined to become one of Africa's outstanding leaders. One of his main problems has been to restrain a fringe of stone-throwing toughs which has attached itself to his big organization and which could hamper the peaceful course he has set for his party.

There are three possible routes ahead of the Federation.

It can continue as presently constituted in a federation. But if it is to achieve peace as a successful, independent nation, the present great wall of African suspicion of the white Rhodesian settlers must be removed. That will call for radical effort on the part of the whites.

Or the Federation might hang together, but in a looser union. The three member territories would become virtually independent states, but voluntarily elect to retain certain economic and other ties with each other.

Or the Federation may disintegrate. The future of the two northern territories of Northern Rhodesia and Nyasaland in that event would be as independent African states on the Ghana pattern. It might be, however, that they would forge a link with each other, or enter a new federation with other African lands.

The future of Southern Rhodesia would be more complex. It is a country in little shape to stand alone. This indeed was the reason for its entry into the present Federation. The only logical quarter to which Southern Rhodesia could look would be South Africa.

In the past, white Rhodesians have vigorously protested the suggestion they might fuse their country with South Africa. They have argued that they could never accept South Africa's race policies and that Southern Rhodesia's are too enlightened for the two countries to find common ground on this key issue.

Yet, in the event of the Federation's breakup, South Africa and Southern Rhodesia would stand alone at Africa's southern tip, confronted by the black millions to the north. It is not inconceivable that they might find mutual advantage in some form of association.

On their part, white Rhodesians probably would require some safeguard against being swallowed up by the more powerful Afrikaner government of South Africa. This is especially so now that South Africa has been excluded from the British Commonwealth, for, although many white Rhodesians criticize Britain on political grounds, many of them are of British descent and still have emotional ties with their British motherland.

On the other hand South Africa's present government, in considering any possible association with Southern Rhodesia, would need some assurance that these white Rhodesians of British stock would not undermine its own political strength, perhaps adding their votes to those of the existing opposition and tipping the scales against the government.

Thus there may be political changes, as well as geographical ones, like the appearance of Lake Kariba, for the mapmakers of the future to record in Central Africa.

SOUTH AFRICA

CHAPTER XIV

South Africa: At the Rainbow's End

AT THE SOUTHERN END of Africa there lies the loveliest, yet the most tragic, land in all the continent.

This is the Republic of South Africa, a country of stunning beauty and enormous wealth but a land which, as is sometimes the case with rich young heiresses, seems to have everything but happiness.

South Africa is bedeviled with a complex problem of political racialism which hangs over it like a mushroom cloud of political fallout. Particularly since the present government assumed power in 1948, this has set faction against faction and made a mockery of national peace and unity with which this nation might go so far.

Were it not for this racial question, South Africa would be the pot of gold at the African rainbow's end.

Gold is the foundation on which it is built. The bulk of the world's gold comes from mines deep beneath South Africa's Witwatersrand, the "Ridge of White Waters," and the new gold fields of the Orange Free State.

This is big business, no job any more for the old-time prospector trudging out over the horizon with his pack horse and clobber. Backed by overseas capital, mainly British, the mining industry is controlled by seven huge business houses which stretch out their tentacles like financial octopi into more than fifty major gold mines. Operating costs are high, but so are profits. It costs $30,-000,000 to establish a new mine. The shaft alone costs between

157

$400 and $500 a foot to sink. But this is the sort of outlay which nets the industry $600,000,000 worth of gold a year and a profit of $150,000,000.

South Africa's economy is keyed to gold but this is not the end of the wealth. Next come diamonds.

Over the years, South African mines have spilled forth a glamorous glitter of gems. The diamond in that engagement ring in Decatur, Alabama, or Wellesley, Massachusetts, may very probably have come from a South African mine. Kimberley was the center of the rip-roaring diamond rush in the old days, but the biggest diamond in the world, the Cullinan, came from Premier Mine, near Pretoria. A company official scuffed it up while strolling through the deserted workings of the mine after the day's work was done. It was as big as a hen's egg and so priceless that the Dutch craftsman chosen to cut it after months of study fainted with his first stroke. Now its various segments sparkle among the British crown jewels.

South African gems enhance the majesty of foreign kings and queens, but the king of diamonds is a shy, brilliant South African Jew named Harry Oppenheimer. One of the richest men in the world, he presides over a vast interlocking empire of diamond, gold and other mines inherited from his father, Sir Ernest Oppenheimer, who died in 1957. The Oppenheimer empire is literally worth many hundreds of millions of dollars. Its annual wage bill runs to more than $100,000,000. By a series of pacts and contracts and deals, the Oppenheimers have canalized the world's flow of diamonds through a central selling organization which Mr. Oppenheimer is able to dominate from his office in the financial district of Johannesburg.

But gold and diamonds are still not the end of the story. South Africa is a major producer of uranium ore, calculated to net $980,000,000 by the time present sales contracts with the United States and Britain expire in 1970.

There is still a long list of other minerals which make South Africa a sort of geological Aladdin's Cave. Altogether, minerals bring in more than $1,000,000,000 a year.

All this is the catalyst for an industrial revolution which has made South Africa the wealthiest and most economically developed nation in Africa.

.   .   .

With all this there goes a delectable, sunny climate. Then there is striking scenery, from the endlessness of the dusty veld with a strange, scrawny beauty all its own, to the cool pines, and the soft blue mountains which come tumbling down to white sandy beaches and the two oceans, Atlantic and Indian, by which South Africa is washed.

This is an open-air country of big distances and many contrasts. It is a thousand miles between the two principal cities of Johannesburg and Cape Town.

Natal is the smallest of South Africa's four provinces and the playground for holiday-makers. Its beaches are fine and its warm coastline is strung with little holiday resorts either side of the province's principal city and port, Durban. Durban is a vivid place, colorful with graceful Indian women in gorgeous saris and a cheerful band of extrovert African ricksha-pullers in fabulous bead robes and headdresses made of feathers (symbolizing speed) and animal horns (for strength).

This is a pleasant city of trailing palms and big, pastel-painted beachfront hotels, and garishly garbed tourists. The air is scented with subtropical blooms and there is a breath of Florida about it all.

Yet hardly a hundred miles away in the Natal midlands are the rolling green meadowlands which remind one of Virginia.

Probe further inland, across the tawny high veld of the Transvaal province and there is Johannesburg, biggest city in the country. Johannesburg is not a little New York, as South Africans sometimes claim, but it is a city of more than a million people and it does have a sense of stimulus, and the thump and bustle of an American city about life in the concrete canyons between its sawn-off skyscrapers.

This is a city built on gold and sensitive to every flicker of the ticker tape from the stock exchange where fortunes are lost and won in gold share dealing. Gold is the reason for Johannesburg's existence. Seventy years ago this was a roisterous mining camp flung up to house the Britons and Australians and Americans and adventurers from all parts of the world who had come to hunt newly discovered gold.

Today the ground deep beneath Johannesburg's main thoroughfares is crisscrossed with the shafts and tunnels of the big mines. Blocks of offices and apartment buildings rise alongside the mine headgears, and the city is ringed with mountains of yellow slime. This is the residue from mining, for, sad to relate, and to the eternal disappointment of visitors, South African gold does not come in the handy nugget size. To get an ounce of gold the size of a pea, the mines must raise and process five tons of rock and gold-bearing ore. The slime is left over after a complex chemical process for the extraction of the gold.

Although they are highly organized, the gold mines still depend for their success and profits on cheap African labor in enormous quantities. About 300,000 African laborers work in the mines. The companies are unable to recruit more than a minority of this number from South Africa itself, so the bulk are recruited in other African territories by agents of the mines established there. Often they are flown into Johannesburg in the mines' own fleet of aircraft.

It is all rather like the army for them. Often straight from simple village life, they are marched goggle-eyed through the neon-bathed streets of Johannesburg to the mines. There they live in barracks, far from their families, while they work out their contracts lasting usually up to 18 months. African miners earn about 40 or 50 American cents per 8-hour underground shift, or something less than $200 a year. White mine officials blanch when one inquires whether trade unionism may not one day raise its head among these docile workers.

On the new gold fields of the Orange Free State there are indications of an attempt to provide better living conditions than exist at the older mines of the Witwatersrand.

Some companies like Mr. Oppenheimer's big Anglo-American Corporation are interested in bringing mine workers' families to live permanently with them near the mines. The companies recognize that a settled labor force is a more efficient one than constantly changing migrant labor. To this end, the Anglo-American group experimented with low-cost housing for their workers. According to company spokesmen, the government has stepped in. In terms of its race segregation policy it has ruled that no more than 3 per cent of the total labor force may settle their families on the mines. This has effectively scuttled the scheme.

One place the African mine workers can let off steam during their contract periods is at the Sunday morning mine "dances." There are men from more than fifty different tribes working on the mines, each with their own tribal dances. Every mine has a dancing arena and on Sundays both white visitors and watching African mine workers gather for the show.

The dances are various. The drums throb and then there come the Shangaans from East Africa and the Mundawo and the Bachopi from the banks of the Limpopo River and all the others. There is one team of bell dancers. They wear tiny bells on their ankles and more on a sort of children's harness arrangement strapped across their chests and they make the whole thing jingle continuously with a series of rippling muscular movements.

But intruding more and more into the weekly ritual are the novelty dancers. There is the team in Western outfits and ten-gallon hats and the boot-slappers, a beautifully synchronized group performing a complicated dance punctuated with many different slaps on their high rubber boots. This is fascinating to watch but a complete prostitution of real African dancing and another reminder that tribalism is on the wane.

And one cannot help suspecting, as one comes away, that it is all getting to be a bit like one of those splendid, ruddy, puffing groups in Europe which dress up in peasant clothes and set about preserving the country dance, or some such other relic from a fast-disappearing age.

Johannesburg is usually the departure point for the Kruger National Park, 200 miles to the east, whose famous wild animals stare out at you from the travel ads in the *New Yorker* and *Holiday* magazines. This is really a slice of raw Africa 200 miles long and 60 miles wide preserved for animals and decreed untouchable in a rapidly industrializing country. The animals are wild and live by the law of the bush. No firearms are allowed but the visitor is safe with observance of two simple rules: Do not leave your car, and stay in one of the park's simple little hutted camps between dusk and dawn.

A tourist who breaks the rules and steps out of his car to photograph lions or elephants in the distance sometimes gets a shock when his films return later from processing. There in the picture, camouflaged in grass six or seven feet way from the photographer, is a peering lion which the tourist never saw at the time.

Some people call the Kruger Park the zoo without bars, but it is really a zoo in reverse, for here the people must stay caged in their cars while the animals run free. Sometimes on a dull Sunday afternoon the lions pad down to one of the dusty tracks to watch the people.

.　.　.

Meanwhile, although Johannesburg is the hub of finance and South Africa's biggest city, it is not the capital. This is Pretoria, a drowsy little town thirty-odd miles away where the jacaranda trees once a year drop a carpet of soft mauve petals over sidewalks and streets.

Pretoria has had many a rendezvous with history. During the Boer War a young and rambunctious British war correspondent by name of Winston Churchill was held prisoner here for a while after his capture by the Boers.

Paul Kruger, president of the old Transvaal Republic, had his capital here and his home still stands. Now government business is conducted in a building of crescent-shaped magnificence set above a tumbling green waterfall of lawns.

South Africa like any other country has its idiosyncracies. Thus, while Pretoria is the administrative capital, Cape Town is the legislative capital where parliamentarians sit for about six months each year. Every six months, government officials and cabinet ministers and members of parliament pack themselves with all their families and luggage and files and documents into what is irreverently dubbed the Zoo Train, and go trundling off the thousand miles between the twin capitals.

On their way from the Transvaal to the Cape province they pass Bloemfontein in the Orange Free State. This, to confuse things a little further, is the seat of the Appeal Court, and thus the judicial capital.

The route from Pretoria and Johannesburg to Cape Town sears straight and monotonous across the Karoo, a desolate, desertlike waste where the whole year's rainfall may drop in a shower of a few minutes. Fall into a Karoo river, says an old South African story with appropriately dry humor, and you can get right up and dust yourself down. There will not be any water in it.

There is a touch of the early American West about the Karoo. There are rickety little hamlets, dust-laden and baking, their corrugated iron roofs glinting in the sun. In some there is a railway station, with never a train in sight, and there are the slowly twirling blades of the aluminum wind pumps, sucking water from a hidden well, and perhaps the put-put-put in the background of an electricity generator.

Sometimes if you half-close your eyes you can almost imagine Roy Rogers or some other cowboy hero swaggering through a pair of swing doors and galloping grandly away on a horse called Trigger or Silver to warn the mail coach in Dead Man's Gulch. But when you open your eyes, there is just the latest Buick or Ford in front of you, giving you a chromium grin, and waiting for one of the wool farmers who have made substantial fortunes out of their rugged Karoo sheep, despite the barrenness of the region.

For many of these farmers the Karoo has its own desolate grandeur. Though many of them are well able to afford to, they will never leave it. Indeed there are breathtaking flashes of beauty to its harshness, as at sunset when its lines begin to soften and a sky, listless blue by day, explodes into crimson, and the flaming orb of the setting sun leaves great streaks of magnificent red, yellow and purple against the first stars in the west.

But eventually we come to the end of the Karoo and the route begins to wind down through the valleys and vineyards of the western Cape province to the city with one of the most beautiful settings in the world, Cape Town.

There are some who say the best approach to Cape Town is from the sea at dawn, creeping through the morning mist into Table Bay to find the city cradled before you in the lap of Table Mountain, which rises like a protective amphitheater behind it.

But whatever the approach, this grand mountain dominates the landscape, unless of course it be one of those days when a fresh wind tugs across its top a tablecloth of cloud, spilling over its edges and down its flanks until it is obscured from view.

In clear weather a cablecar zooms to the top of the mountain. The top is flat and broad and you can spend hours rambling across it. There, stretching away to the south, is the rest of the peninsula on which Cape Town is situated. Eventually it narrows to the Cape of Good Hope, Drake's "fairest cape in the whole circumference of the earth," where the warm currents of the Indian Ocean meet the cold of the Atlantic.

Cape Town is the mother city, a mellow sort of old lady whose lusty youngsters like Johannesburg to the north have outgrown her grasp. The pace here is more leisurely. There is the stuff of history about the city's old oaks, and the peeling little houses on cobbled streets in the Malay quarter. People of different cultures and races have been living together here for more than three hundred years. This is the seat of South African history, for it was here, under the lee of Table Mountain, that white settlement began more than three turbulent centuries ago.

. . .

For years, ships voyaging around the Cape of Good Hope on their long journeys between east and west had sought a few days' haven in sheltered Table Bay. But it was not until 1652, thirty-two years after the Mayflower grounded at Plymouth, that the Dutch East India Company established a revictualing station for its ships on the site where Cape Town now stands.

Originally the company's Dutch employees were charged only with laying out vegetable gardens and providing fresh water for the company's ships. Eventually, however, they became permanent settlers. Later they were reinforced by Huguenots fleeing religious persecution in France.

With war in Europe, the Cape became a strategic base, bouncing like a shuttlecock from one maritime power to another through the late eighteenth and early nineteenth centuries. Eventually it became a colony of Britain.

The territory which Britain won was a sprawling one, trailing

along the coast and inland to ill-defined boundaries. Besides
the white foreign settlers, it encompassed the original Hottentots
and Bushmen of the area as well as Malay and other slaves imported from the east.

Beyond its boundaries lay the African tribes which had traveled
southward down the continent, and with whom the Dutch fron-
tiersmen edging out and away from British rule at the Cape were
clashing.

Interbreeding between these white and diverse nonwhite groups
produced the first of those people of mixed racial descent now
known as "coloreds" in South Africa who total some 1,500,000.

In 1833, Britain abolished slavery. This with other British
reforms and irritations was more than some Dutchmen could
bear. One in five left the Cape and struck inland on the epic
Great Trek.

In the face of tremendous hardship including wild animals
and wars with African tribes they ground onward to create the
republics of the Transvaal and the Orange Free State. Britain
retained control of the coast, the Cape and Natal. Thus were
aligned the protagonists eventually to become roiled in the Boer
War of 1899-1902. Thus too was laid the foundation of an Afrikaner nation, people who shrugged off their Dutch descent and
ties with Europe to become Afrikaners, with their own rugged
individualism and their own language called Afrikaans, derived
from Dutch.

These were the Boers, men of the land, who staked out vast
farms and were happiest with their horizons undefiled by the
smoke of a neighbor's fire.

Their isolation was short-lived. Diamond strikes at Kimberley in
the 1860's and gold strikes in the Transvaal in the 1870's and
1880's shattered the peace of the veld. New waves of trekkers of
all nationalities swarmed in searching for riches. Soon the country-
side was transformed with the clatter of mining camps.

Giants of the age were men like Barney Barnato, Alfred Beit
and Cecil Rhodes, the vicar's son who made his millions out of
diamonds before his thirties, founded the Rhodes scholarships and
dreamed of a British Africa.

Meanwhile, the importation of coolie labor from India to work the sugar plantations of Natal was laying the foundation for yet another of South Africa's racial groups. These are the Asians who have multiplied their numbers and wealth to become an economically influential community of some 450,000.

Eventually the thrusting, ambitious imperialism of Rhodes clashed head-on with the suspicious isolation of the Transvaal's President Kruger. Boer and Briton were engulfed in the Boer War which the British ultimately won.

By 1910 the former antagonists had come together to create the Union of South Africa. Its first political leaders were the defeated Boer generals of the recent war, and South Africa's prime ministers have been Afrikaners ever since. The first prime minister, General Louis Botha, brought along with him another Boer leader by name of Jan Christiaan Smuts. After Botha's death, Smuts became prime minister but was overthrown by an alliance headed by yet another Boer general, James Barry Munnik Hertzog.

In time, Smuts and Hertzog formed a coalition called the United Party. Some of Hertzog's followers could not stomach the fusion. They split and departed for the political wilderness under the leadership of a clergyman named Daniel F. Malan.

With the advent of World War II came political crisis. As in World War I, many Afrikaners deplored South Africa's participation in a "British" war. Many of their fellow Afrikaners thought differently and fought valiantly with the Allies. But the differences split the Hertzog-Smuts coalition and Smuts as prime minister took the country into war after the slimmest of majorities in parliament favoring such action.

Smuts, the Boer War enemy of Britain, was a confidant of Churchill during World War II and a man of stature among the Allies despite the smallness of his own nation. His pointed little beard and clipped accent were familiar features at wartime conferences and he was always warmly welcomed by the British people. As a boy in the early 1940's in Britain I can remember my father shushing the family to listen rapt and silent whenever Smuts made one of his wartime broadcasts over the BBC. At war's end, Smuts was prominent in the foundation of the United Nations organization where his country's present government now stands condemned.

Perhaps Smuts was more at home in the halls of international statesmanship than he was in the basement brawling of South African politics. During his preoccupation with world affairs, the Malanites were nibbling away at the foundations of his party. In the postwar general election of 1948, Dr. Malan's Nationalist party, reinforced by Hertzog supporters who had broken with Smuts at the war's beginning, displaced the Smuts government with a small majority of parliamentary seats.

Over the intervening years, the party has entrenched itself solidly. Dr. Malan was in time succeeded as prime minister by Johannes G. Strijdom, a Transvaal lawyer. Upon Mr. Strijdom's death in 1958, Dr. Hendrik F. Verwoerd, a former psychology professor, assumed leadership of the Nationalist party and prime ministership of the country.

Establishment of a republican form of government, severed from links with the British Commonwealth, had long been a goal of the Nationalist party. Under Dr. Verwoerd's regime it has become a reality. In a 1960 referendum confined to whites, a majority of 74,000 voters gave Dr. Verwoerd a narrow mandate to declare a republic. During the referendum campaign, numbers of government spokesmen assured the white electorate that such a republic would remain a member of the British Commonwealth, of which South Africa was then a member.

Dr. Verwoerd presented South Africa's application for continued Commonwealth membership at a meeting of the Commonwealth prime ministers in London in 1961. South Africa's race policies, abhorrent to various Commonwealth member nations, particularly those in Africa and Asia, came under critical discussion. Eventually Dr. Verwoerd withdrew South Africa's application. On May 31, 1961, the former Union of South Africa became a lonely republic, outside the Commonwealth.

·   ·   ·

It is against this historical background that the 16,000,000 polyglot peoples of South Africa live today.

Only 3,000,000 of them are white. These are split roughly 60–40 between Afrikaners and South Africans of British descent, and this is a country with two official languages, English and Afrikaans.

It is from the land that the Afrikaners spring. These are big, bluff, farming people, dispensing an earthy hospitality, and with a strong Calvinistic sense of religion threaded through their Dutch Reformed Church.

English-speaking South Africans are centered predominantly in the towns and cities, and although there is a steady migration of Afrikaners to the urban areas, the cities are mainly English strongholds and it is the English-speaking South Africans who have primarily built up the gold mining and other industries, of course with black labor.

White South Africa has one of the highest living standards in the world. In the homes of Johannesburg's rich northern suburbs there are two or three African servants, bridge parties in the afternoon, two cars in the garage and a swimming pool in the grounds. Even in humbler homes there is usually a servant to mind the baby and clean the house. With an abundance of black servants at less than $28 a month this is a society without a white lower class. However poor the poorest whites, they are always a bracket above the nonwhites. Thus the white lower class becomes middle, the middle class becomes upper, and the upper becomes upper upper.

Many whites find it difficult to believe that this world of privilege is drifting toward its end. Hovering over the white man's shoulder, demanding a share in all this, are the country's 13,000,-000 nonwhites. Of these, nearly 11,000,000 are Africans. They range from primitive, blanketed tribesmen in the Transkei to sophisticated city lawyers and teachers. About 30 per cent of them live in the cities.

For this latter group the main attraction is Johannesburg. They keep on flooding in there, crowding into the African townships and locations which are flung like an encircling black paw around the white man's suburbs.

Johannesburg is the cruelest and the most exciting city for Africans all rolled into one. This is the city of slums and harshness and passes and policemen and jails. Yet South Africa's black men bubble, fizz and froth with noise, music, good humor and an endless capacity for fun. Amid the grimness they somehow plug in this natural gaiety to all the novelties and wonders and diversion of Johannesburg and light up a little world all their own. This is the threadbare but hilarious world of jazz and shanty-town jive haunts, of American ties and wide-brimmed hats and boxing bouts and African beauty queen contests.

By contrast the 1,500,000 coloreds (of mixed race) are a more complex people. In their blood is much of the music and laughter of the African. Each New Year in Cape Town, where their numbers are strongest, the streets run gay with a streaming, seething riot of color and melody. This is the time when colored minstrel troupes in candy-striped trousers and exotic costumes cavort to the twang of banjo bands. It is carnival time for the coloreds and competing among others are the Hollywood Palm Beach Serenaders, the Original Seven-Up Jazz Singers, the Star-Spangled Crooning Minstrels and the Ethiopian Hollywood Jazz Singers. All this is supposed to have been inspired by the visit to Cape Town in 1887 of an American Christy Minstrel Show.

But this is a time for letting off steam and there is a gloomy, brooding streak to the colored community, living as it does in a twilight, rootless world between Africans and whites. More akin in their culture to whites than Africans, the coloreds have never-theless been spurned by the present white government. Perhaps in unhappy reflex, some of them in turn adopt a patronizing superiority toward Africans. But while many Africans are confident that numbers and history are on their side, the coloreds are divided, without allegiance, and know not where their future lies.

Lastly there are the Indians, perhaps the unhappiest people in all South Africa, confined mainly to Natal and clinging to their possessions against the next menace to their security. Recently one government legislator told parliament that the Indian monopoly of trade and commerce in Natal should be gradually broken up so that a fair redistribution could take place.

Since their importation as plantation laborers, the Indians have multiplied vastly and spread out into many occupations. They are canny traders, keeping overheads to a minimum and ready to work all hours, which makes them tough competitors for white traders. Some have amassed substantial fortunes and much of Durban's business property is Indian-owned.

Strangely, it was in this city that the weapon of *Satyagraha*, passive resistance, was forged which later was to free India. Mahatma Gandhi, a young Indian lawyer living in Durban at the turn of the century, experimented with passive resistance in a campaign to improve the lot of his people. Later he transplanted it to India and perfected it. One of Gandhi's sons, Manilal, lived on in Natal, editing an Indian newspaper founded by his father. However, Indians in South Africa remain in political oblivion.

CHAPTER XV

South Africa: White Wonderland

THE MAN with the most difficult job in South Africa is Mr. Piet Meiring. Mr. Meiring is head of the government's propaganda bureau, the State Information Service, and his task is an impossible one.

Somehow he has to gloss over all the heartbreak and present South Africa as an idyllic land where all the races gambol contentedly, if separately, in the sun.

The government has allocated more and more money for publicity as its reputation overseas has grown worse and worse. Mr. Meiring has an extensive publicity machine. South African press officers are stationed in major capitals throughout the world. The department churns out pamphlets and brochures and magazines. It invites foreign notables for carefully conducted tours. Lately it has been making expensive television films about South Africa for whichever foreign stations will screen them. There is a tinge of hypocrisy about this, however, for at home the government has barred television, ostensibly because it is a corrupting medium, but actually for political reasons.

But even with Madison Avenue's resources at his disposal, Mr. Meiring's assignment would be doomed to failure. It is no fault of his. It is the fact that both his employers and the product they are trying to sell are unacceptable throughout most of the world.

The employers are the present South African government. The product upon which they have staked their reputation is apartheid. This is a policy designed to preserve South Africa as a sort of white wonderland. In its present stage of application it means

171

racial discrimination in its most degrading and possibly dangerous form.

The name itself, pronounced "apart-hate," has an unhappily sinister ring. One wonders, in these days when even the name of a new detergent gets exhaustive testing before it is inflicted on the public, why the government chose and pursued this dismal label.

However, if it was a mistake it was but one of a string of actions since 1948 which have wrought a drastic change in South Africa's world standing.

The color problem in South Africa is not, of course, the creation of the present Nationalist party government. It had been snow-balling over the years and the present government inherited it. Yet despite rumblings of trouble to come, South Africa at the end of World War II was a country well-remembered for its gener-osity and hospitality to thousands of servicemen who had called there. It had credit in the bank, so to speak, for its wartime con-tribution. Under a less rigid government throughout the 1950's, willing to negotiate and compromise on the color question, it might have gained a more sympathetic hearing by the world in later years.

Instead, the Nationalist government has inflamed the problem and brought it to a head.

There are figures to show, of course, that the present govern-ment has spent millions of dollars on the material well being of nonwhites, perhaps even more so proportionately than previous governments. It is possible to catalog the government's achieve-ments in African housing, and the number of dams it has built and the amount it spends on African schooling and health.

It is true that there is a migration of Africans from neighboring countries who flow to South Africa for the higher wages they can earn in its cities. But these, in a way, are like the Americans or Britons who travel to far countries of which they are not particu-larly enamored for the sake of high financial rewards. And when the job is done they, like "foreign" Africans in South Africa, can go back to their homelands.

However, although financial opportunity for Africans may be greater in industrialized South Africa than it is, say, in poverty-stricken Nyasaland, there is a ceiling to it, a cutoff point beyond which Africans may not advance into jobs held by whites. And all this takes place within a framework of political and social repression which has roused world antagonism.

Members of the present white government sometimes express puzzlement that South Africa's policies of racial discrimination are singled out for world attack when, they say, there is segregation in the American South, and in Southern Rhodesia, and even the Smuts government before them practiced it, yet all without the deluge of criticism which pours over Dr. Verwoerd's government.

But South Africa's white Afrikaner government is not, of course, the subject of a Machiavellian world plot. The fact which worries the world is that South Africa seems to be going in the opposite direction. Segregation there may be in the American South, but the law of the United States federal government enshrines racial equality. Discrimination there may be in the Rhodesias, but the official policy is partnership, however ill-defined that may be. These countries are moving away from racial inequality, whereas the present South African government is entrenching it. And though Smuts too practiced discrimination, there were not in those days the oppressive laws on the statute book which have since been introduced by the present government.

It is this South African unwillingness to yield just a little, this persistent and flagrant denial of human rights despite world-wide appeals from statesmen, scientists, philosophers, professors, entertainers and countless nations, which has roused world ire.

Said Britain's Prime Minister Harold Macmillan, after that fateful Commonwealth premiers' conference which saw South Africa excluded from membership: "Had Dr. Verwoerd shown the smallest move toward understanding of the views of his Commonwealth colleagues or made any concession; had he given us anything to hold on to or any grounds for hope; I still think the conference would have looked beyond the immediate difficulties to the possibilities of the future."

South Africa's policy of racial discrimination was the sole reason for the hostility of other Commonwealth premiers toward South Africa, and for South Africa's consequent exclusion from the Commonwealth. Various nonwhite leaders have indicated they would have no objection to South Africa's returning to the Commonwealth once it abandons its present race policy.

Over South Africa's departure from the Commonwealth there were pangs of regret among those who had hoped to keep it in the Commonwealth, while placing on record the Commonwealth's disagreement with South African race policy. Among others, however, and particularly throughout the Afro-Asian world there was widespread rejoicing "not only," as one correspondent cabled from India, "because justice has triumphed but because the Commonwealth has emerged from this crisis, in Indian eyes, stronger and cleaner."

The fact is that the question of race has become a dominant issue in a world increasingly influenced by Afro-Asian opinion. South Africa, on account of its race policy, has become an embarrassment on one side of the Iron Curtain and a weapon for anti-Western propaganda on the other. Each year, the pressure mounts more and more upon South Africa at the UN, and the day may come when South Africa leaves that organization too. In the meantime correspondents from every major newspaper and news organization have flocked to South Africa, a country which ordinarily would not be high on the newsman's itinerary. It features in the headlines of the world. And after his last visit, the United States' present ambassador to the United Nations, Mr. Adlai Stevenson, declared: "I leave this beautiful land with grave doubts for the future."

A government to turn the world against it and make Moscow rumble and Washington splutter must have a fearsome look about it, you might think. Yet there is nothing particularly startling about the cabinet as it sits on the green leather benches in parliament. They might be directors at a board meeting. There is Finance Minister Donges, suave and smiling, and a dab with the bat in parliamentary cricket games; Eric Louw, the prickly little minister of external affairs; Paul Sauer, a round, Easter egg-ish sort of man, and all the others. Even Prime Minister Verwoerd (pronounced "fair-voort") himself, broad and tall with a shock of white hair, might be taken at first glimpse for a successful stockbroker.

But in the heat of political harangue, Dr. Verwoerd is transformed. The eyes are those of the fanatic, the hair becomes ruffled
and a displaced lock drops down over the brow. The right arm
reaches heavenward and the forefinger makes angry stabbing
movements. He becomes a sort of human lightning conductor,
crackling with oratorical static, hurling verbal thunderbolts and
calling down political brimstone in a voice that gets tighter and
higher with excitement.

Zeal is the key to Dr. Verwoerd. He has an awesome dedication
and fervor. When other cabinet ministers have gone home, Verwoerd works on, sometimes sixteen and seventeen hours a day.
When his colleagues are on holiday, Dr. Verwoerd is at his desk.
He pores over files and documents in his car between residence
and office.

Behind this energy there is a self-confidence, almost a sense of
divine mission, sobering to see. If a rebel movement rears its
head in his party, the rebels are wrong. If the government-supporting Dutch Reformed Church questions an aspect of his policy, the
church is wrong. If the United Nations, with the moral weight of
the whole world behind it, condemns apartheid, then the whole
world is wrong.

Once when a reporter asked him whether he never got tired or
taxed, Verwoerd snapped back: "No. I do not have the nagging
doubt of ever wondering whether perhaps I am wrong."

Thus when two bullets from a would-be assassin's gun thudded
into his head at close range in 1960, an event which might have
given pause to a lesser man, perhaps even caused his retirement
from politics, Dr. Verwoerd recovered to return vibrant to the
political scene, and, if anything, more unyielding than before.

What is the goal of all this zeal? What is Dr. Verwoerd dedicated to? The driving force behind him is a passionate dedication
to the "nasie" (nation), the "volk" (people). But this is the Afrikaner nation, and the Afrikaner people. Of Afrikaner nationalism
he says: "There are forces that are unconquerable. This is one of
them." For Dr. Verwoerd the Afrikaners are South Africa's master
race, destined for mystic supremacy in a land where other races
are privileged to dwell.

Dr. Verwoerd himself is not an Afrikaner by birth. He was born in Holland and brought to South Africa as a baby. But he has steeped himself in the spirit of Afrikanerdom and its lore. His student days were spent at the great Afrikaner university of Stellenbosch and after further study in Germany he returned there to become professor of applied psychology.

In 1936 he achieved minor prominence with a group of other Stellenbosch professors by protesting the admission to South Africa of Jewish refugees from Hitler's Germany.

Soon after, Dr. Verwoerd forsook the academic world for politics and the editorship of the *Transvaler,* official newspaper of the Nationalist party in the Transvaal province. Numbers of Afrikaners, imbued with anti-British hatred, hoped and actively worked for a German victory in World War II, confident that this would bring them their Afrikaner republic and freedom from ties with Britain. During the war years Verwoerd followed an extremist line with his paper. He lost a Supreme Court action in which the judge held that he "made his newspaper a tool of the Nazis in South Africa, and he knew it."

With the end of war, the Smuts government invited the British royal family to tour South Africa in 1947. Not a line of coverage appeared in Verwoerd's newspaper, although the biggest crowds in history disrupted Johannesburg where the paper was published.

For the postwar election of 1948, Dr. Verwoerd organized intensively in the Transvaal. After the Nationalist party won it he became minister of native [African] affairs in the Malan cabinet. He flung himself into the task of segregating the country's nonwhites, reducing them by legislation and decree to the point where they could not imperil the white man's supremacy. "If the stream [of Africans] into the towns continues unstemmed, we [whites] will be drowned in a black sea," he warned. And again: "Mixed racial development will lead to the most terrible clashes of interest imaginable."

Somewhere over the horizon lay Dr. Verwoerd's theoretical goal of a country neatly compartmentalized into racial groups. In an attempt to get there he created a governmental machine which ground over human rights with relentless detachment, oblivious to the misery of uprooted families and businesses and racial groups, and wives and children separated from husbands, and all the grisly tragedy of apartheid. The machine marked out where a man might live and love and work and travel and see his children.

In informal conversation Dr. Verwoerd declares a paternalistic sort of affection to the primitive, tribal African, modeled something after the patriarchal relationship of the pioneer Afrikaner *voortrekkers* to their African servants. "The *voortrekkers* knew how to combine strictness with benevolence," he says. But as a dedicated nationalist himself he has a peculiarly blind spot where the African nationalism and frustrations of urban Africans are concerned. These are the Africans, many of them second- or third-generation city dwellers, who are at the root of the color problem. Yet he dismisses them and their leaders and rambles on with a chilling unreality in the world of tribal legend and folklore which millions of Africans have forsaken.

Listening to him talk, one cannot avoid the impression that he regards all Africans as ciphers, or pieces to be moved hither and thither in a vast game of chess which the white men always win.

.   .   .

With Mr. Strijdom's death in 1958, the Nationalist party was thrown into a short, sharp struggle for leadership. The contenders were Dr. Verwoerd, architect of apartheid, Dr. Donges, now minister of finance, and Mr. Charles R. Swart, then minister of justice, who, during an American tour in his youth, once played the part of a long lean cowboy in Hollywood. From the caucus room where the Nationalist party legislators met to choose their new leader, Dr. Donges emerged somber, Mr. Swart in tears. Dr. Verwoerd was to be the new prime minister of South Africa.

To many outsiders, the puzzle about this government is how it has lasted through three prime ministers and all the years since 1948. Not only is most of the world against it, but most of South Africa too, for it rules with the consent of only a fraction of the population.

The fact is that the government needs only the votes of its own white Afrikaners to remain in power. Nonwhites are voteless and the government is returned by a purely white electorate. To win a majority of the seats in the House of Assembly and thus become the government, the Nationalist party does not need the votes of English-speaking South Africans. It can be confident of victory as long as it has the support of the majority of the Afrikaners, who comprise 60 per cent of the white population.

It does not even need the votes of all the Afrikaners, nor even a clear majority of all votes cast. Under the South African electoral system, city seats are loaded against rural seats, where the present government's supporters are strong. There is provision for a 15 per cent variation either side of a constituency's normal population. Thus a rural constituency with up to 15 per cent less voters than the norm can put a man into parliament. A city constituency may be loaded up to 15 per cent the other side of the norm. There may be a disparity in the numbers of voters in rural and city seats of up to 30 per cent, yet each put one man into parliament.

The Nationalist party's main preoccupation is with the Afrikaner loyalist without which the fortress of Afrikanerdom would crumble. Within its ramparts the ranks of the party are drilled and organized and regimented. The generals crack down ruthlessly on the defaulter who questions. If he cannot be reformed he is flung beyond the walls to social and other types of ostracism. Talk to an Afrikaner professor or churchman or journalist who has turned upon the party and one realizes what courage they need to stick to their views in the face of all the pressures brought to bear upon them. And always in the background there is the Broederbond, a secret Afrikaner brotherhood, to crack the whip of Afrikaner racialism. It is the Broederbond which is dedicated to the destruction of British symbols in South Africa. One after another they have disappeared, the British crowns and flag and anthem and emblems, to be climaxed by the republic, the severance of bonds with the British Queen who before the republic was Queen of South Africa too, and finally South Africa's exclusion from the British Commonwealth.

The party juggernaut the Afrikaner nationalists have built is a formidable one but it might never have rolled to triumph without one thing more. This is the streak of unscrupulous party genius which has built the black man into a figure of menace for the white voters. This is a government with a mastery of the psychology of fear. It is the cornerstone on which apartheid is built. Time

after time the party extremists have ensured victory by presenting
to election audiences the image of the black tide which will engulf
them unless they elect a strong government that knows how to
deal with the blacks.

With each electoral victory the government has consolidated
itself further by a variety of maneuvers. It shut off the stream of
immigrants from Britain because they voted against it. It made
South African citizenship, and the vote, more difficult to achieve
for foreigners. It lowered the voting age from twenty-one to eighteen to pick up the votes of Afrikaner youth. It stripped coloreds
of the common vote they once had, a vote which influenced the
results in a dozen constituencies, in return for four separate seats
in parliament. It awarded undue representation to safely progovernment South-West Africa.

So today government members sit in a solid phalanx along two-
thirds of the benches in parliament. The parliamentary opposition
has steadily dwindled away.

The official, or biggest, opposition group is the United party,
which sits dreaming sadly of its former glories under Smuts.
Smuts' successor as party leader was a slight Johannesburg lawyer
named Johannes G. N. Strauss. Strauss stepped into the shoes of
a world-famous figure to lead a defeated party. Dissatisfied with
his failure to regalvanize it and bring it victory, the United party
replaced him with a handsome, wealthy lawyer and farmer, Sir
de Villiers Graaff. But under Graaff too the party has retrogressed
from one defeat to another.

The United party's problem is that it has got to win that decisive fringe of Afrikaner voters if ever it is to be returned to power
by a white electorate. The party is opposed to the excesses of
apartheid but at the same time it is terrified lest a hint of liberalism attach itself to its policy. Its policy has thus become a pale
image of the government's. Sir de Villiers has described it as
"white leadership with justice." This has so far failed to attract
the out and out segregationists who support the government and
neither does it satisfy those white South Africans who have turned
their backs on segregation.

Thus has emerged a new opposition group, the Progressive
party. This has splintered from its parent United party on grounds

this is not progressive enough on the color question, and the opposition is thus fragmented into two small parties neither of which has much prospect of ousting the government in the immediate future.

However, the Progressives have been putting up a fiery fight in parliament. At times it is they who have assumed the mantle of real opposition to the government, as in the somber emergency days of 1960 when the United party sat in embarrased silence and watched the Progressive party fight the battle of the beaten and arrested thousands. The Progressives were aided by two members of the tiny Liberal party whose seats the government has since abolished.

The Progressives have a cautious plan for limited enfranchisement of nonwhites, and if this were 1930, or even 1940, and they had twenty years ahead of them and a fund of nonwhite good will, their future might look brighter than it does at present. For the moment, however, perhaps the best they can hope for from a conservative white electorate is to scratch enough seats together to become the official opposition. Even this is an optimistic goal.

All in all there is a strangely unreal air about this parliament as one looks down upon it from the press gallery in Cape Town's pink brick parliamentary buildings. It is the parliament of a country whose population is four-fifths nonwhite, yet there is not a single black face among the ranks of white legislators.

Across the country outside there is the rumble and mutter of the frustrated African. In 1960, 30,000 of them marched to the environs of parliament, where the government hastily summoned a protective cordon of machine guns and armored cars. All up the vast bulk of Africa there is the crackle and stir of new black power and influence.

Yet here in this chamber at the continent's southern tip, in a little white world of fantasy, you would hardly know all that. Endlessly the debate drones on about the never-never land of apartheid, like a stuck gramophone record after the party's gone home.

.   .   .

The real opposition to the government is not in parliament at all of course, but outside in the ranks of African nationalism and the handful of its white supporters who would allow nonwhites an equal say in the running of their country.

These are the black millions in extraparliamentary opposition to the government, barred from orthodox political expression in parliament, whose voice the government tries to stifle.

They have leaders like Albert John Luthuli, an African chief stripped of his office by the government for refusing to cooperate with it.

Mr. Luthuli was educated by American missionaries in South Africa and in 1948 was invited by the Congregational Church in the United States to make a nine-month lecture tour from head-quarters in Boston. Now he is not allowed out of the country, is confined to the environs of his home, and the African National Congress of which he is leader has been banned by the govern-ment since 1960. Mr. Luthuli has suffered many indignities and much suffering for the cause of his African people over the years, including such provocations as the one at a Pretoria meeting when shouting whites kicked him until he lay silent. None of this ap-pears to have impaired either his Christianity or his quiet con-fidence in the justice of the African case.

Not a single member of the government has ever met Mr. Luthuli. Yet they have branded him on the one hand as unrepre-sentative of any body of African opinion, and somewhat contra-dictorily on the other as a formidable agitator liable to plunge the country into chaos. In either case, he is dismissed as an "extremist."

The irony of Mr. Luthuli's extremism is that it has come to look like sweet reasonableness with the emergence of new and more militant African leaders such as Robert Mangaliso Sobukwe. The government's consistent rejection of such men as Mr. Luthuli has now spawned a new and perhaps genuinely extreme organization like Mr. Sobukwe's Pan Africanist Congress. This is the militant organ of a tough and aggressive corps of young men impatient with moderation and anxious for action. Like the African National Congress it has been banned by the government. Mr. Sobukwe, who forsook his job as a university lecturer to lead it, is serving a three-year jail term for his political activities. But the spirit of the organization lives on. Nobody knows whether it has outstripped in popularity the African National Congress which was hitherto the prime organ of African political expression.

In addition to the forces of black nationalism, there is the fringe of whites who are bitter foes of apartheid and who sympathize with the African cause, though not necessarily supporting the platforms of specific nationalist organizations. There are the churchmen like Father Trevor Huddlestone and Bishop Ambrose Reeves and Anglican Archbishop Joost de Blank. There are the professors and intellectuals, among them some Afrikaners. There are the journalists and writers like Patrick Duncan and Alan Paton and the liberals like Margaret Ballinger. There is even Mr. Paton's little Liberal party of whites and nonwhites which cannot get a member into parliament with a white electorate because it demands equality for each race. There are the unnamed others but they are a small band.

All these are the black and white South Africans whom the government must rule increasingly with the bayonet and the secret policeman, with the deportation order and the warrant for arrest, for they will never be ruled by the present government with their consent. Thus the African Nationalist Congress and the Pan Africanist Congress are banned. Mr. Luthuli, in and out of jails for years, is restricted in movement. Sobukwe is behind bars. Patrick Duncan has been too. Alan Paton has had his passport seized. Bishop Reeves has been deported. This is the penalty for real opposition in South Africa as distinct from the droning debate of a parliamentary party which has no prospect of overthrowing the government.

These sound like police state measures. Is South Africa a police state? The answer to that depends on one's point of view.

To the cruise-liner tourist, spending a day ashore in lovely Cape Town, there is little sinister about South Africa. There are no jack-booted blackshirts wielding machine guns at every street corner. Africans are not being publicly flogged.

There is a press highly critical of the government. The prime minister is lampooned by its cartoonist almost daily. There are South Africans both black and white who are vocal in their denunciation of the government. This is not police state stuff.

Most of South Africa's whites, ignorant of life in the African locations, probably would join in rejection of the police state theory.

The African sees things differently. He is told where he may travel and what class; where he may live and how long; what type of restricted job he may take; whether his wife and children may live with him. He is confronted by a maze of controls, restrictions, curfews and penalties. He may go to jail if he does not have on his person at every hour of day and night a "reference book" with an official and up-to-date record of his life. He may serve his sentence in a farm jail where convicts become bondsmen for white farmers. And in the locations beyond the white public's eye there are policemen with machine guns and Africans do get slashed and beaten. Few whites believe this, but then few whites have witnessed a baton-wielding police raid for illegal liquor or to check up on the validity of reference books in the middle of the night. Many Africans I know have no doubt in their minds that for them South Africa is a police state.

.   .   .

To crush those who challenge its omnipotence the government has resorted to increasingly authoritarian methods. Over the foreigner it brandishes the deportation order. Over the nonwhite South African there hangs the banishment order to a desolate spot, and over the white South African the threat of restriction to home and banning from meetings. To keep its own critical citizens in it seizes their passports, and to keep too-curious visitors out it refuses them visas.

It has passed one piece of tough legislation after another, bestowed wide powers upon its cabinet ministers and prescribed flogging as a legal punishment.

It makes extensive use of the police Special Branch, which is a force of plain-clothes political policemen. They swoop at dawn, probe through private documents, and peer and pry into the lives of those suspected of challenging the government's rule. They have hidden behind cupboards at trade union meetings, planted their informers in political and other organizations throughout the country and encouraged young students to spy on their university lecturers and colleagues.

In 1960, the government scooped up 2,000 political prisoners and held them for several months without trial under emergency rule. Fathers were separated from children, and even wives imprisoned while their husbands went free. One woman came sobbing at dawn on our doorstep, her two children at her skirts. The political police had just taken her husband from his bed. She did not know where, nor for how long. One of the regulations in force at this time forbade a citizen to reveal to any other the name of anyone arrested.

For those engaged in liberal politics there is little belief any more in the privacy of the telephone or the mails. On various occasions when I have interviewed a nonwhite political leader I have found him sitting at his desk with a towel stuffed into the telephone mouthpiece throughout the conversation, or perhaps with a portable radio playing softly beside it to confuse tappers. There is nothing subversive about the conversation, but nonwhites suspect that the Special Branch is listening in to their tactics and plans with a device which operates through the telephone even when it is not in use and on its hook.

Most foreign newsmen suspect that their telephones are tapped, not always efficiently, for their calls are often interrupted by a remarkable amount of audible interference and "line failure." Some diplomats, including those at the American Embassy, have similar suspicions.

The mails are also suspect. On one occasion the government was embarrassed by parliamentary discussion of a case in which two letters had obviously been opened, but sealed again with the wrong letters inside. A student group in Cape Town addressed a letter to a similar body in Europe. The Liberal party in Cape Town addressed a letter to its Johannesburg branch. The student letter turned up in the envelope addressed to the Johannesburg Liberal party, and a puzzled university group in Europe received a letter for the Johannesburg Liberals in an envelope addressed to itself.

To prevent the influence of "sickly, sentimental liberalism" from abroad, as one government member calls it, the government bars nonwhites from foreign study, even when awarded handsome scholarships from schools like Kent and universities like Harvard.

Television is banned because it would bring a breath of fresh air from the world outside. Newsreels screened in South African movie houses are innocuous. Relays of news bulletins from the British Broadcasting Corporation have been dropped by the state-influenced South African Broadcasting Corporation, and the corporation's own news editorship often seems to be stamped with voluntary political censorship and slanting where issues affecting South Africa are concerned.

The government imposes sweeping censorship on imported books. In South Africa it is a crime punishable by a fine of up to $2,800 or five years imprisonment to be in possession of the American magazine *Boxing Life*, presumably because it depicts black men fighting white, or *The Complete Life Story of Harry Belafonte* or the UNESCO pamphlet *Behind the Color Bar*. Banned authors range through John O'Hara, Ernest Hemingway, John Steinbeck and Carson McCullers in a long list of publications, 3,500 titles in the last four years alone, prohibited by the official censor.

Once the customs men seized a consignment of books by that dangerous Bolshevik trio, Tolstoy, Dostoyevsky and Turgenev, only to release them later after a little embarrassed classical research. On another occasion they pounced on a book called *Black Beauty*. But it was not a sinister volume on color, just a children's book about a horse. Sadly, they let it go.

This sort of thing, and other examples of official ham-handedness, must make Mr. Meiring's public relations men in foreign capitals tear their hair.

In 1960 the government arrested Norman Phillips, foreign editor of the *Toronto Star*, and withheld from transmission a cable he had attempted to file while in South Africa. That was a sure way to get South Africa big black adverse headlines around the world. After a few days in jail, Mr. Phillips was released on condition he left the country immediately. Yet when he was first arrested, Mr. Phillips was on his way out of the country anyway. It was difficult to see what the government had gained except a bad press.

Then there are all the other little human dramas which have been flashed to the ends of the earth. A government that refuses an entry visa to Louis Armstrong or seizes the passport of Alan Paton can hardly expect to avoid publicity.

There was the case of Mr. and Mrs. Frank Beecher, an English couple who had settled in Cape Town. They loved and cared for and tried to adopt a two-year-old baby called Thomas who had come into their possession. There was just one problem. Thomas was a foundling and officials who looked at him declared he had some colored blood in him. A government department tried to take him away, but the Beechers hid and refused to give him up. In a blaze of publicity, and after many trials, they fled to England, a country which would allow them to keep baby Thomas.

There was George Kaschke, a German immigrant who had a child by a South African colored girl and wanted to marry her. Instead, he and she were prosecuted under South Africa's immorality laws which prohibit intercourse or marriage between different races and given a suspended jail sentence. They fled to Germany and marriage in another blaze of publicity.

In February, 1961, the government informed Victor Niedermayer, a German schoolteacher, that his visa valid for one year would not be renewed, although he had come to South Africa on a five-year teaching contract. Mr. and Mrs. Niedermayer's apparent crime was that they had allowed their three children to stay with their African nurse in an African hut during their holidays. The government action was widely publicized.

One of the most headlined cases was that of Hans Beukes. Beukes was a mild little colored student who won a scholarship to Oslo University. After a long wait he was surprisingly given a passport. But government officials had second thoughts and when he boarded his ship they pounced, confiscating his new passport and confining him to South Africa.

Beukes fled the country by a secret route and turned up at the United Nations to give evidence against South Africa's race policies. Before the passport incident, nobody had heard of him, but the government itself established him as a martyred victim of political oppression.

The government cloaks many of its actions in the guise of anticommunism. It has taken sweeping powers against communism but the International Commission of Jurists and other legal organizations have expressed concern over the wide definition of communism under which any South African can be named a Communist by the government without appeal to the courts.

Even with these powers, however, the government has been able to list by its own definition only some 600 people out of a population of nearly 16,000,000 as Communists.

The Communist party is illegal and in 1956 the government expelled the small consular mission which the Soviets had till then maintained in Cape Town.

The main attraction in the anti-Communist drama has been the treason trial, a mass trial which began with the dramatic dawn arrests of 156 South Africans of all races in December, 1956. In early proceedings the prosecutor hinted at revelations of a plot to establish an eastern European-style Peoples Democracy in South Africa.

To gain equal rights, went the argument, the African National Congress, many of whose leaders were involved in the trial, must have contemplated a violent overthrowal of a government which had no intention of granting them voluntarily.

The trial dragged on and on, and in a way became a symbol of the struggle between the government and its African nationalist opposition.

Over the years the accused were whittled down as the case collapsed against them, and finally more than four years later the last twenty-eight were acquitted and from the whole long drama the government had secured not a single conviction. The special treason court of three judges ruled unanimously that it was not proved that the African National Congress had become a Communist organization. Further, it was "impossible for the court to conclude that the African National Congress had acquired or adopted a policy to overthrow the State by violence."

What the trial did do was ruin financially some of the trialists who lost their jobs, or whose businesses collapsed, while they sat month after month in court.

Perhaps it was felt in some circles that the trial would also crush opposition to the government, for coincidentally the original 156 included almost everybody prominent in the African "freedom" movement in the country. As we know from later events, the spirit of the opposition has not been crushed, and some African leaders believe the trial coupled with government intransigeance has been a major stimulus to African nationalism.

The trial went through many interesting facets. In its early stages, for example, an African political detective was under cross-examination by defense counsel:

COUNSEL: You say a speaker said, "It is time to shoot Malan [a former prime minister]"?

DETECTIVE: Yes.

COUNSEL: How do you spell shoot?

DETECTIVE: S-H-O-O-T.

COUNSEL: Now read the letters you have written down in your notes. Is it not C-H-E-C-K?

DETECTIVE: Yes.

COUNSEL: Does that spell shoot?

DETECTIVE: No.

COUNSEL: In fact your notes show the speaker said "It is time to check Malan"?

DETECTIVE: Yes.

COUNSEL: Then why did you say shoot?

DETECTIVE: It was a mistake.

That is how the government of South Africa hunts its Communists.

CHAPTER XVI

South Africa: Black Tragedy

FOR MORE THAN a decade the word "apartheid" has dotted newspaper headlines the world over.

Translated from the Afrikaans it means "apart-ness," and it is the label for the present South African government's racial policy.

Yet still it puzzles the man struggling with his morning paper in the New York subway train. His perplexity is excusable, for apartheid is a confusing blanket term for racial separation open to a variety of interpretations even by those who apply it.

Thus to an audience of white bigots on election eve it becomes a policy to stop black men marrying their daughters. Yet to the inquirer from overseas it is represented as a costly program to give Africans self-rule in their own partitioned sector of the country.

Actually there is no doubt about the basic object of apartheid. This is to preserve the supremacy of whites in a land where nonwhites outnumber them four to one. Government members have reiterated it time and again.

Ultimately, and within this framework of white supremacy for South Africa, the Verwoerd government holds out the prospect of responsibility and progress for Africans in those tribal areas reserved for them. This is the "positive" side of apartheid as distinct from the "negative" humiliations of race discrimination in the cities. But for the moment all this is on paper. Both the political and economic development of the tribal reserves to date is negligible against the dimensions of their needs. The government's sincerity, and its ability to develop the reserves, must be largely taken on trust by Africans.

At its present stage of application, apartheid consigns them to social, economic and political inferiority. It entrenches their inequality before the law.

Over the years there has been in South Africa what is called traditional segregation of the races. In some instances this has been voluntary, as when nonwhites preferred their own company or were unable to afford that of whites. But nonwhites have not been allowed in white movie houses, hotels and so forth.

Then, for example, there is the recent case of the Cape Town yacht club with an exclusive white membership which without any compulsion from the government refused moorings to a nonwhite doctor. The nonwhite had bought a boat from one of the club's members, but the club decided that the same boat could not have the same anchorage with a new, nonwhite owner.

This traditional segregation was inevitably destined to cause trouble in a fast-changing world, under whatever white government assumed power in South Africa. Yet it is difficult to see how any government could have eroded the good will and phenomenal patience of the nonwhite more effectively than the present government during its tenure of office.

With its accession in 1948, race phobia ran wild.

Throughout government buildings and on the railways and in telephone booths and upon park benches government workmen hammered up a rash of signs segregating them for "Europeans" and "Non-Europeans." The non-European signs confused more than one American tourist who used the facilities so marked, only to be warned that non-European in South African parlance means nonwhite.

Government buildings were ripped apart to provide separate entrances for whites and nonwhites. Separate witness boxes were built in many courts. In some cases costly tunnels have been built to funnel blacks away from whites.

Each parliamentary session the government introduced a new crop of laws to seal off the races and throw up the barricades.

To curb the flow of Africans to the cities, the government tightened up influx regulations and consolidated pass laws, rooting out of the towns Africans who had no legal right to be there.

In 1950 came the most oppressive legislation of all in the shape of the Group Areas Act, the kernel of apartheid. This was designed to reshuffle property holdings throughout the country, consolidating various races in various blocs. The Group Areas Act has lost Africans the few freehold land rights they enjoy, uprooted Indian families after half a century's trading on one spot, and sent colored couples looking for new homes after fifty and sixty years residence in their battered cottages. It has caused untold misery and almost always works to the disadvantage of the nonwhites. The human tragedy and destruction left in the wake of the Group Areas Act would fill a grim book all by itself.

Early in its career the government extended bans on intercourse between whites and nonwhites, then legislated to prevent marriage between whites and nonwhites. Although such marriages had been socially frowned on, they had not previously been illegal. They had totaled less than a hundred a year.

With all this new legislation and the string of new offenses it was creating for specific racial groups, the government was confronted by a new problem. How was it to keep track of the various races and make sure a member of one race did not cross the line to become assimilated as a member of another group? With intermarriage over the generations, for example, some light-skinned coloreds were able to pass for white.

The government's answer was a national population register to classify all the country's citizens by race. At considerable cost over many years, millions of South Africans were photographed and labeled and issued with identity cards proclaiming their race.

Inevitably this led to race classification investigations in borderline cases. Tribunals probed and uncovered and laid bare secrets sometimes unknown to those being investigated. Government officials, at times acting upon the information of informers, would examine and perhaps tag as colored a man or woman who had considered himself or herself white since birth. Sometimes this led to family upheavals, the shocked separation of husband and wife, the adjustment of reclassified children, or social ostracism, the loss of a job or the necessity to move to another area.

The government's preoccupation with segregation extended to all institutions it could compel to conform. It reached into the courts and the universities, to the municipalities which were or-

dered to impose segregation, and even into the Cape Town bus
company which had always carried mixed passenger loads.

Government interference with the universities was a particularly controversial action which brought searing criticism from
students and universities around the world. Only two English-
speaking South African universities were admitting a small percentage of nonwhite students, who worked quietly and peacefully
alongside the white students with never a hint of trouble. The
government could not tolerate it. At a time when the United States
was struggling with the integration of segregated universities, the
South African government passed a law to segregate these universities which already were happily integrated.

Perhaps it is in the sphere of the church that the government
has been least successful with its segregation policies. The Dutch
Reformed churches in South Africa claim the allegiance of more
than half the white population and they have consistently supported the government. From other Protestant churches and the
Roman Catholic church, however, there has come opposition in
varying degrees to different aspects of government policy. Outside the Anglican cathedral in Cape Town just a few yards from
parliament a poster proclaims defiantly, for example: "This church
is open at all times to all men and women of all races."

Not all churchmen share this militancy. At an interdenomina-
tional church conference in Johannesburg on one occasion, whites
separated themselves on one side of the hall and African clergy-
men on the other. Before the conference began an African cleric
rose to ask solemnly: "If Jesus walked into this hall now, on which
side would he sit?"

But as Mr. J. P. Duminy, principal of the University of Cape
Town, told a conference on race relations, there can be no doubt
that Christ would have rejected South Africa's racial laws. Thus
the churches have moved more and more toward critical self-
examination on the racial question.

Even in the Dutch Reformed churches there has developed a
crisis of conscience over the more extreme aspects of apartheid
which is not yet resolved.

Meanwhile, apartheid has reached into the trade unions and
industry. Africans are prohibited from striking and, while it is not

illegal for them to form trade unions, these are not recognized or included in the official conciliation machinery.

One American congressman visiting South Africa was fascinated by the story of Mrs. Elizabeth Mafekeng. Mrs. Mafekeng, the mother of eleven children, was the highly active president of the nonwhite Food and Canning Workers Union in the little fruit-farming town of Paarl, near Cape Town. Hinting darkly at visits by her to Communist countries, the government announced it would banish her to a remote area. Before it could do so, Mrs. Mafekeng fled to the British protectorate of Basutoland with her baby in arms, leaving her other ten children and husband behind her. In disbelief, the congressman shook his head. "Just what," he said, "do you think would happen in the States if the government decided to banish our canning workers union boss to remote northern Maine!"

The key to the government's program for separation in industry is the Industrial Conciliation Act which empowers it to reserve various occupations for individual racial groups. Read with other legislation this effectively prohibits the advancement of Africans into skilled jobs where they might challenge whites.

Sometimes there has been a dash of the Gilbert and Sullivan about implementation of apartheid. Once the government ordered a ban on hand-shaking between white officials and Africans. Government ministers have fussed over whether white or colored traffic policemen should direct the flow of traffic in Cape Town, and whether an accident case lying in the street should be driven to hospital by a white or nonwhite ambulance driver.

Once, after the government had legislated to segregate South Africa's beaches, it discovered a loophole. Although white beaches were reserved to the high-water mark, nonwhites could bathe below this when the tide was out. Quickly the government passed a new law to segregate the sea water right out to the territorial three-mile limit.

.   .   .

With all this new legislation it is not surprising that thousands of Africans become enmeshed in a web of technical crime and petty offense. More than a million Africans a year are convicted

for nonserious crime in South Africa. One African in ten in the
city of Johannesburg can expect to go to jail during the year. For
petty crimes such as these, there is no stigma attached to them in
their own communities.

The bulk of the offenses are for contravention of the pass laws
controlling the movement of Africans. In a normal year, as distinct from 1960 and 1961 when thousands more Africans were
picked up under emergency regulations, more than a thousand
Africans for every day of the year including Saturdays and Sundays are convicted for breaking these laws. Either they do not
have their reference book on their person at the very minute a
policeman asks for it, or they have infringed the regulations in
some way. Even an African who was born and has lived in a city
for fifty years needs the proper documentation to return there
even after a short absence.

To the Africans their passes are the most hated symbols of their
inferiority and a source of constant friction between themselves
and authority.

The face of authority is generally that of the South African
police, for this is the agency which has the unfortunate task of
enforcing the pass laws and all the government's other regulations
which are unpopular with Africans.

The acts and attitudes of the police force are at the root of
many problems in South Africa. Partly because of the character
of the laws they enforce, and partly because of the way in which
they enforce them, the police are regarded by Africans with a
deep-rooted bitterness.

Early in 1960, nine policemen, both white and African, were
hacked to death in the Durban African township of Cato Manor.
That was a barbarous and savage action against the police. Yet
it might have been foreseen for in 1957 the present commissioner
of the force, Lieutenant General H. J. du Plooy, who was then
head of the Criminal Investigation Department, had warned that
the very type of raid which the policemen were conducting when
the African crowds set upon them was the sort of operation which
led to policemen being branded as oppressors.

Lieutenant General du Plooy now has succeeded as police chief
Major General C. I. Rademeyer, the force's tough-talking former

chief who retired on sick leave during the 1960 emergency. There are signs that he intends generating a more precise respect for the preservation of law and order among members of the force than has previously appeared to exist. He has raised the educational qualifications for entry, and demanded that his men exhibit more courtesy to members of the public. These moves will hearten some of those officers who have privately expressed concern at the deterioration of the force's reputation and its relations with the African public.

There are good men in the force, but the rot has gone far. Bad pay and low entry standards have encouraged admission of many teenage constables of abysmal education and ability. Crumpled and unkempt, they shuffle along their city beats, sometimes surreptitiously smoking cigarettes on duty.

The force is really a paramilitary one, for, although each constable carries a revolver, the force is issued rifles and equipped in addition with automatic weapons, such as the Sten gun, and armored cars.

It is a somber business when the police conduct a midnight raid for pass offenders or illegal possession of liquor by Africans. The pick-up vans roar into the African township and the policemen jump out and crunch from door to door. There is the rap of a truncheon and the occupants are roused from their beds. When they are tardy, the door is sometimes broken in or a window smashed. Sometimes their possessions are strewn about. Those people the police decide to take are herded into the pick-up vans. Sometimes there is the wail behind of crying children.

This is a routine raid, but in time of emergency the atmosphere is much grimmer.

During the emergency of 1960, editor Patrick Duncan testified he saw ten policemen armed with whips made from strips of rubber tires chase and beat three Africans. This was a day of widespread beatings. Newspaper offices were flooded with reports of assaults in Cape Town which shocked many whites to the point of protest. A man who saw Africans beaten by police in the suburb of Maitland telephoned: "I could not stand their screaming."

During these days, white troops and sailors cordoned off Cape Town's African locations. Snarling security men kept newspaper correspondents and photographers away at the point of the gun. Inside, the police went on a door to door rampage to persuade Africans to return to work. Cause of the emergency was the Africans' revolt against pass and other apartheid laws and their decision to stay at home.

Later a young girl showed foreign newsmen the bruises from a beating she said she suffered when she flung herself across an aged, invalid relative threatened by the police. Heart-rending calls for help filtered through the dust of the operation inside and out through the cordon. One group of screaming Africans ran to the top of a dune, flung their arms wide and shouted to the police: "Shoot us. What more can you do to us now. . . ." From excellent authority I heard the story of the young white army officer, shaken at the vision before him, who warned police officers he could not be responsible for the conduct of his white troops unless the police stopped their brutality.

Some black chapters were written in South African history during these days in the Cape Town African locations of Langa and Nyanga. Yet most of white South Africa still does not know they exist. White friends of ours living a mile from Langa never knew what went on there.

In another stay-at-home strike, on the eve of the 1948 general election, I saw Africans in the Johannesburg suburb of Sophiatown beaten by white policemen. These were Africans standing or walking in the streets and involved in no crime. One African was slashed across the back with a rawhide whip by a policeman on top of a cruising truck. The weals showed on his bare back after he had taken off his shirt and leather jacket. Another was cracked on the head with a wooden truncheon by a white policeman leaning out of a patrol car as it turned a corner.

Two other newspapermen witnessed the assaults with me, yet when I told acquaintances in the governing Nationalist party of the incidents they listened with polite disbelief. "Are you sure it wasn't a rope the policeman hit the native with?" one lady asked me.

In 1959, the last year for which figures are available, a total of 311 men in the South African police force were convicted in the courts of assault. Only twenty-nine of these men were discharged from the force.

In one case involving the police, there was evidence that a colored prisoner was lashed between two police trucks. The trucks were driven apart. The prisoner died later. One policeman was jailed for four years, another for eighteen months.

In 1960 a white detective sergeant was sentenced to four years imprisonment and an African detective to two years for beating an African suspect to death.

This is not government policy. The guilty policemen were brought to court and tried. But it is against this present legacy of human misery that the African must weigh apartheid and the government's promises for the future.

.   .   .

The positive side of apartheid revolves around certain African tribal areas, land allocated for African use, in extent a little less than 13 per cent of the total area of South Africa. With the exception of concentrated urban areas, these African reserves are more densely populated than any other part of South Africa. They must support at present about 40 per cent of the total African population. Yet they are backward, undeveloped, plagued by soil erosion and often badly farmed.

Clearly, development of these areas is desirable and there is an urgent need for it. But it is the political rather than the economic future of the reserves which has been the center of speculation since Dr. Verwoerd's accession to the prime ministership in 1958.

Dr. Verwoerd, like Nationalist party prime ministers before him, is dedicated to the preservation of white rule in South Africa. Again in his New Year's message for 1961 he warned: "Any form of political multi-racialism, or so-called partnership, would ultimately rob the white man of his rightful heritage."

Yet under his administration the future of these reserves has been given a new interpretation. Dr. Verwoerd says they are to be given increased autonomy to the point where ultimately they will be self-governing under African rule. This is a considerable advance on the thinking of previous premiers, and on that of many of today's supporters of the Nationalist party. Does it not mean, inevitably, that these reserves would one day seek independence and secession from the rest of South Africa? When I asked him this question Dr. Verwoerd indicated he had considered even that prospect, but he said he hoped that wise white statesmanship would persuade the African territories to remain bound to the central white state.

The essence of the idea then is to build African or Bantu home-lands, "Bantustans" as they are called, where Africans will run their own affairs. This is a move designed to give apartheid some moral basis, to offset the denial of rights to Africans in the rest of the country, to answer foreign criticism that Africans have no opportunities, and to still the consciences of another wing of the governing party troubled over apartheid's vast negative panoply.

With additional promised land the reserves would total a little more than 13 per cent of the total area of South Africa. Thus Dr. Verwoerd is offering 11,000,000 Africans ultimate autonomy in 13 per cent of the country as the price for continued suprem-acy for 3,000,000 whites in the remaining 87 per cent.

The 87 per cent contains all the gold, diamond and uranium mines, all the industry and commerce, all the big cities, ports, railways and communications networks and an overwhelming per-centage of the nation's resources.

Whatever the plans for the future, the 13 per cent which the Africans hold is at present backward, undeveloped, unindustrial-ized and used for peasant farming.

To many observers it has seemed a top-heavy arrangement, although Dr. Verwoerd has brushed aside protestations about the inequality of the division. But the glaring flaw in it all is that the reserves cannot possibly carry the African population of South Africa in their 13 per cent area.

The proof of this is tucked away in a dusty government volume which nobody talks about any more. It is dryly titled *The Report of the Commission for the Socio-Economic Development of the Bantu Areas within the Union of South Africa.* It is better known as the Tomlinson Report, after the name of its chairman, Professor F. R. Tomlinson.

This was to have been the government's blueprint for development of the reserves. Composed of a body of experts, the commission made an exhaustive investigation of the state and potential of the reserves. Its conclusion was an unpalatable one for the government. In essence, it reported that to develop the reserves to their utmost reasonable potential, the government must launch a crash program of development costing nearly $300,000,000 in the next ten years.

Next came the bombshell. With such a program, reported the commission, the carrying capacity of the already overcrowded reserves might be developed to the point where they could absorb 60 per cent of the total African population by 1981, and a maximum 70 per cent by the year 2000.

The conclusion was clear. If the government developed the reserves to their utmost, and siphoned off from the rest of the country as many Africans as the reserves could take, it would still have left in the so-called white areas between one and two Africans for every white man by the turn of the century.

In fact the dream of total territorial segregation had never been taken very seriously. If all the Africans were crowded into the reserves there would be none left to work the white man's mines and industries and clean the white housewife's floors. But now finally and indisputably the Tomlinson Report had demolished the prospect of a country completely boxed into black and white compartments.

The government balked even at the crash program recommended by the commission to settle a greater percentage of Africans in the reserves. It has spent nothing like the $30,000,000 a year on the reserves which the commission suggested. The report has been quietly dropped.

Thus South Africa is confronted by the immovable fact that there will always be more Africans than whites in the so-called white areas, whatever the future of the reserves.

Dr. Verwoerd persists in the reasoning that these are transient Africans, that they are not really detribalized and that they can be persuaded to look upon the reserves as their true homelands. This is despite the fact that many of these city dwellers now would be as much use back on the land as the average New Yorker pitchforked into a Western rodeo, and that their whole lives are spent in urban areas.

From this reasoning stems Dr. Verwoerd's stubborn refusal to recognize the presence or demands of urban Africans.

Will these millions be content with their voteless, rightless, eternally transient state? Will even the millions in the reserves be content with promised control of 13 per cent of the country? These are the questions which swirl around the Bantustan scheme.

Overriding all other considerations is the question of the government's sincerity in implementing the Bantustan program. Already the economic recommendations of the Tomlinson Report have been shelved and political autonomy is something which must remain on paper alone for many years.

Some critics of the government, like doughty Margaret Ballinger, who, as a white, represented Africans in parliament expertly for many years until the government abolished her seat, label the Bantustan scheme a complete sham. She charges the government has no intention of implementing it. In any case, she maintains, the tribal lands are far too scattered and fragmented ever to be cemented into viable states.

Mr. Luthuli opposes the scheme on grounds it gives Africans "neither freedom in the white man's areas nor independence in their own."

Critics such as these are extremely skeptical of the amount of political power which actually will be given to the African people. Their suspicion is traceable directly to the network of Bantu, or African, "Authorities" which the government has established in the reserves. These are the local authorities which are supposed to be the first step toward African self-rule. Yet they are limited in power and subservient to the government. The government has extensive control over them and appoints and can dismiss their members.

From the early proposal of the scheme, Mr. Luthuli had warned: "They [the Bantu Authorities] make the tribe's chief and his inner council absolute dictators over the tribe. They will make all decisions for the tribe but will not be responsible to the

tribe since they are all appointees of the government and not
elected by the people. This is not at all in conformity with our
traditions."

The government did not heed him. Soon there came the rumblings of trouble in reserves where tribesmen protested the nomi-
nation of certain chiefs to the Authorities. The tribesmen claimed
the chiefs had become stooges of the government.

Then in 1960, and into 1961, Pondoland exploded in revolt
against the rule of its chiefs who had cooperated in the Bantu
Authorities scheme. Pondoland had been one of the quietest reserves in South Africa, tucked away on the southeast coastline.
Ironically the government had imposed the new system en bloc
throughout Pondoland, so acquiescent did the Pondo tribe seem.
Pondoland had been selected to become a Bantustan showpiece.

Yet the tribesmen murdered some of their leaders, fired their
huts and kept white police, shock troops, armored cars and planes
and helicopters of the South African Air Force in the area for
months on end. Only just recovering from the earlier emergency
of 1960, the government was compelled to impose emergency
rule again in Pondoland. It was a bitter blow for Dr. Verwoerd.

African confidence in the Bantustan concept has not been
encouraged by contradictions in official statements. For instance,
while Dr. Verwoerd talks of self-government for the reserves, one
of the government's chief theoreticians of apartheid, Dr. W. W. M.
Eiselen, had earlier written in the Anglo-American Corporation's
magazine *Optima:* "The utmost degree of autonomy in administrative matters which parliament is likely to be prepared to concede to these [African] areas will stop short of actual surrender
of sovereignty by the European trustee."

Within the ruling Nationalist party, Dr. Verwoerd must also
reconcile the views of those party radicals to whom African rule
even in the Bantustans is unpalatable, and those intellectuals on
the other hand whose reserve on the question of Dr. Verwoerd's
sincerity is no secret.

It is in this atmosphere that the African has been asked to
accept the Bantustan plan as a promise of better things to come.
Yet the daily frustrations of apartheid have whittled away what-

ever trust most Africans may have had in the present government. As an African woman asked at a rare multiracial meeting in the South African city of East London: "I would like to be frank— must we really believe in white people?"

CHAPTER XVII

South Africa: Five Past Midnight?

WHAT IS South Africa's future? Can the whites resist the roaring tide of African nationalism, even push it back as the present government is trying to do?

On the face of things, the government is politically entrenched. It has no intention of surrendering political power to nonwhites. It commands the guns and tanks and planes with which to beat them back.

Elsewhere throughout the continent, Africans are governing themselves. Ironically here, where nonwhites have had the longest contact with the white man's civilizing influence, there looms no prospect of independence freely bestowed by whites.

Yet there is an air of disastrous inevitability about the course of events under the Verwoerd government. It has dug itself in, but there is an air of Hitlerian, last-ditch ecstasy about it all. Unless it is given to these few Afrikaners to divert the whole flood of history down the ages, they will be overtaken by the African revolution.

The most dangerous fallacy about South Africa today is that the African is a passive, stagnant force and that the white man still controls the direction of events. The white man may still be able to check the pace here and there, for even the ramparts of a sandcastle hold back the incoming tide for a while. But eventually it builds up and overruns them, as will the restless, rippling force of the African one day breach the fortress of Afrikanerdom and with it white supremacy. The questions are when, and how.

Some optimistic South African whites who have faced the

prospect believe there may be another twenty-five years of exclusive white rule. Others think the whites will be lucky with
five. Still others would not be surprised if the news tickers
started chattering the story of upheaval tomorrow.

How will it come? Perhaps it will begin with nation-wide industrial strikes and the stoppage of nonwhite labor. The millions
of nonwhites need only to stop work in concert for a week or two
to bring the economy grinding to a standstill. South Africa had a
brief foretaste of this during the 1960 emergency. Only part of
the labor force stayed at home and they could hold out for
only a few days, for there is no strike pay, or the resources of the
AFL-CIO, behind them. Yet it was enough to agitate the government, clog harbors with unworked cargo, leave factories empty
and in confusion and imperil essential services.

The police finally smashed that strike, but in one way it was
the end of an era, for the black man had flexed his muscles and
found them powerful. On the surface, the government triumphed,
but there were many elements of victory for the nonwhites. They
discovered their capacity to frighten the government itself, and
to force concessions such as the suspension of the pass laws, even
though these were reinforced within a few days.

It began with Sharpeville, that name etched upon the memory
of the world. The police fired on crowds thousands strong demon-
strating against the pass laws. More than seventy were killed and
many others injured in the massacre. It triggered off African protests and demonstrations across the country. Thousands of African
workers stayed home. There was violence in the big cities. The
white territorials were called to arms and the police and army
moved into action on a massive scale to crush the forces of African
opposition to the government. Thousands of South Africans of all
races were arrested and imprisoned for months without trial. The
country was under emergency rule for five months. The stock
market collapsed and the flow of capital into South Africa dried
up. Millions of dollars already in the country were whisked back
overseas by nervous investors who saw the country teetering on
the edge of revolution.

The end of an era perhaps. But it has made little difference to
the Verwoerd government. There may be a desire to avoid another

massacre like Sharpeville lest it unleash a new wave of international reaction against South Africa. There is a stirring of conscience among some clerics of the progovernment Dutch Reformed Church, and there is questioning and concern among the Afrikaner intellectuals.

However, the government has not seized the opportunity for negotiation and compromise with African leaders which offered itself once unrest had been quelled. There has been no new deal for nonwhites. Since his recovery from an assassination attempt during the emergency (the would-be assassin, a white farmer named David Beresford Pratt, is confined in a mental institution), Dr. Verwoerd has been more intransigent and unyielding than ever. He has if anything hardened government attitudes.

But African opinion is hardening too. Reaction sets up counter-reaction. The gap is widening. The emergence of the more extreme Pan Africanist Congress to challenge the African National Congress was an early warning signal of a more militant African outlook. Though both organizations are banned, the forces of African nationalism are active underground. In the African locations the people are not cowed. They talk of success "the next time."

Will "the next time," or perhaps the time after that, or even the time after that, be nonviolent? Or must there be an explosion in South Africa?

The government has left nonwhites with no orthodox political weapons. Yet if you stoke up a pressure cooker and screw down the safety valves, something must explode. The sadness of it all if this happens in South Africa is that many nice people may get hurt in the process.

.   .   .

Time is something of which South Africa has least to spare. Yet the tragedy of contemporary South African politics is that the present government has frittered away the past thirteen years in the cul-de-sac of apartheid.

This is a country with the largest white population in Africa. It is the most industrialized and prosperous. If contact with the white man is the criterion, then its nonwhites who have lived alongside whites for more than three hundred years are better fitted for responsibility than those elsewhere in Africa with less than a century under colonial rule. Clearly, South Africa offered the white man his best chance in all the continent of creating a truly successful multiracial state. He has turned his back upon it.

Is there still time for whites to retrace their steps and work out a deal with nonwhites which would avert a racial clash? Or is it five minutes past midnight and are the whites living on borrowed time? Nobody has a simple blueprint for a new South Africa. If there is still time for a peaceful solution, it is no easy one. The changes and adjustments and the sacrifices of white privilege must be radical, extensive and probably painful. At the moment there is no sign that anything but a small minority of whites is prepared to make them. This is what leads some spectators to declare that South Africa's real problem is a white one, not a nonwhite one.

It is dangerous to generalize about any race, and white South Africans are no exception. There are white segregationists who treat their nonwhite servants and employees impeccably, and there are liberals who exploit theirs. There are whites who treat Africans with outrageous arrogance, and others who are sensitive in the extreme to their dignity.

The circles from which my wife and I drew our white friends in South Africa were the sort in which there generally would be sympathy and kindliness toward African employees. Within the narrow confines of the master-servant relationship there is often good will and even affection. There are stories of nonwhite loyalty to white employers in time of danger, and of formidable battles waged against police and authority by whites defending their nonwhite employees.

Yet having said all this, it is impossible to overlook the curious amalgam of fear, ignorance and blatant self-interest in which much of white South Africa is steeped. Except for a few lone voices and organizations, white South Africa allows to continue unchecked exploitation, indignity and cruelty on a massive scale where nonwhites are concerned. Infringement of nonwhite rights frequently laps over and erodes those of whites as well. Democracy is raped every day in South Africa. Yet the assaults on freedom which would see the universities of America ablaze with righteous anger, the cobblestones of Paris torn up and the duffle-coated youth of London marching on Downing Street, were they to occur in those countries, pass with barely a blink of the white man's eye in South Africa.

Of course fear has much of the population in its grip. Fear looms large in the armory of the government. It has ruthlessly exploited white fears of the outnumbering nonwhites, and the white way of life has become impregnated with many other fears besides. It is surprising how many white South Africans are afraid to sign with their own names a letter to a newspaper critical of the government, or to discuss politics over the telephone.

One striking thing about South Africa today is that it is the white man, not the African, who is afraid. With all the oppression and penalties loaded against him, the African somehow emerges cheerfully confident of his future. In Johannesburg it is the white men who retire at night behind their grilled and guarded windows, with their big dogs, and sometimes a revolver under the pillow.

Thus fear of being swamped by the outnumbering nonwhite millions hinders the white political and other concessions which perhaps might avert violence.

Another hurdle is extreme white ignorance of the facts of life in South Africa.

White South Africans complain that Americans and Britons and others who criticize South African racial policies might very soon change their views if transplanted to the South African situation. There is something in this, for there are immigrants whose views have undergone a radical change.

Another complaint is that all white South Africans are blamed for the government's racial atrocities, although they do not all support the government. There is something in this too; however, it must be said that there is broad white support for racial discrimination and segregation although some whites disagree with specific aspects of government policy.

The most frequent complaint, however, is that South Africa's problems are distorted and sensationalized by the foreign press. Perhaps there are incidents of misrepresentation. The foreign correspondents I know lean over backward to present the facts accurately. You can hardly blame them if the facts are almost always ugly ones.

Most of the complainants really have no idea what the foreign press reports about South Africa. They never see an American or a British newspaper from one year's end to another. They have fallen into the dangerous habit of parroting the government's charges. And the validity of the government's attacks on the foreign press depends upon one's standards of news evaluation and interpretation.

In the way of things, the massacre of seventy Africans at Sharpeville with all its implications is assured far bigger headlines than the fact that the government spends $28,000,000 a year on African education. Even this latter fact loses some of its luster when one discovers that eight times as much is spent on the education of a white child as on an African. Also that a third of the funds for African education come from direct African taxation. These are the subsidiary facts which white South Africans rarely know.

Many South African whites are self-appointed experts on the color question. And rightly, it is they, not the criticizing Americans or Britons, who have to live in the midst of the problem. Yet not one in a hundred has been inside an African location. Not one in a thousand has been in an African home. Their actual knowledge of African living conditions, habits and customs is of a most limited kind. Few ordinary white South Africans have ever had a conversation with an African lawyer or doctor. Their assessment of African capacity is all too often based on the performance of an African servant, and it is only fair to state that such performance can be irritating at times. However, even at this level, many whites employ Africans without ever learning their proper names, their tribes, their religions, their homes, their ambitions, their frustrations. Sometimes this association lasts for years without whites ever finding out what their African servants really think about the world in which they live.

Aside from the chiefs appointed to the Bantu Authorities, it is probable that no single member of the cabinet has in his whole life had a heart to heart talk with a genuine African nationalist politician.

This interracial contact is neither wanted nor encouraged by the government. The government has barred whites from visiting the African townships and the African reserves. It does not want the races to mingle, or the whites to see how white authority controls the African areas. It wants the two worlds separate. This barrier to understanding is one of apartheid's most bitter bequests.

So friends of ours in New York and London, reading their newspapers and viewing the television news films, are often better informed on South African affairs than our white South African friends living a mile or two from the African locations.

Much of white South Africa's ignorance is genuine. But one cannot avoid the suspicion that it is feigned in some instances, just as some Germans denied knowledge of the incidents that were taking place in the Nazi concentration camps. There are whites who feel deeply for the sufferings and hardship of the nonwhites. But there are many others who know things in their hearts but dare not admit them. To do so would mean action, and that might mean the end of white privilege.

Self-interest and white conservatism is naturally most deeply rooted among the lower classes of whites in economic competition with nonwhites. This is not to say that there is not prejudice threaded right through and up to the polo-playing clubmen. But the whites in lowly jobs, dubious of their ability to hold them in free competition with nonwhites, are those who cling most steadfastly to protection on racial grounds and who resist reform.

Often these are the Afrikaners who are the sheet anchor of the ruling Nationalist party, and whose nationalism has clashed with that of the African. Both Afrikaners and Africans are from the land, and are poor and unskilled as they come flooding into the cities for economic betterment. Both are becoming urbanized, and in the process are nudging each other for the jobs which each might do. Afrikaner nationalism is one of the continent's most early nationalisms, and in many respects the Afrikaner struggle against the British has resembled the struggle of indigenous Africans against colonialism. Perhaps one day someone will conduct a fascinating study into the parallels between African and Afrikaner nationalism. However, to some students of Afrikaner history it seems as though the Afrikaner has been conducting a trek from the racial realities in his midst, from the time he left

British rule at the Cape to his latest defection from the Common-wealth. Now there are not many places left to trek to.

Of course, there is some leavening on the South African scene. The captains of industry are often the first to see the writing on the wall. Some like Mr. Oppenheimer probably would support political concessions to nonwhites within a framework providing checks and balances and guarantees of white security. Others, not prepared to go this far, are nevertheless urging higher wages and economic reforms.

One must hope this will all have some effect, but often the outlook in South Africa seems so dark that one is in danger of overestimating the occasional faint gleam of light. On the basis of concrete evidence, there is little indication that the walls of white prejudice will crumble except by duress.

.   .   .

It is impossible to believe that South Africa can escape the African revolution which has swept across most of the continent. Whether the revolution in this country will be peaceful as in much of Africa, whether it will have the sharp edge of militancy, or whether it will even border on the chaos of the Congo, remains to be seen.

Despite the present catastrophic trend, there are imponderables. Dr. Verwoerd might be overthrown by an internal party revolt, although to date he has been strikingly successful in quelling the occasional rumbles of dissent. The nation might be hit by a slump, which it is in little shape to weather. There are mounting pres-sures in the world outside South Africa, of which South Africa's exclusion from the Commonwealth, and increasing attacks at the UN are symptomatic.

All or any of these could affect the course of upheaval. How-ever, once it has effectively begun, it is difficult to see how non-whites with their considerable numbers, can ultimately fail to gain political control. On the other hand, unless there is an un-imaginable holocaust, it is difficult to conceive of an overnight white abdication of power.

Thus there may be an interim period of drastic readjustment; of mounting nonwhite demands and white compromises; of crumbling color barriers, rising nonwhite wages, and the emergence of class rather than color divisions; of lowered white living standards and increased taxes to meet new demands for nonwhite housing and improved state services.

It is a period into which few observers are prepared to probe. They are occupied enough with the immediate course of events and the shape of the upheaval they see impending. The days thereafter will be critical. White and African statesmanship will be at a premium. South Africa has been fortunate to date with its African leaders although the whites have rejected them. Future leaders may not be so moderate. Events may not be orderly and reasonable. The clash, if there is one, may not be short and sharp, but may extend over a string of worsening disorders. Some people are convinced the United Nations flag will yet fly over South Africa after the international organization has been called in to restore order.

All this can only be speculation. Some type of accord is inevitable unless South Africa's races are to live in perpetual disorder. Beside the African majority, there are 3,000,000 whites rooted in an industrial society. Some are already leaving and others will too. But the removal of the bulk of them is a physical impossibility. Then there are the half million Indians and the 1,500,000 coloreds inextricably interwoven in the life of South Africa.

For the moment, South Africa seems a bastion of white rule, out of character with the rest of the changed map of Africa. Yet if all the lessons of the African revolution mean anything, Africans will guide the force of change here too. And it will come quicker than any of us imagine.

CHAPTER XVIII

Southern Africa: Verwoerdian Heel?

WE HAVE lingered long in South Africa, for it is the most potentially explosive country in the continent, which might pose even graver challenges than the Congo.

Colonialism is in its twilight stages. It is rapidly disappearing as an issue for the emergent African states, together with those of the Asian and Arab worlds. But apartheid drags on in South Africa. This is becoming a new focal issue for the nonwhite nations.

In some of these territories around South Africa, these states believe they see the chinks in apartheid's armor.

Before leaving southern Africa, we must pause for a quick look at these territories which might appear in the headlines.

First of all there is South-West Africa, which abuts South Africa on its western flank. For all its size, this is a dry, drab, forlorn corner of Africa, not particularly likely, one might think, to become a world flashpoint and the center of international crisis.

Yet South-West Africa could well prove Dr. Verwoerd's Achilles heel. Some imaginative observers believe the day may come when the landing ramps will drop down and American marines will come splashing ashore on this coastline as part of a United Nations task force. Whether it will come to that is perhaps doubtful, but it is conceivable that the Verwoerd government might face other world pressures on South-West Africa which could jar it to the point of collapse.

Why South-West Africa? The territory is a blank to ordinary citizens the world over. Once a year there is a debate on it at the United Nations. A team of petitioners headed by a stubborn and controversial and dedicated English clergyman called Michael Scott appears before the Trusteeship Committee. It pleads the case of the Hereros and other South-West African tribes for United Nations trusteeship instead of rule by the present South African government. It relists the Africans' grievances and record of oppression under white rule. Each year the Trusteeship Committee passes another resolution, makes another plea to South Africa and nothing happens till the following year again.

Yet it is at just such a debate as these that the trouble could start, and lately the resolutions are getting tougher.

South-West Africa is the cause of a major dispute between the United Nations and the South African government. Each claims jurisdiction over it. Before World War I, the territory was part of Germany's colonial empire. This chapter in the territory's history lives long in the memory of its people today. In thirty years, the Herero population had been "reduced" by German rule from 80,000 to 15,000.

During the war, South African forces under Smuts and Botha trounced the Germans and at war's end South-West Africa became a League of Nations mandate under South African rule.

Now the United Nations claims that it inherited the old League's mandates and that South-West Africa should be a trusteeship territory. South Africa maintains the mandate has lapsed and South-West Africa now is virtually part of South Africa.

For more than fifteen years the weary tug-of-war has continued although South Africa has been in effective control of the territory. But in the past year or two, the composition of the United Nations has changed. New African states angrily opposed to South Africa's race policies have come bustling into membership. They are determined to smash apartheid, and in South-West Africa they believe they see the instrument to deal the Verwoerd government a mortal political blow.

South Africa has steadfastly refused to recognize the authority of the United Nations to interfere in its internal racial affairs. Although United Nations Secretary General Dag Hammarskjöld visited South Africa in 1961, this was on the clear understanding that this did not prejudice the government's rejection of United

Nations authority. The government still stoutly adheres to its argument that apartheid is a domestic matter, beyond United Nations jurisdiction.

However, in South-West Africa, where the same system of apartheid is applied, the Verwoerd government is vulnerable to outside intervention.

This, at any rate, is the belief of Dr. Verwoerd's opponents elsewhere in Africa and they are intent on bringing the issue to a head.

Liberia and Ethiopia have taken South Africa to the International Court of Justice over South-West Africa. They are the only black African states which were members of the old League of Nations, and they are entitled to take a mandate dispute to the International Court at The Hague.

In the past the United Nations General Assembly has sought advisory opinions from the International Court but South Africa has not responded to them. A new and compulsory judgment would be a very different thing, however, especially if it were adverse to South Africa and ruled that South-West Africa must be returned to United Nations supervision.

South African intransigence in this event would entitle Liberia and Ethiopia to seek enforcement of the judgment by the United Nations Security Council. This is when the United Nations might take serious action against South Africa, perhaps in the form of sanctions or a combination of diplomatic and economic pressures. This too is when some observers see the prospect of a United Nations military expedition on the march.

At first glimpse, it is difficult to imagine why anybody would quarrel over this arid, unattractive land which stretches for miles of desert emptiness from the Namib Desert along its western seaboard to the Kalahari Desert and Bechuanaland in the east. Yet seized it was from the Bushmen, the little Stone Age people who are supposed to be the earliest inhabitants of southern Africa, but who were decimated by African tribes sweeping southward down the continent, and by whites marching up from the Cape. Today there are just the rock paintings of the early Bushmen left, and a few thousand Bushmen living a razor's edge sort of existence in the desolate Kalahari. South-West Africa's present population of about 450,000 is predominantly African. Half of these are Ovambo tribesmen, big, strong men much in demand by the mining companies at work along the coast.

Perhaps the Germans alone would have had the tenacity to colonize South-West Africa, and they set about it thoroughly as soon as they marched in in the late nineteenth century. The evidence of their presence lingers in the capital of Windhoek today, and in a mainly Afrikaner population of 73,000 whites, there are 15,000 people of German descent. Thus there are German shops and cuckoo clocks from Bavaria, and beer gardens and *lederhosen* and even a newspaper called the *Allgemeine Zeitung*. The local government is housed in a building called, with straight-faced German practicality, the Tintenpalast, the Ink Palace. There are knobbly little castles like the Schweringsburg and the Heintzburg and the Sanderburg, and you can almost imagine yourself in the Rhineland, if the Rhine flowed sand, that is, like the South-West African rivers which are dry for much of the year.

Although the Germans never found them, there are rich rewards beneath South-West Africa's desert dunes. Buried along the Namib coast where the Atlantic sends cool fingers of foam rippling up over the blistering beaches are the diamonds fit for a royal tiara. This is the Diamond Coast and it is the preserve of Consolidated Diamond Mines, another tentacle of the Oppenheimer financial octopus, which reaches out and scoops up $60,000,000 in diamonds every year here.

There is a lot of scooping involved. The diamond-bearing gravels are hidden under the coastal dunes within sight and sound of the surf, and although this is not deep mining, a mechanized army of giant earth-moving machines must nevertheless shift twenty tons of sand and gravel for every ounce of diamonds recovered.

There are other diamonds in South-West Africa, the "black diamonds" which the farmers call their curly black Karakul sheep. The Germans imported the sheep as an experiment and now the export of their pelts is a money-spinning industry. The pelts earn the farmers about six dollars each and are much in demand by overseas fashion houses for manufacture into "Persian

Lamb" or "Astrakhan" coats. Most of the pelts go to the United States. To satisfy fashion's whim, some 3,000,000 Karakul lambs are slaughtered every year in South-West Africa at birth. They must be killed almost immediately otherwise the wool does not retain its curliness.

South-West Africa's other contribution to the world of fashion comes from Cape Cross. Hundreds of baby seals basking on the rocky beach here are clubbed to death each year to provide expensive sealskin coats for women. The young pup seals are selected because the skins of full-grown seals are covered with coarse hair. Again, most of the skins go to the United States.

In South-West Africa are some of the most restricted and closely guarded areas in the world, open to visitors only after exhaustive investigation and with official documents. Partly this is to seal off the diamond areas from smugglers, partly to stop travelers penetrating the dangerous deserts where only camels and specially equipped desert vehicles can move and partly to keep the politically curious away from the big African reserves. The police Special Branch exhibits an extraordinary sensitivity where these latter areas are concerned. They fall under the jurisdiction of the South African native [African] affairs minister. Even for illegal entry of an African location on the outskirts of the capital of Windhoek, New York *Times* reporter Milton Bracker was given a comprehensive grilling about his political contacts, as well as being fined.

Thus apart from the annual testimony of petitioners at the United Nations, much of South-West Africa remains a closed book. Occasionally one gets a peep at official thinking, as during an exchange of correspondence on African labor conditions recently in the South African magazine *Financial Mail*. One reader wrote to say that he had "never seen labor exploited the way it is" in Walvis Bay, where there is a substantial canning industry to absorb the product of the port's fishing fleet. The following are extracts from a letter from the territory's chief government official in rebuttal of the charges: "The contracts made with the Ovambo labor allow 48 hours a week in eight-hour shifts a day at a minimum rate of 1s 3d [17 American cents] a shift.

"This rate is never adhered to and the minimum a shift is

1s 6d [21 cents]. Good laborers are often paid at 2s 6d [35 cents] and even 3s 6d [49 cents] a shift. They get 6d [7 cents] an hour overtime.

"Normally Ovambo labor works an average of 12–13 hours a day for six days a week."

. . .

Three other neighbors of South Africa are the British protectorates of Bechuanaland, Swaziland and Basutoland. These are territories ruled by Britain, either adjacent to South Africa or, in the case of Basutoland, completely encircled by it.

Bechuanaland is a flat, desert country bigger than France and containing much of the same Kalahari Desert which spills over into neighboring South-West Africa. It has a long common border with South Africa on the latter's northern frontier.

Swaziland is a pocket kingdom hardly bigger than Connecticut, set snugly within South Africa's eastern boundaries beyond a parapet of jagged mountain tips. Although Swaziland fronts South Africa on three sides, its eastern border is a common one with Portuguese Mozambique.

Basutoland, the Switzerland of Africa as it is sometimes called, is a remote and relatively inaccessible mountain enclave entirely surrounded by South Africa. This is a land of soaring, snow-capped peaks, much of it penetrated only by Basuto pony over winding bridle trails.

The three are wards of Britain and are run by British officials under the jurisdiction of a British high commissioner to the territories.

South Africa for many years argued that the three territories should be included within South Africa. The argument was that the states were already economically bound to South Africa, and were too weak to become viable independent nations. In many respects the territories already are treated as part of the South African economy, sharing various services. Thousands of laborers from these little lands are dependent for their livelihoods on work in South Africa's mines and industries.

There was, in fact, provision for the cession of Basutoland, Swaziland and Bechuanaland to South Africa provided two conditions were fulfilled. The populations of the territories, which are overwhelmingly African, had to agree. Also required was the consent of the British parliament.

With the advent of an apartheid-minded government in South Africa in 1948, the prospects of either the Africans or the British government agreeing to absorption of the three protectorates by South Africa grew more and more remote.

Then Britain began constitutional reforms and advances in the protectorates entirely out of character with the political pattern for Africans in South Africa. Basutoland and Bechuanaland were given legislative councils, or local parliaments.

Finally South Africa's exclusion from the Commonwealth shattered any ideas that the protectorates would one day be handed over to South Africa.

In the meantime the protectorates offer sanctuary to political refugees who have fled the arm of the South African government. Many of the entry points are unguarded and it is relatively easy to slip across the border from South Africa under the protection of the British flag.

Sometimes the refugees wait for the clamor to die down, then return to South Africa. If they are permanent exiles they use the protectorates as a staging point on their journeys north either to other African lands or even to Europe or the United States.

All this angers the South African government considerably. Ministers have racked their brains for a method to block the escape route, but this is no easy task when one considers the enormousness of the borders.

.   .   .

The protectorates are peaceful backwaters, far from cities and crowds. Swaziland has a population of 240,000, only 6,000 of them white. The territory needs no military force and only a modest police detachment of 27 whites and 122 Africans for the whole country.

Even when someone does commit a crime, prison life is not too trying. Convicts serving less than six months' imprisonment are sometimes permitted to live at home and come and do their prison chores during working hours.

Taxation for Africans is $4.90 a year for each man who is un-married, or who if married has limited himself to one wife. For each additional wife, states the tax table solemnly, there is an additional tax of $4.20 to a ceiling of $12.60. Wives after that come tax free.

There is provision for trade unions but nobody has formed one. There is only one political party.

The price of all this seclusion from the buffetings of the outside world is considerable backwardness. Swaziland has no railway, no air service and not a single tarred road. As one British official put it: "If South Africa really did take over Swaziland we would get some bridges and fine new roads and really get things rolling." Then wistfully: "But it would rather spoil it all, wouldn't it?"

Spoil it all or not, progress is on the way. Swazi soil will soon be bearing the biggest man-made forests in the world. Britain's Colonial Development Corporation has a big scheme under way in Swaziland's Usutu Forest and there are other company proj-ects. Next must come the railway to ship the timber out and open the country to development.

Political progress must come too, as it has in Bechuanaland and Basutoland. Till now a British resident commissioner, next down the line of command from the high commissioner for the three territories, has listened with one ear to a white elected advisory council, and with the other to Sobhuza II, the Ingwenyama, or Lion, who is paramount chief, and thus king, of the Swazis. Backed by a council of chiefs and headmen, Sobhuza wields ex-tensive rule over his countrymen, dispensing tribal justice and controlling a Swazi national treasury. The system has worked with tranquillity but now the Swaziland Progressive party has called for independence within five years and the country is stirring. Inevitably there must come a legislative council and the paraphernalia of parliamentary rule.

Bechuanaland too has a strong tribal background. There are only 3,000 whites in the territory, but 300,000 Africans. Of these the biggest tribe is the Bamangwato which lived for many years under the enlightened rule of an outstanding African leader, Tshekedi Khama. Tshekedi was regent for his young nephew, Seretse Khama, whose marriage to a white English girl he met during his university studies in Britain was splashed across the world's press.

The mixed marriage drew stormy protests from whites in South Africa and Southern Rhodesia. Britain deposed both Tshekedi and Seretse and sent Seretse into exile in Britain. The Bamangwato became the tribe that lost its head.

As is always the pattern with Britain's African exiles, Seretse was permitted to return to the territory, where he has lived quietly with his wife for some years. Tshekedi died in 1959. Ostensibly, Seretse is aloof from politics and Britain has attempted to fill the vacuum left by the deposal of both Seretse and Tshekedi with a government-appointed tribal authority. But the Bamangwato recognize Seretse as their leader and his white wife, who caused controversy among the tribe itself at first, is now accepted.

All this has impeded Bechuanaland's constitutional development but Britain announced reforms to give the territory its own legislative council in the second half of 1961, and, though it is not clear what role Seretse will play, the territory is on the move again.

Meantime, the Rhodesian Selection Trust group of mining companies has signed a ten-year agreement with the Bamangwato tribe to prospect for minerals over 40,000 square miles of the tribe's lands. The tribe would get royalties on any mineral mined. A big strike would put Bechuanaland on the map.

In Basutoland too the hunt is on for treasures beneath the earth. The South African De Beers group—Mr. Oppenheimer once again. —is hunting for diamonds. Diamond mining on a substantial scale would pour some badly needed funds into the treasury of this poverty-stricken little land, but it would not provide work for all the Basutos who must trek to the gold mines of South Africa to earn their livelihood. Although the mines pay little, between 40 and 50 per cent of Basutoland's able-bodied men are constantly away on the twelve-to-eighteen-months-long contracts which give them the money they cannot earn in their own rugged land. Of Basutoland's 600,000 people, about 60,000 men are at the mines each year. With few crops and no industries, Basutoland's principal export is black labor.

This is a land of mystic mountain splendor and wild, plunging valleys. Existence is precarious. Winter after bleak winter, the Basutos go to ground in their stone, wind-tugged huts, huddled in their exotic blankets. When the first sign of spring thrusts through the melting winter snows, they are out to tend their staple crop of mealies (corn).

The climate has produced a sturdily independent people, as tough as their ponies, which are the principal transport. These ponies are of Arab and Persian stock, first imported from Java and later Andalusia, by white settlers in South Africa. The men of the mountains are one of the world's last races of horsemen and the stores in the capital of Maseru are cluttered with saddles and leatherware and other horsy gear.

Maseru is really only a village. Here live most of the 2,000 whites in the protectorate, many of them government officials in the administration. All of Basutoland's imports must travel the long overland route from the ports of South Africa and there is scope for improvisation. Some of the filing trays in the government offices are sawn-down gasoline cans.

Basutoland is the poorest of the three protectorates and is confronted by several cruel dilemmas.

On the one hand its economic future seems inextricably bound up with that of South Africa. Yet being completely surrounded by South Africa, its people are more apprehensive of South African political influence than those in the two other protectorates, and are the most vigorous in their determination to prevent it seeping into Basutoland.

Many Basutos recognize that their best protection against South Africa is Britain's continued presence in the territory. Yet on the other hand this is the most politically developed of the protectorates and the one with an African nationalist organization which is active. Its leader is Ntsu Mokhehle, who has aligned himself with Dr. Nkrumah's pan-Africanism and who is well-known in Accra and other African capitals.

The elected leaders are balanced in Basutoland's legislative council, however, by tribal chiefs and their nominees. Basutoland's paramount chief is Bereng Seeiso who recently won a struggle for the chieftainship against the regent, Mantsebo Seeiso, senior wife of the previous paramount chief. Mantsebo ruled during the childhood of Bereng, the legitimate heir, but yielded the chief-tainship to Bereng only after a struggle in which he flew home from studies at Oxford's Corpus Christi college and refused to return to England until he had secured the tribal throne.

For all the politicking, however, the Basutos remain an un-spoiled people up in their mountain redoubt. Once when I was photographing a group of them in their traditional colored blankets in Maseru, I felt a heavy tap on my shoulder. There stood a huge African policeman. He wanted me for no crime. He just wondered, he said with a shy smile, whether I would include him in the picture and send him a copy.

We stood in the middle of the street and he chuckled as, for a change, *he* had *his* name and address written down in some-body *else's* notebook. His first name, he told me, was Peacock.

EAST AFRICA

CHAPTER XIX

Tanganyika: Haven of Peace

THE EAST COAST of Africa is where all the tropical travel posters come true.

The coastline of Tanganyika and Kenya is one of immense charm. The colors are vivid, the sky is bright blue. If you are fortunate enough to come by sea, the Indian Ocean sparkles under tropical sun by day, and shimmers under a pale yellow African moon by night.

Porpoises dip and dive in the wake and phosphorescence of your liner. Sometimes you sight a shark, the garbage man of the deep, sorting through the ship's trash. Once when I sailed this coast, a flying fish came whizzing through an open porthole in the dining room to plop squarely in the soup plate of a startled English matron. If it had arrived with the fish course, it would have made an even better story.

To shore beyond the surf lie the creamy beaches and the forests of palms and the wooden outrigger canoes drawn up upon the sand. Here and there are little creeks and inlets with huts on stilts and perhaps a fishing boat stranded dry and helpless for scraping and caulking.

The ports of call are fascinating. Offshore there is Zanzibar, a romantic little island which is the source of the world's cloves. Capital and principal port of Tanganyika is Dar es Salaam, where the lavender-hulled mailship swings at anchor in a grand tropical harbor in a frame of coconut palms. Then there is Mombasa, Kenya's port, and a polyglot town of white shipping men and African laborers and Indian and Arab traders. Here is a complete

225

Arab quarter with its narrow cobbled streets and soaring minarets, for Arab influence is strong along this coast.

An annual event along this coast is the arrival of the great fleet of Arab sailing dhows which come foaming out of the sea haze as they have for centuries past on their yearly voyage to East Africa. From Arabia, and the ports of the Persian Gulf and the Red Sea they come, strung out over the Indian Ocean for 3,000 miles, scudding before the annual monsoon from the northeast.

They seek haven along the coast and for the next six months the ports and harbors are cluttered with dhow captains and their crews, selling and bartering their cargoes of dates and figs, salt, dried fish, building tiles, carpets and ornaments. The dhow harbor at Mombasa is crammed with a forest of tall masts as the dhow captains hold court in the sterns of their vessels, dispensing coffee to guests and traders seated on Persian carpets who have come to traffic with them.

The dhows on the East African run are mainly "booms" and "baggalas," the latter built with a high poop, frequently beautifully carved, and resembling the old-time galleons in hull design despite the single mat sail which they use.

No cockleshell coastal or river dhows are these, but sturdy oceangoers of 200 tons and more, built by Arabs expert in the business, although they are often sailed with a minimum of navigating equipment and charts.

Finally, when the last deals have been clinched, the formalities exchanged, and the homeward-bound cargoes of mangrove building poles and sometimes cotton goods and light machinery have been stowed away, the dhows are ready. When the palm trees are ruffled by the first monsoon winds from the south, gusting in the opposite direction to those which brought them down from Arabia, the longboats haul them out to sea, the big lateen sails are rigged and the dhows speed away again till next year.

.   .   .

Compared with the black anarchy of the Congo or the strident white nationalism of South Africa, Tanganyika is a haven of peace. The name of its capital, Dar es Salaam, means just this, "haven of peace," and Tanganyika has been a tranquil land, rarely the subject of international attention.

There has been no outbreak of African violence here, no intertribal caterwauling, nor even defiant resistance by a white minority to African rule. Spared such sensational events, Tanganyika has been overlooked in much the same way as the quiet African giant of Nigeria in West Africa.

All this should not delude one that Tanganyika is unimportant, or that the African revolution has passed it by. Advance here may have been achieved with a minimum of fuss and a maximum of good will, but Tanganyika has struck out along the independence road as vigorously as any other African nation. Among the countries of East Africa it has come from behind to lead the race to African self-government, winning it before Kenya and Uganda. Tanganyika's role in the future may be an important one, perhaps as the kingpin of a projected East African federation.

Various reasons are advanced for Tanganyika's peaceful progress. A main one is that, although Tanganyika was brought to African rule under a British administration, it was a trusteeship territory of the United Nations. The international organization sent regular investigating missions to the territory, took evidence from African politicians and prodded Britain regularly to set a date for self-government.

Another factor is the smallness of the white population—only some 20,000 compared with an African population of 8,700,000 and 100,000 Indians and Arabs. The prospect of so tiny a group preserving white rule in Tanganyika was ludicrous. African rule was inevitable. Thus, although there have been white groans and moans, there has been no serious obstruction of African ambitions. Some whites have in fact cooperated in the African campaign for independence.

However, the principal reason for Tanganyika's success to date has been the outstanding ability of its African leader, Julius Nyerere. Mr. Nyerere is rated as one of the ablest politicians in Africa. He is respected by all races in Tanganyika, white and nonwhite, and is lauded as a man of moderation. Remarkably, he has survived that label in a continent where among Africans it often means political oblivion.

But Mr. Nyerere is no favor-currier with the immigrant races despite his friendliness and moderation toward them. He is as quietly tough an African nationalist as many another, who has proved his willingness to turn on the pressure during his campaign for African rule.

A small, slight African with a toothbrush mustache, Nyerere was born near Lake Victoria and became a teacher in a Roman Catholic mission school (to which faith he is himself a convert), after study at Makerere College in Uganda. Later he won a master's degree in history and economics at Scotland's Edinburgh University and returned to his country to throw himself into the organization of the Tanganyika African National Union. This is the dominating political party in Tanganyika, and as its leader Mr. Nyerere argued the case for Tanganyika's independence at the United Nations, and swept his party to electoral victory at home when constitutional reforms were introduced.

Prime minister of an African government, Mr. Nyerere has shown his willingness to recruit both Indians and whites for his cabinet. His finance minister, for example, has been Sir Ernest A. Vasey, an able white and formerly finance minister in Kenya's government. One of Tanganyika's problems is to find enough qualified Africans to fill top governmental posts.

For the present, Mr. Nyerere enjoys widespread popularity throughout the territory and his Tanganyika African National Union is clearly in control. There is an opposition party, the Tanganyika African National Congress, whose president, Mr. Zuberi Mtemvu, surprised everybody recently by making a trip to Peking. The Congress has attacked Nyerere for not going far enough fast enough, but in the light of Nyerere's achievement the ground has been cut from beneath it.

In time, Mr. Nyerere expects the emergence of a stronger African political opposition, perhaps swelled by a splinter group from his own party. Thus like most African leaders he is anxious to consolidate his position by producing for his people tangible economic benefits from his rule.

As an economist he is well aware of the economic problems

which for the moment loom larger than political ones in Tanganyika.

Despite the lushness of the coastal belt, Tanganyika is a vast arid territory more than twice the size of California with nothing but empty bush and the tang of the African dust through great sections of it.

This is Africa in the raw. This is the land which Henry Morton Stanley, that famous Welshman-turned-American, tramped across when the *New York Herald* sent him to find Dr. Livingstone. Stanley was best remembered by his newspaper for his fabulous expense accounts for the trip which have roused the awed admiration of every African correspondent since. However he has become immortalized in the public's memory for that statement of glorious British reserve when he found Livingstone at Ujiji, on Lake Tanganyika, after a grueling trek: "Dr. Livingstone, I presume?"

Stanley found Livingstone in 1871, and, soon after, the Germans began their colonial conquest of Tanganyika. They held it until the First World War, then they were squeezed out by Allied forces under the command of South Africa's Smuts at one time. From war's end the British ran Tanganyika until Africans took over the government more than forty years later.

Under British rule as under German, Tanganyika drifted on in isolation.

This was storybook Africa. Young British district commissioners sat in kingly rule over vast slices of territory and thousands of tribal Africans. There in their lonely outposts, once the stones marking the square had been whitewashed, and the Union Jack hauled to the top of its pole until sunset, their thoughts would wander to Devonshire cream and girls in Cheltenham and next month's tattered shipment of the London *Times*. And sometimes the *bwana* would be called out to deal with a rogue elephant trampling down somebody's corn patch.

Once after World War II, the British government attempted an ambitious colonial project to grow groundnuts in Tanganyika, but the scheme collapsed with the loss of many millions of dollars.

And so Tanganyika has remained poor and undeveloped with most of its people engaged in peasant agriculture. Some tribes, like the arrogant Masai, do not exert themselves even thus far, and drift with their cattle which are their wealth and sustenance across the country. Where the game plains tip upward and rise to the foothills of famous Mount Kilimanjaro, on Tanganyika's northern boundary, there is a notable exception. This is the Chagga tribe of about 310,000, which has been building something of a prosperous middle class in this fertile area with high-powered production of coffee for the export market. The Chagga tribe had achieved a considerable degree of economic independence even under British rule, running their own affairs from a modern administrative building, levying their own taxes on the tribe, printing their own newspaper, administering their own clinics and construction projects and marketing their coffee crop through their own cooperative, said to be the largest in Africa.

This is only a corner of the country, however, and average per capita income has remained less than one-third that of the citizen of Ghana, and about one-fiftieth that of the average American.

When my wife and I drove across the country some years ago on a trip from Kenya to South Africa the backwardness was apparent. In parts the Great North Road which the trans-African motorists must travel was no more than a rutted, dusty track, turning to impassable red mud in the rains. There was heavy sand, drifts to be forded and rivers to be crossed on rickety pontoons. The route wound over the hot, endless plains of Tanganyika many miles from a gasoline point, and up through rocky passes occasionally blocked by a landslide or by a tree felled by an elephant. Over some lonely sections the whole day passed without our seeing another car.

On several occasions we passed the road graders at work. Sometimes a grader was a log dragged behind a tractor in an attempt to flatten the corrugations in the track. Incredibly, at other times it was a bundle of stout twigs dragged mile upon mile over the surface of the road by barefooted Africans.

To lift Tanganyika out of this tropical economic torpor, Mr. Nyerere's government hopes to double the national income within ten years. Currently the main export income comes from sisal, grown by white plantation owners, and coffee and cotton grown by Africans, while a steady money spinner is Tanganyika's

diamond mine at Mwadui. This is the famous mine developed by
a Canadian geologist, Dr. John Thoburn Williamson. Williamson
had an abiding faith that a rich diamond pipe existed in Tanganyika and in 1940 he struck it.

The mine which Dr. Williamson developed lay remote in the
African bush, guarded by dogs and a private police force behind
barbed wire, and inaccessible accept by his fleet of private aircraft. Dr. Williamson himself was a shy and retiring man but
over the years he was built, probably much to his distaste, into
the figure of a romantic and mysterious millionaire.

He made large but unobtrusive bequests to various charities,
and gave to Queen Elizabeth II a 56-carat diamond, the "Princess
Pink," valued at $300,000. To Princess Margaret he presented a
250-stone diamond brooch valued at between $40,000 and $55,000.

Dr. Williamson died in 1958 and the mine has been jointly
acquired by the De Beers diamond group of South African
financier, Harry Oppenheimer, and the Tanganyika government.
They work it, and share the profits.

Mr. Nyerere has two hopes for an economic uplift. One is that
the United Nations, in view of its past connections with Tanganyika, will look with favorable eye on the territory's requests for
technical assistance and expert advice. The second is that Tanganyika's record of tranquillity will be an attraction for foreign
investors.

Economic factors have largely motivated Mr. Nyerere's campaign for a federation of East African territories. "The boundaries
of East Africa," he says, "are artificial ones. They divide peoples
united by language, by custom and by a history of [British]
colonial administration based on the same principles. A Federation of East Africa could bring new economic strength to all the
parts of it; could destroy the possibility of any territory losing
the reality of its independence through its need for economic
assistance. The arguments for this federation are so strong that
in fact the only remaining questions are how and when it can be
established."

Thus he is working for a federation of those territories in East
Africa which have been under British control. These are Tanganyika, Kenya, Uganda and the island of Zanzibar.

Ironically, such a federation was long a goal of the British when they ruled these lands as colonial units. However, it was always obstructed by the Africans, who were suspicious of a white-dominated federation after the style of the federation of the Rhodesias and Nyasaland.

In spite of African fears, various services were pooled by the territories. Thus railways and harbors, civil aviation, posts and telegraphs, and a number of medical and agricultural research projects were administered by an East African high commission. Clearly, it has been much more economical to run them jointly than to have each territory fund the identical services individually.

Mr. Nyerere recognizes this and envisages the extension of such pooling, although of course in a federation run by Africans. Similarly, he feels it is an unnecessary cost for each of the African territories in his proposed federation to dispatch separate ambassadors to world capitals, build up individual diplomatic corps and pay separate dues at the United Nations when they might finance such activities jointly as a federation.

With Tanganyika achieving complete independence in December, 1961, we now may expect to see an accelerated campaign for an East African federation.

Whether an East African federation is more likely to emerge under African control than under white remains to be seen. In Tanganyika support for the idea is strong. Kenya's Tom Mboya has announced he favors it. Uganda, as we shall see in the next chapter, is one of the most confused and unpredictable little states in Africa; however, Mr. Nyerere has indicated his willingness to launch the federation without Uganda in the first instance.

If the federation gets under way it is suggested that its membership might be swelled ultimately by Northern Rhodesia and Nyasaland in the event they break away from the federation of the Rhodesias and Nyasaland as it is presently constituted. Indeed, a coordinating movement known as the Pan African Freedom Movement for East and Central Africa (PAFMECA) already exists.

The hurdles are many but perhaps one day a federation of former British territories may weld millions of Africans from

Central and East Africa into a single bloc which the British themselves failed to build.

. . .

Zanzibar, the offshore island which may feature in a federation, is a glorious refuge from the cares and bustle of the everyday world. The scent of its cloves wafts out across the water as your boat nudges into shore and perfumes the island. Here is tropical romance, with all its deserted sandy coves and clear blue water and lazily waving palms, and white beaches with melodious names like Mangapwani.

In unhappier days, Zanzibar was the center of the vast slave trade conducted along the east coast of Africa by the Arabs. That has been stamped out but still the Arab atmosphere predominates, although the population of 300,000 is 75 per cent African.

Britain has been the power behind the throne for many years, but the legitimate ruler is the Sultan of Zanzibar, Seyyid Sir Abdulla Bin Khalifa, whose plain red flag flies above his palace on the waterfront.

The present Sultan succeeded to the throne in 1960 after the death of his father, Seyyid Sir Khalifa Bin Harub, who ruled for forty-nine years, longer than any other monarch in the world.

The little principal town on the fifty-mile long island is of Arab architecture with a maze of narrow winding alleys cluttered with tiny shops where craftsmen hammer out silverware and other metal work for tourists. Arab vendors jog through the streets selling everything from peanuts to bitter black coffee in brass pots kept hot by a little undercarriage filled with smoldering charcoal, and announced by the tinkling sound of two coffee cups whirred skillfully together.

One of the most magnificent sights on the island are the huge, handsome carved Arab doors, studded with big brass nails after the Indian fashion to repel invading war elephants. Apparently the tourists thought these doors were magnificent too, for they had them ripped out with their giant frames in such numbers to take home with them that there now is an official ban on their export.

It is perhaps tedious to divert to politics in such idyllic sur-roundings, but they have become increasingly important in recent years. Two main parties are in the field, the predominantly African Afro-Shirazi party and the Arab-led Zanzibar Nationalist party.

The Arabs are perhaps more politically conscious than the Africans, whipped up by the propaganda of Cairo Radio which blares from the shops night and day. It is they who are pressing for independence while the Africans, suspicious of Arab domina-tion despite their own numbers, have been rather more lukewarm to the idea.

In what must be one of the most dramatic elections in history, the Zanzibar Nationalist party lost by one vote the one decisive seat in elections held early in 1961. The elections were held again, but were marred by savage rioting.

A thorny issue in which Zanzibar plays a central role is the lease to Kenya of a vital strip of land, ten miles wide and fifty-two miles long, and including Kenya's principal port of Mombasa, on the mainland. Besides the island of Zanzibar, the sultan also reigns over the neighboring island of Pemba, some other islets and the strip of territory on the mainland. His "dominion" over the Kenya strip, however, is of a very nominal kind, for it is ad-ministered to all intents and purposes as part of Kenya, and the sultan has leased it to that country for a mere $28,000 a year since 1895. Obviously the territory is worth many millions of dollars and comprises most of Kenya's vital front to the sea. African nationalists charge that the treaty should be abrogated and the coastal strip be handed to Kenya. The Arabs, however, say that if the treaty is abrogated the belt should be returned to the Sultan of Zanzibar.

CHAPTER XX

Uganda: Up the Beanstalk

"UGANDA IS A FAIRY TALE. You climb up a railway instead of a beanstalk, and at the end there is a wonderful new world. The scenery is different, the vegetation is different, the climate is different, and, most of all, the people are different from anything elsewhere to be seen in the whole of Africa."

That is Winston Churchill speaking more than fifty years ago. Of course today you do not necessarily have to chug up the 870 miles of railway line from Mombasa, on the Kenya coast. You can fly in by jet, jinking over the Ruwenzori Mountains which skirt Uganda in the west, to land at the capital of Entebbe. But still Uganda remains a sort of rooftop fantasia, high on its sunny green plateau.

Here are tall forests of mahogany and other tropical trees, strung with monkey-rope tinsel, and shimmering with thousands of brilliant butterflies which smother your car's windshield thick as flakes in a heavy fall of snow when you drive through them.

Orchids and hothouse blooms grow wild.

Out of the undergrowth and across the roads come tramping all the animals Walt Disney ever painted, elephant and antelope and buffalo and the rest. On several occasions when driving through Uganda we have been halted by herds of elephant roaming at large across the track or breakfasting in the scrub beside it.

The plains are dotted with extinct volcanoes and interwoven with swamps and lakes and rivers. One-seventh of Uganda is open water, and, for all the fact that it straddles the equator, Uganda is a lush little country, particularly in the south where it borders Lake Victoria.

The great lake is the source of the Nile, which has been trapped and sent roaring through a big hydroelectric dam at the lakeside town of Jinja. When last I was there, Egyptian officials were stationed permanently at the side of the dam to measure the flow of the Nile so vital for their own country many hundreds of miles further on. Lower down in Uganda the Victoria Nile calms and goes meandering across the country until it links up with the Albert Nile from Lake Albert. The elephants come down to paddle in it and sometimes to squirt each other with it through their trunks like oversized schoolboys in a water-pistol fight. Now and then they flap their ears at the river steamers which go churning by. If the fancy so takes you and you have about three weeks to spare, you can take one of these steamers and follow the Nile all the way to Cairo, changing to train and bus over the unnavigable stretches of the river.

Around the lake's fertile shores agriculture is easy and banana trees grow in profusion. Thus bananas are the staple item on the menu, and dinner grows just outside the kitchen door. One choice banana recipe goes like this: Take about one hundred bananas (which sell for about twenty-five American cents). Wrap in broad green banana leaves, tying bundle securely with same. Boil to a mash in a pot with a little water in the bottom. Finally, smoke-cook over an open fire for about an hour. Serve on a banana leaf.

Uganda is primarily an agricultural country and is likely to remain so. Cotton and coffee are easy to grow in its rich black soil and have developed to the point where they are the two main export crops earning millions of dollars annually. Thus Africans here are much wealthier than those in surrounding, and more barren, territories. Some own expensive motor cars, some pay income tax on five-figure salaries, and some farm on such a scale that they employ migrant laborers from the neighboring territory of Ruanda-Urundi.

. . .

If Uganda is a fairy-tale country, its politics are fairy-tale politics too. This is a black African country with an overwhelmingly African population of some 6,500,000 as against a white population of about 11,000 and 70,000 Asians. White settlement is barred and the whites are transient, mainly officials of the British administration which governs Uganda as a British protectorate. Of Britain's three territories in East Africa, Uganda has always been regarded as a purely African state, destined for African self-government, with no complicating white settlers.

Yet this little state where the land is African-owned, where the population is overwhelmingly African, and whose right to govern has been least in question in colonial Africa, has been having one of the most arduous struggles to achieve African independence.

In this case this is not so much the fault of Britain as of the peoples of Uganda themselves. Britain is not particularly reluctant to hand over authority to a representative African government. Indeed the British governor of Uganda for a number of crucial years was Sir Andrew Cohen, believed by many to be one of Britain's ablest and most progressive colonial administrators. But the Ugandans themselves are riven by intertribal and interregional jealousies and dissent which has hindered the emergence of a representative government to which responsibility might be transferred.

In this country about the size of Britain there are thirteen main tribes. The most glaring contrast is between northern Uganda, which is peopled by Nilotics and Nilo-Hamites, and southern Uganda, whose people are primarily of Bantu stock. The south, however, contains the four important tribal kingdoms of Bunyoro, Toro, Ankole and Buganda, each with its own hereditary ruler enjoying considerable prestige and authority within the over-all framework of Uganda.

It is the kingdom of Buganda which is at the seat of Uganda's problems. This is the rich territory spread about the shores of Lake Victoria, site of the official capital of Entebbe and the biggest city of Kampala, center of Uganda's administration and communications and home of the biggest tribe in the country, the Baganda, numbering more than a million.

Perhaps it is time to pause and explain once again that the Baganda are a tribe living in Buganda, which is a kingdom within the country of Uganda. To add to this confusion a little, the Baganda speak a language called Luganda, and a single member of the Baganda tribe is a Muganda!

The Baganda are the biggest and most advanced tribe in Uganda, envied and feared by other tribes. Some of these other tribesmen in the northern territories wear only a few leaves. When they heard our car in this remote area, some of them threw themselves into the bush. They are perhaps no match for the relatively sophisticated Baganda and thus various tribal leaders have sought safeguards against their domination by the Baganda once Uganda becomes independent.

Some Baganda find this prospect of politically and economically dominating the rest of the country an attractive one. Other Baganda, however, believe that the less-developed bulk of the country would be a drain on Buganda in an independent Uganda and hold it back. This has led to Buganda's refusal to cooperate in a central government and reforms introduced by Britain, and a determination to make Buganda an independent country separate from the rest of Uganda.

The Baganda already have their own parliament, the Lukiko, with considerable authority over local affairs, and in recent years this local government has consistently refused to participate or allow Buganda's participation in a national elected government.

This stand led to a much-publicized clash in 1953 between Buganda's Kabaka, or king, and the British government. For his refusal to cooperate, the Kabaka was whisked away to exile in Britain, being allowed to return in 1955. During his absence his people went into mourning, many refused to cut their hair and performed similar acts of protest and loyalty, until he was returned to a capital delirious with excitement.

However, the problem has dragged on and early in 1961 Buganda declared itself independent. This was an inconclusive touch, for, while Buganda maintained it was independent, Britain maintained it was not. Life in Uganda drifted on as before.

Although it cannot be dismissed entirely as such, for the almost mystic attachment and loyalty of the Baganda to their king is a powerful factor in Uganda politics, much of the problem revolves around the same old clash in Africa between traditional tribal leadership, which sees its influence slipping, and the new threatening nationalism.

Thus the Kabaka's court and government ministers have resisted the democratizing reforms which they believe might erode the power of the Buganda throne.

Perhaps fortunately for them, they have not been confronted by a national leader, capable of overriding tribal divisions and welding the opposition into formidable unity with the fire of a Kwame Nkrumah or a Sekou Touré.

There is a welter of political parties but in national elections to the legislature in 1961, the Uganda Democratic party won a majority of the seats. However, Uganda political parties are subject to many shifts and changes.

In his middle-thirties, the Kabaka of Buganda, Mutesa II, is a youthful-looking ruler with an impeccable English accent and manner from his days at Cambridge University and a spell with the British brigade of guards.

Kampala, although its name means "hill of the antelope," is in fact built on a number of hills. The Kabaka's palace, fenced with elephant grass, stands on one of them, Mengo. The drums beat each day when he is in residence and a fire burns night and day at the palace gates, to be doused only upon the Kabaka's death.

When I met him in his study the Kabaka was dressed in an English-cut suit and wore an old school tie. There was an "Anna and the King of Siam" touch about the interview, however, for all the Kabaka's informality. The royal attendant who ushered me in did so on all fours, prostrated himself, and retired in the same manner with his face always towards his sovereign.

At first sight this was a normal room with ordinary furniture. But the Kabaka's chair was constructed so that it increased his height, while all other chairs in the room had tiny legs. This ensured that the Kabaka's head was always higher than those of his visitors and that he always looked down upon them although he is himself a fairly short man.

Many influences are at work in Uganda today. On one of Kampala's other hills there is the excellent Makerere College, East

Africa's principal university, turning out the country's new young intellectuals. Elsewhere in the city political parties are plotting and maneuvering and campaigning. Despite the loyalty of his own Baganda people, the tide of change is lapping at the Kabaka's throne. Whether he can continue to keep his head high and above the water up on Mengo hill remains to be seen.

. . . .

If Uganda is a fairy tale, Ruanda-Urundi is a postscript to the story.

Wedged between Uganda's southern border and Lake Tanganyika, this is the home of the Watutsis, those slender, aristocratic giants up to eight feet tall who drifted south from Ethiopia four or five hundred years ago. By contrast, although most of Africa's pygmies live over Ruanda-Urundi's western border in the Congo, there are still a few of the little people here to accentuate the Watutsis great height.

Until independence scheduled for 1962 this little country about the size of New Hampshire and Vermont put together is a United Nations trusteeship territory under Belgian administration. Before the Congo became independent it was administered much as part of the Congo, although visiting UN missions made periodic inspections and calls for progress. Since postindependence chaos in the Congo, however, the territory has looked more and more to stable East Africa. There is a possibility that Ruanda-Urundi, or at least part of it, might merge in a federation of former British territories in East Africa.

Ruanda-Urundi has problems both economic and political.

For Africa, this is a crowded country. Its 4,000,000 people are packed into a poor and undeveloped land with the highest population density in the continent. The economy is keyed to coffee, and thus dependent on prices on the world market. There is a shortage of trained men to fill the 1,200 administrative jobs presently held by Belgians. The outlook after independence is shaky and Ruanda-Urundi will need outside aid just to keep going, let alone progress.

Although the Belgians have administered Ruanda-Urundi as a single country from the present capital of Usumbura, it in fact is two separate units, Ruanda and Urundi, which might yet go separate ways after government has been decentralized to their own capitals.

Political problems revolve around the long domination by the Watutsis of the other nonwhite peoples of the territory. The Watutsis number 15 per cent of the population but have imposed their feudal rule over the other 85 per cent, who are 84 per cent Hutus, a Bantu tribe, and 1 per cent pygmies.

The Germans, during their thirty years of colonial rule in Ruanda-Urundi before World War I, encouraged the system, ruling indirectly through the Watutsi chiefs. Belgium conquered the country in World War I and acquired it as a League of Nations mandate but the system lingered on until recent years.

In 1959 the Watutsis and the Hutus clashed in Ruanda in a brief explosion of violence. Ruanda had discovered politics and the Watutsis campaigned for immediate independence in the belief they could emerge from it with their power entrenched, while the Parmehutu party of the Hutus demanded "democracy before independence" in a bid to loosen the Watutsis' grip and forestall Watutsi domination of an independent Ruanda. The Hutus have emerged on top. Early in 1961 they declared Ruanda a republic, though one with a sympathetic relationship with Belgium. The young new Mwami, or king, of the Ruanda Watutsis, is in exile, campaigning in Leopoldville and New York and elsewhere for his reinstatement.

In the southern state of Urundi, meanwhile, the Watutsi minority remains in control for the moment.

CHAPTER XXI

Kenya: Kingdom of Animals

NAIROBI IS the safari capital of the world.

From here the safaris trundle out all over East Africa. Of course these days they are motorized. No more of that *New Yorker* cartoon stuff, where a white man with a pith helmet and knobbly knees goes trudging off at the head of a score of African porters. Today the whites ride out in powerful safari wagons while trucks bring up the baggage and the rear.

Most of the safaris are in search of big game for foreign tourists who want to hunt. The tourists are mainly Americans. They have the money for this costly pastime and they provide a major slice of East Africa's tourist income.

Under the protective eye of a white professional hunter, they shoot down as much as they can or want under a licensing system which limits the hunter to a maximum of two elephants, two rhinos, one cheetah, one leopard, one hippopotamus, three buffalo and so on.

Eventually the heads of these animals are stuffed and shipped back to the United States to hang on walls as far more expensive decorations than anything bought on Fifth Avenue.

Happy to report, there is an increasing number of safaris for clients who balk at this slaughter and prefer to hunt only with the camera. They face the same dangers, get the same thrills, but the animal keeps his head. Some of these safaris are led by old white hunters who have themselves sickened of killing and laid up their guns except in self-defense.

Then too there are safaris commissioned by such clients as movie companies. They require guides and protection by white

242

hunters while they are on location in the African bush. Stars like William Holden and Rock Hudson and Clark Gable and Ava Gardner have all been in Kenya, with a string of others, and the average Kenyan probably sees more movie stars in a workaday year than the average New Yorker. Sometimes the bronzed professional hunters get parts in these films. Often they provide animals or assist with animal stunt shots.

Then there is another unique type of safari client such as the wealthy American businessman who comes back time and again "to get away from it all." He brings his movie projector and a stack of films and books from the United States. He employs a safari team and a white hunter for protection, sets up camp deep in the bush and rarely moves out of it. That way, he says, he is free of interruptions.

An African safari may bring remoteness, but these days there is no need to rough it in the African bush. The professional safari firms which arrange your expedition ensure that every reasonable comfort is to hand. You may sleep in a tent, but it will be on a soft mattress and there will be a hot bath whenever you want it. There will be ice clinking in glasses, the food comes straight from the camp refrigerator and a radio will provide soft music if you wish it. On the menu will be anything you desire, together with a checklist itemizing ten different choices of pickles and sauces.

There will be a dozen African servants at your command, ranging from the porters and the cook and the cook's assistant to your personal tent servant and the laundryman. If it is a hunting safari there will be gunbearers and animal skinners and cleaners.

Nobody will blink an eye if the client calls for caviar in camp, but, if he has not checked in advance, the client may blink when he gets the bill for the safari when it is over. For a 30-day safari the bill would be around $3,000 for transport, tentage, food and the white hunter's salary. Four clients on a 90-day safari should expect to pay $25,000 between them for basic costs.

The organization of all this is a major business, and indeed one of the white hunters we met was an American who had been a Harvard Business School man before taking up his novel profession in Kenya. The way he told it, and the way he explained all the paper work and organization that lay behind a long safari, his studies at Harvard in business administration did not seem such an unusual grounding for safari work after all.

Nairobi is the capital of the safari business, but it is of course a city of many varied businesses and industries. Since World War II it has grown and developed rapidly. Nevertheless, despite the secondhand car marts and the five-and-ten-cent stores, it has retained a colorful tang which makes it one of the most fascinating cities in Africa. It is a multiracial city, for Kenya is a British colony peopled by whites and Asians and Arabs as well as the overwhelmingly African population.

In the hotel lounges, African politicians thus rub shoulders with Hollywood script-writers and actors. Farmers in khaki bush jackets who have driven in for the day chat with Nairobi businessmen in city suits. Then there are the white hunters, tanned, with their wide-brimmed hats trimmed with leopard-skin bands. African waiters in long white khanzus and red fezzes bustle between the tables. And there goes an African bellhop, plucking a bicycle bell screwed to the base of a long pole which bears a blackboard with the name of some wanted party chalked upon it.

. . .

Kenya is animal country. Of course the neighboring East African countries of Tanganyika and Uganda are roamed by big game too. It is perhaps an injustice to them to lump all the animal stories in a chapter on Kenya, and gloss over their own magnificent animal parks and reserves such as the Queen Elizabeth and Murchison Falls parks in Uganda, and Tanganyika's Serengeti plains where vast, breathtaking herds of game graze beneath your safari lodge on the rim of the famed Ngorongoro Crater.

Nevertheless, Nairobi is the arrival point for visitors to East Africa, and here seem to be collected the widest variety of white hunters and game experts and veteran swoppers of animal tales.

Once we saw the dented army boot of a private in a British regiment who, while on anti-Mau Mau patrol, was surprised, charged and trodden on by a rhinoceros and lived to tell the tale. With a fine sense of the drama of the situation, the army allowed him to keep the boot as a souvenir, while issuing him with new ones.

When I accompanied one such British patrol on a Mau Mau operation, the unit's tracker dog picked up a hot scent and led us swiftly down a narrow path through tangled bush. We retraced our route at speed when an African tracker working with the dog became increasingly suspicious, then announced tensely that the dog was tracking a full-grown buffalo—not the sweetest-tempered of animals to meet in thick bush.

Once my wife and I were having tea at the pleasant home in Nairobi of a Kenya government information officer. In the middle of it, an enormous ostrich walked in. Our host and hostess were unconcerned, but for our part we found it difficult to hide our surprise. "Oh yes," said our hostess, "someone gave it to my husband when it was small. But it's getting a bit big now." Then brightly: "I suppose *you* wouldn't like it, would you?"

In fact, it would not have been difficult to acquire a variety of animals in Kenya. At one time, a wealthy Asian businessman in Nairobi announced with a grand gesture his intention of presenting my wife with a young but substantial cheetah. I listened dubiously as he explained: "He is really still too wild to be called a pet. But on the other hand he's too tame to let loose to fend for himself in the bush." Somehow I could not see us continuing our journey across Kenya in the Volkswagen we were driving at that time with a wild-tame cheetah breathing down my neck—especially as the back seat was already occupied by our large Labrador retriever dog. With as much grace as possible, and some reluctance on the part of my wife, we declined the kind offer.

On another journey through Kenya we met an engineer waging a small war against wild animals. He had been given an unusual task. He had to tap the snows of Mount Kilimanjaro and pipe them nearly a hundred miles across the Nyiri Desert to fill water supply tanks for steam locomotives panting up the railway line from the port of Mombasa to Kenya's capital of Nairobi.

In the years after World War II, traffic over this railway line increased substantially. However, bore holes which had previously supplied water for the locomotives were inadequate to meet the new demands. Some were drying up altogether. The railway authorities had to have water, and so they spent more than $2,000,000 on a scheme to pipe water from a spring on the slopes of Kilimanjaro, fed by the melting snow which caps the former volcano's stubby 19,340-foot peak, to a reservoir at a point on the railway line called Sultan Hamud. In addition to giving the railway locomotives their needed water, the scheme brought drinking water to thousands of cattle owned by the Masai and Kamba tribes at runoff points along the pipeline.

But the wild animals of the area proved a constant harassment to our engineer friend. On occasion herds of elephants fifty-strong would carry out an inspection of the works, sending off both African work gangs and white supervisors until the animals left the site. Sometimes elephants tore up part of the seven-inch-diameter pipeline which had been laid eighteen inches below ground.

To track down such mishaps, our engineer had a telephone line strung along the length of the pipeline. But cruising elephants and giraffes knocked it down and it had to be restrung on abnormally high poles.

Once a two-ton rhinoceros halted work when it charged a trailer laden with pipes and sent them flying. It did not make quite such an impression on a heavy tractor which it subsequently charged, but the tractor was out of action for some days nonetheless.

Finally the project was finished, and without any serious accident to any of the 500 African laborers or the dozen whites employed on it, despite the curiosity and occasional antagonism of animals in the area. Then it all seemed worth-while to the engineer in charge, even that dark night during the middle of the project when he walked into his makeshift garage on the site to find a large, snarling leopard there.

Beside the pipeline there runs a rough motor track for maintenance vehicles and if you follow it you arrive at Amboseli, one of East Africa's splendid game reserves.

Within the reserve at a spot called Ol Tukai there is a simple lodge for visitors. There is nothing else there but this little group of huts where you find a bed and a stack of wood to cook the food you have brought with you.

In many ways Amboseli is the most satisfying of all East Africa's game reserves and parks, for it is a flat, hard salt pan

over which you can roam freely by car for miles, unfettered by
the need to keep to tracks and motor paths. Thus you can get to
very close quarters with the game.

Here we got some of our finest and closest-ever lion pictures in
Africa. One morning we chugged out of the lodge at dawn with
an African askari, who knew the reserve, acting as guide from
the rear seat. Long before us he spotted what seemed to be two
rocks in the middle of an empty stretch of the salt pan. Off we
went to investigate and, as our guide knew all the time, the rocks
turned out to be lions.

Closer and closer we drove as the first light of day streaked the
sky. Each moment I imagined the lions would make off and so we
stopped frequently to take what I was sure would be our last picture of them before they moved. They saw us, but lay there barely
interested in our approach.

Fifty feet, forty feet, thirty feet, twenty feet. Then I halted
the car. "Closer, closer," urged our guide. Slowly we edged in
until I stopped the car five feet from the nearest lion. He was so
big that his head was on a line with ours although his body lay
flat on the ground. For a few long seconds he looked at us
squarely with his big, cold, yellow eyes. They say that there are
some animals that a lion fears, but in that instant it did not seem
to me that the lion was afraid of anything in the whole wide
world. After a few seconds he dismissed us and turned his gaze
away.

Long before this, I had rolled up my driver's window, however
fragile a protection it might seem against such a beast, and I had
been taking pictures through a minute crack at the top. To our
askari, wise all his life to the ways of animals, this was clearly
sissy stuff. "Quite safe to wind down the window, master," he
assured me, "they've just killed and eaten." Somehow I could not
entirely rid myself of the suspicion that they might care for one
of us for dessert. But I did wind down the window—a little. And
for twenty minutes we photographed the lions stretching and
yawning and scratching. When the pictures came out later, they
showed the lions so clearly and closely that you could pick out
the flies upon their backs.

Eventually the lions grew bored with us and stalked off. But we were not done with lions yet. For, explained our guide, he knew where a lioness and her cubs had made their lair in a thicket not far away.

We found the place and ground gingerly in through grass perhaps eighteen inches high. There, sitting on a fallen tree trunk, sunning itself like an outsized kitten, was a pert lion cub which watched us fearlessly as we drove nearer.

"And now," said our African guide, "we must pass behind that log, and about here we should see . . ." And there they were, three more cubs peeping quaintly through the blades of grass, with a lioness lying close by, crouched and with teeth bared and eyes angry and suspicious. All were superbly camouflaged in the undergrowth so that one might have come on foot within twenty feet of them without seeing them.

This, of course, was a far different encounter to our earlier one with the two lions. This was a jealous lioness guarding her cubs and we stayed only a minute or two before leaving her in peace.

The animals of Africa roam all through Amboseli, and of course beyond its borders, although outside the reserves and game parks they are the prey of hunters and even inside the reserves they are hunted by poachers. Thus at any moment you may come upon a dozen elephants sploshing about in a water hole, or a giraffe nibbling daintily from the topmost branches of a tree, or a herd of many different kinds of buck. One dawn as we were driving off from our hut we found two rhinos trotting through the grounds of the lodge not fifty yards from our door. One dark night, when my wife called me to investigate strange noises in the "garden" in front of our hut, my flashlight picked out the startling bulk of an elephant, champing through the shrubbery.

Meanwhile, about a hundred miles from Amboseli lies the Tsavo National Park, the largest in the world, about the size of Massachusetts. Lions are the main attraction here and, says the East African Tourist Travel Association's brochure blandly, "they still display some of the aggressive characteristics of their ancestors made famous in the book 'The Man-eaters of Tsavo.'" The man-eaters of Tsavo were two famous lions which brought the building of the Mombasa-Nairobi railway line to a standstill at the turn of the century when the construction gangs reached Tsavo. Thousands of Indian laborers had been imported to build the line, and, although it was they who originated East Africa's substantial Asian community today, they nevertheless suffered heavy casualties from sickness while working on the line. At Tsavo, however, work stopped completely until the rampaging man-eating lions, which pounced on and killed twenty-eight Indians and many Africans, were eventually shot.

The highlight for us in the Tsavo park was the subterranean tank set in the edge of a hippo pool at Mzima Springs. We were told the tank had been built by a Walt Disney camera crew which had come to photograph wild life in East Africa. You climbed down into it and there through the wall of underwater glass which was one side of it you could watch the clumsy underwater ballet of the hippos, and the crocodiles sliding past shifty-eyed and all the other pool life.

Kenya's most unique game park, however, is the Nairobi National Park just five miles from the center of Nairobi. Though only forty square miles in size, this is the home of hippos and crocodiles and lions and even a few rhinos, all roaming free and wild within the unfenced park, and all within taxi distance from the center of Nairobi.

It is not so long ago since a lion from the park walked into the city to seat itself on the steps of the cathedral. Pilots using a near-by airfield have long made a routine check to satisfy themselves they will meet no lumbering animal coming up the runway as they touch down.

Thus you may drive out to the park at dusk and perhaps photograph a pride of lions snarling over a kill, all against the background of Nairobi's modern skyline with its modern office blocks and apartment houses.

Yet this little scene symbolizes in a way the clash between the new face of Africa and the old, and the inroads which are being made in the world of wildlife.

East Africa is the last great haunt of Africa's wild animals. Elsewhere, apart from a few game reserves in South Africa, the Rhodesias and the Congo, Africa's animals have virtually disappeared in bulk in the face of the population explosion, progress, and the onward march of cities and highways and smelters and factories and hydroelectric projects and jet runways.

In East Africa there remain the great herds, but even here there is serious thinning out and interruption of the old migration trails, and the animals are becoming increasingly restricted and confined.

There are still thousands of animals in the plains and forests of East Africa, but game experts say that compared with the previous abundance of Africa, these represent only between a tenth and a twentieth of the numbers of thirty years ago. Many of these experts believe that preservation of today's herds is at a desperate stage and that some varieties will die out within the next ten to twenty years unless conservation campaigns are expanded and galvanized.

Donald Ker, one of Africa's best-known hunters and director of a leading Nairobi safari company, believes there is as yet no shortage of elephant, and that buffalo have seemed on the increase in recent years. But the position with rhino and lion is much more serious from the conservationist's point of view. Leopards "have taken a considerable beating," and cheetahs are "decidedly scarce."

The "phenomenon of human expansion" in Africa has been the major over-all cause of declining numbers of game, says Mr. Ker, but over the past decade "poaching has been the greatest scourge that African animals have ever had to face." He estimates the poaching toll in East Africa in the past few years in excess of three hundred animals per day.

In former days, Africans killed wild animals either to eat, or to provide clothing and weapons and utensils, or to protect their families and homes. But in recent times, poaching has become "highly and viciously commercialized," according to Mr. Ker.

Nowadays there is a tremendous black market in ivory elephant tusks and rhino horn, hacked by African tribesmen out of slaughtered animals, passed on to middlemen, then smuggled out of Kenya's coastal ports to Asia where it fetches high prices.

Poisoned arrows and muzzle-loaders and deep pits are the old poaching weapons, but today cruel steel wire snares are widely used by poachers to trap animals. The poachers have become highly organized, with transport at their command, and are backed by illegal traders skilled in law evasion.

The authorities have not been idle. Dedicated game rangers, sometimes risking their lives against violent and ruthless poachers, have declared war, and are supported by police and other government officials in an attempt to stamp out poaching and smuggling.

But the task is immense and they are handicapped, as is the over-all program of wildlife preservation in East Africa, by lack of men and money. "This point—sheer lack of money—has been a massive and enduring problem," says Mr. Ker. "It has frustrated so many of the efforts and disheartened the staffs of the game departments and national parks. It has held up water schemes and road building and all forms of development. It has vastly hindered antipoaching forays. It has loomed over game affairs with the awful logic of young and poor communities in which so many other things have seemed essential first."

Now of course these programs for game preservation will be passing to the hands of new African governments in East Africa. For the income provided from tourism alone, and particularly the inflow of American dollars, preservation of wildlife is a project highly worth-while.

CHAPTER XXII

Kenya: Jungle of Politics

SINCE THE BEGINNING of the century when the railway opened up the country and settlers moved in to carve out their estates, Kenya had been the most "British" of all Britain's colonies.

Some of the young settlers were the wilder sons of aristocratic English families, sent out to cool off for a while in Africa. Others were sporting young men attracted by the prospect of adventure and wide open spaces in Kenya. For all the tough job of working up a farm from the African bush, many of Kenya's settlers have retained a huntin', shootin' and fishin' air about them over the years.

Still today, titles and links with the landed dukedoms and earldoms of Britain are not uncommon here in East Africa, and in the years after World War II there was an influx of British army officers and wartime pilots seeking a new life in the bracing highlands of Kenya.

There are hunt balls and horse shows against a background clatter of teacups. The neat cottage farmhouses in the lush greenness of the Kenya highlands look more English than African. About it all there often seems a smack of English county life.

A billboard outside a news agent's shop in Nairobi proclaims with an exclamation mark: "English Magazines—Arrived Today From Home!" There inside are the *Illustrated London News* and *Country Life* and young men with enormous Royal Air Force-style mustaches buying airmail copies of the London *Daily Telegraph*. There is cricket every Saturday, although Nairobi is only eighty-seven miles from the equator. Peter Sellers is at the movies. The Nairobi Welsh Society is staging a grand rugby football dance. And in the main street of Nairobi, an English schoolgirl voice shrills: "Have you got my netball kit, Penelope?"

Yet for all these British touches imposed upon Kenya during the last sixty years, this is an African country with an overwhelmingly African population of 6,000,000 outnumbering the 65,000 white settlers by more than ninety to one. Now after more than half a century of white rule, Kenya is within sight of independence under black African government.

No country in Africa perhaps, with the exception of the Congo, has seen such a dramatic somersault in political trends as Kenya in just a few brief years. Five years ago the colony was still emerging from the horrors of Mau Mau terrorism. With the revolt put down by British troops and white rule firmly established again, there seemed little prospect of concessions to Africans, or compromise. Officially, the state of emergency declared in 1952 lingered on until early 1960. Yet today Britain has given Africans widespread voting powers, although not without objections from the local white settlers, and Africans have put an African majority into the legislative council, or local parliament. Such has been the speed of change in Kenya.

Inevitably with the approach of African government and independence the "white highlands," long the sacrosanct preserve of whites, have been opened to African farmers. Land is a subject of emotional intensity in Kenya. The extent of white land ownership and African land hunger lie at the root of many problems. Frustration among the principal Kikuyu tribe over land shortage and overcrowding was one of the principal reasons underlying Mau Mau terrorism.

Long at the center of African frustration have been these white highlands. In area they total only some 16,000 square miles out of Kenya's total of 220,000 square miles. But the bulk of Kenya is arid and difficult to farm. The highlands have a crisp, clear climate and are green and fresh like Virginia or the English Downs. Here is the most fertile land in the country, and about one quarter of the total 68,000 square miles of arable land. The whites have till recently monopolized it, refusing to permit African ownership.

Naturally this has infuriated Africans living in the vicinity of the white highlands who have observed these spacious acres from their own desperately overcrowded land. Further, the original ownership of these highlands is an issue of intense controversy which probably will never be settled to the satisfaction of both sides.

The whites claim that when they or their ancestors arrived in the early 1900's they found the land vacant, and therefore stole it from nobody. The Africans say it was theirs, and that, even if they were not in physical possession of it at the time, they were only temporarily absent and never surrendered their rightful ownership.

White explorers in the late 1880's and 1890's reported intensive cultivation by the Kikuyu of the highlands in the vicinity of what is today Nairobi.

However, experts on the Kikuyu like Dr. L. S. B. Leakey, a white man who grew up among the tribe, speaks the Kikuyu language perfectly and was made a first-grade elder of the tribe, maintain that a smallpox epidemic, a rinderpest outbreak, an intense drought and famine and a devastating locust invasion all had reduced the area to virtually uninhabited bushland by 1902 and the time of white settlement.

An official British commission concluded in 1934 that actual land alienated by the first white settlers from the Kikuyu came to 106¾ square miles out of the total 16,000 square miles of the white highlands.

The Kikuyu have never accepted this. They maintain that most, if not all, the white-occupied land was stolen from them.

Whatever the truth of the matter, it is apparent from subsequent official reports that, although the white population of Kenya is today about 65,000, there are only about 4,000 actual farm-owners among them. These hold about one-quarter of the finest land in the country, while 6,000,000 Africans are crowded onto the remainder. Whatever the legality of the Kikuyu claims, it is easy to understand the explosiveness of the situation as the Kikuyu looked out covetously from their own poor plots over white lands which they claimed were not always intensively developed. And aside from the issue of original ownership, Africans of course have till recently been barred by law from buying into the highlands to relieve their overcrowding.

Experts like Dr. Leakey charge that the leaders of Mau Mau terrorism deliberately misrepresented the land question and fomented further frustration to whip Africans into an orgy of violence.

.   .   .

For some months before, despite official denials and pooh-poohing, there had been whispers and reports of secret oath-taking among the Kikuyu. Then in the autumn of 1952 the first savage incidents began. White farmers' cattle were slashed to death with *pangas*, the heavy, all-purpose knives used by Africans. Then Africans who refused to submit to the authority of Mau Mau were murdered, and the first whites were found cut to death on their lonely farms. Kenya was face to face with Mau Mau terrorism.

To this day, nobody is sure what the name "Mau Mau" means. But the organization resorted to savagery in keeping with the sinister ring of its name.

Basically Mau Mau was anti-Christian and antiwhite. Despite long investigation, evidence was never uncovered linking it with communism or indeed with any outside influence. It was an African, and primarily Kikuyu, organization through and through.

It derived its strength from a series of ghastly, binding oaths. Often these were forcibly administered in rituals of barbarism involving blood, excrement, animal organs and mutilation of animals. In an ascending series the oaths compelled the initiate to complete loyalty to Mau Mau, even to the point of producing a white man's head if so ordered. Having taken the oath, the initiate was the captive of Mau Mau, betraying it only at the price of sudden death.

The oathing spread far. A friend of ours had employed for thirty years a loyal Kikuyu cook, trusted implicitly even when other servants and workers on her farm were discovered to have taken Mau Mau oaths. Yet one day the police arrived and carried him off to jail nonetheless as the master oath-giver for the area.

Mau Mau members were discovered on the personal staff of the British governor of the colony, and among employees in the American consulate.

Yet many thousands of Kikuyu Christians and loyalists refused to take the oath or to obey Mau Mau. Some were armed and fought back against Mau Mau. Many hundreds, including chiefs and elders of the tribe, paid for their opposition with their lives. For although Mau Mau was basically antiwhite, it lashed out at Africans who refused to conform and support it, and Africans bore the brunt of the fatalities.

British officials believed that Mau Mau was somehow an undercover offshoot of at least a wing of the Kenya African Union (KAU). The KAU was headed by a fiery African nationalist, Jomo Kenyatta, who also ran a network of independent Kikuyu schools through the Kikuyu area. However, although the KAU was eventually banned, it included in its membership various prominent Africans and politicians who have remained above suspicion of complicity in Mau Mau. Kenya's leading African nationalist in recent years, Tom Mboya, was a young member of the KAU in his early twenties, for example.

The Kikuyu schools were centers for the propagation of African nationalism and antiwhite feeling and the British charge that, although Kenyatta issued appeals, at government request, for an end to Mau Mau, he slyly gave it his approval.

Kenyatta's original name was Kamau wa Ngengi, and as an orphan he was brought up at a Church of Scotland mission. At an early age he became immersed in Kikuyu politics and was a founder-member, and later president, of the Kikuyu Central Association. The association sent him to London and he spent more than fifteen years there studying, and airing the Kikuyu grievances over land and protesting white rule. There he emerged with the name of Jomo Kenyatta and the nickname "Burning Spear." There too he married an English girl in 1943 and had a son, although he has had no contact with them for years.

In 1929, 1932 and 1933 he paid visits to the Soviet Union, and perhaps inevitably has been accused by Kenya white settlers of links with communism, but in the intervening years there has been no tangible evidence of this. After World War II, during which he worked for a time as a farm laborer in England, Kenyatta returned to Kenya. Soon after Mau Mau's emergence he was arrested, tried, convicted on a charge of complicity in managing Mau Mau, and sentenced to seven years' imprisonment. Throughout the trial, Kenyatta steadfastly denied the charge, and refuted knowledge of antiwhite propaganda disseminated through his Kikuyu school system.

Now Britain concentrated on smashing Mau Mau. Thousands of British tommies were shipped and flown in and plodded through the dense Kenya forests hunting Mau Mau gangs. Planes of the Royal Air Force bombed what they believed to be Mau Mau hideouts. This was full-scale war and it cost many millions of dollars. But for all the might ranged against the terrorists, they waged a guerilla campaign from the forests, living on little, moving off at the approach of patrols and slipping out in gangs to slash their victims and burn homesteads at night. They blew up bridges, blocked roads, attacked and overran posts and garrisons where they knew they could find arms and ammunition.

They were backed by a network of supporters across the country, bound by the Mau Mau oath to supply information, food, money. Nobody knew who was a Mau Mau or not. Thus, even in the restaurants and night clubs of Nairobi, women in evening dresses would wear revolvers strapped around their waists, and the men would park their Sten guns underneath the tables.

The British command resorted to a variety of methods to smash the terrorist campaign from amnesties to de-oathing ceremonies conducted by Kikuyu loyalist witch doctors in the pay of the government. Brave sorties were made by white officers into the forests, with bodies blackened and disguised as terrorists themselves, to pinpoint terrorist positions and destroy them. For many miles Kikuyu villagers working under government orders dug a wide ditch, almost a moat, cluttered with sharpened stakes at the bottom, around the forests to prevent terrorists coming out or supporters taking food in. Thousands of Kikuyu tribesmen were uprooted and collected in new villages where they were shut in at night and kept under watch and guard. There was collective punishment for Mau Mau crimes and other measures which roused strong criticism from some sections of the public in Britain. However, many white settlers themselves advocated much harsher measures in a sort of eye-for-an-eye campaign.

Eventually the troops turned the tide and after three years the real power of Mau Mau in the military sphere was smashed. Many thousands died in the war, the vast majority of them Africans, and the great bulk of these being terrorists killed by police and soldiers. Many thousands more were arrested and detained without trial under the emergency regulations. Slowly these made their way up the pipeline to freedom via a series of rehabilitation and work camps engaged in a massive prisoner-reform program. Hard-core Mau Mau fanatics, classified in prison jargon as "blacks," stayed on in maximum security camps. "Greys," or passive Mau Mau supporters, and "whites," on probation and ready for reclassification as "cleared," moved on and eventually out to local work camps in their home areas where they underwent a final screening by loyalist tribal elders before returning to their own villages. Object of the program was to make the prisoners confess their crimes and break with the Mau Mau oaths, while "instructing" and educating them.

However, although the large-scale war against Mau Mau was largely won by the end of 1955, isolated pockets of terrorists remained and tension lingered on for several further years. When we rented a cottage for a while just outside Nairobi in 1956, our landlord remarked that three of his cattle guards had been found with their throats slit in a ditch just behind it. He and his family had awakened one night at the height of terrorism to find the thatched roof of their house afire, and had run from it with our landlord, an ex-army officer, firing his pistol into the dark before them.

Meanwhile, a British army patrol which I accompanied had recently put on a show for a visiting American television camera crew. As military activity seemed to be drawing to a standstill, the cameramen arranged to film the patrol charging across an open piece of ground and firing live ammunition into a thicket ahead of them. The movie operation was duly staged, but to the surprise of everybody the troops flushed—but failed to catch, in all the excitement—a small band of real terrorists hidden there. Either they had been unaware of the troops near them, or had laid low in the hopes they would go undetected.

· · ·

With the end of military warfare, it would have been unrealistic to imagine that Kenya Africans would not resort to a more orthodox, political campaign for redress of their grievances. Many African leaders, however, were in jail or restricted in political activity, and members of the Kikuyu tribe, with Embu and Meru tribesmen also affected by Mau Mau, were dissuaded by various decrees from public politics.

To the fore at this time there leapt a deceptively sleepy-eyed young man by name of Tom Mboya. Mboya came not from the Kikuyu tribe suspect in official eyes, but the next-biggest tribe in Kenya, the Luo.

With the KAU banned, an African trade union group, the Kenya Federation of Labor, became the focal point of African activity. By the time he was twenty-three, Mboya had fought his way to the leadership of this organization as its secretary general. In the vacuum left by the removal of African leadership during Mau Mau and its aftermath, Mboya quickly soared to a position of influence and stature among Kenya Africans.

By any standards, Mboya has had a remarkable career. Now still in his very early thirties, he has long years of politics ahead of him and could become one of Africa's most important figures.

Schooled by Roman Catholics at Kenya mission stations, Mr. Mboya was born on a sisal estate, the son of a humble Luo headman earning seven dollars a month. There was no prospect of university for the young man, but he qualified as a sanitary inspector, working for the Nairobi City Council, and from there graduated to trade unionism, and eventually politics.

Early in his career as a unionist, Mboya attracted the attention of local representatives of the anti-Communist International Confederation of Free Trade Unions and he has since become an important figure in that organization. During several visits to the

United States he has also forged strong links with organized American labor leaders and from one trip took back $35,000 from the AFL-CIO to build a new union headquarters in Nairobi.

Mr. Mboya has made a particular hit in the United States, having paid a number of visits there and addressed large audiences and met such leaders as former Vice-President Nixon and President Kennedy. Aside from his tours of the United States he has traveled extensively, both earlier as a student on a year's scholarship to Oxford's Ruskin College, and later as an up-and-coming politician whose potential is widely recognized in other lands both inside and outside Africa.

Although he has kept up his connection with trade unionism, as Africans have been permitted more and more participation in Kenya politics, he has become a member of the legislative council, which eventually will become the parliament of an independent Kenya, and a leader of the principal African political organization, the Kenya African National Union (KANU).

With the resumption and development of political activity after Mau Mau, Mboya's membership of the Luo tribe, which had initially given him an advantage during the political neutralization of the Kikuyu, seemed to loom as a handicap. With the Kikuyu returning to politics, would they accept as a leader a man like Mboya from the rival Luo tribe?

Mboya set about removing this disability in a number of ways. He adopted a tougher and more extreme line toward white rule than anybody. He won widespread African support by personally arranging airlifts of Kenya students to the United States for university study there—a particularly striking achievement in the eyes of Africans who prize education above all else. He saw to it that news of his standing elsewhere in Africa and the world seeped back to Kenya. He cloaked himself in the aura of Nkrumah-ism, adopted at Nkrumah's suggestion tribal costume to titillate the imagination of the crowds.

Despite all this effort to make himself a national figure, thus cutting across tribal rivalries, probably Mr. Mboya's shrewdest political move was to fling himself on the Kenyatta bandwagon.

After serving five years of his seven-year sentence, Kenyatta had been released but confined to Lodwar in the most inaccessible area of Kenya, which made him virtually still a prisoner. Though the prospect of his return to public life was bitterly resented by the white settlers whose memories of Mau Mau were still fresh, he was still the mystical leader of the Kikuyu.

Mboya recognized that Kenyatta was the hottest political issue in Kenya. To oppose his return, even appear lukewarm about it, might mean the loss of Kikuyu support and political suicide. So he campaigned for Kenyatta's release more vigorously than any other politician. In speech after speech he demanded Kenyatta's return. As secretary general of KANU, he declared the party lived for the moment when Kenyatta would return to lead it, presumably replacing the caretaker leader, James Gichuru, an ex-headmaster.

At first glimpse, Kenyatta's return would appear to stymie Mboya's own ambitions for national leadership. But Kenyatta is now an elderly man. Clearly, Mboya's strategy was to ride to power on Kenyatta's coattails, and carve for himself a role as Kenyatta's political heir come the time when the old leader stepped down.

Mr. Mboya's tactics appear to have brought him success where Kikuyu support is concerned. In general elections in 1961 giving Africans a majority in the legislative council, Mboya had to fight a Nairobi constituency with a predominantly Kikuyu electorate. His opponents ran a Kikuyu doctor against him. Yet Mboya swamped the poll with 31,407 votes to 2,668.

After the elections both KANU and its principal African opposition party, the Kenya African Democratic Union (KADU), led by Ronald Ngala, refused to participate in a new government until Kenyatta was completely free. The British governor, Sir Patrick Renison, rejected this demand but agreed to move Kenyatta nearer Nairobi. Thereupon, KADU agreed to participate in the new government amid jeers from KANU that it was "selling out" on the Kenyatta issue.

At the time of writing the outcome of the controversy was unsettled but Kenyatta's release appears inevitable ultimately, and perhaps by the time this book is published he will be free.

Although Mboya as a shrewd African politician may be expected to keep up his harangue against white authority in these last lingering days of colonial rule in Kenya, his real challenge comes from fellow African politicians. Besides Mr. Gichuru there are wilder members of KANU such as Mr. A. O. Oginga-Odinga who have little love for Mboya, as well as political enemies outside the party. Further, Mboya is relatively unknown to Kenyatta, who may have different ideas about the selection of a political heir. Some of Mboya's opponents have also tried to make capital out of his apparent pro-Americanism and conceivably Mr. Mboya for the sake of political expediency might have to go through a phase of disengagement from his association with various American friends.

One of the principal challenges to the combined African leadership of Kenya, however, will come in its attitude toward the white minority, and too to the important minority of Asian traders and businessmen, after independence.

Among the more pessimistic settlers the stories are circulating that their land may become subject to expropriation, that Mau Mau oath-taking is again rife, and that once Africans are in control of the government, whites can look to a grim time ahead.

Kenya is an African territory where a sizable body of permanent white settlers who have resisted African advance will come under African rule. For Africans this presents a striking opportunity for the exercise of tolerance and good will which they claim was not always shown them by whites.

If there is injustice and discrimination against Kenya's racial minorities, it will harden still further white opinion in those countries at the southern end of Africa like South Africa and Southern Rhodesia.

But if the transition is a peaceful one and whites find they still have a place in the sun under African rule, it may do a great deal to wipe out the catastrophe of the Congo which has done so much to sully the African record.

CHAPTER XXIII

Ethiopia: The Lion's Tale

Beyond the waterless wastes of Kenya's Northern Frontier Province, the desert track grinds up over a mountain range 8,000 feet high to the mountain plateau of Ethiopia.

This is a difficult and sometimes dangerous journey not often undertaken. The motorist's guidebook to Africa's "trunk" roads is full of bleak little warnings and footnotes about it. Much of the route is impassable between June and September. Traffic over a certain section is "nonexistent." Over another section "no water, provisions or petrol [gasoline] are available." At one point, notes the guidebook, "an armed escort is considered necessary."

Thus for many years Ethiopia, or Abyssinia as it used to be called, has remained apart from the rest of Africa like an inaccessible land of the Lost Horizon.

This is not a black African state at all in the strictly Negro sense. Its ruling Amharas, with a feudal royal house which they claim is descended from Solomon and the Queen of Sheba, derive from a Semitic-Hamitic compound and have long held themselves arrogantly aloof from the Negro tribes of Africa.

Yet recently there has been a significant change. Ethiopia's government has sensed the import of the African revolution swirling about it and descended from its mountain redoubt to play an important role in pan-African politics.

"Government" is really just another name for Ethiopia's absolute monarch, Emperor Haile Selassie, Conquering Lion of the Tribe of Judah, Negusa Negast (King of Kings), for there is no doubt that it is he who runs Ethiopia.

For all his slightness of build and the remoteness of his domain, the bearded little emperor has been a remarkable figure on the world's stage since the early days of his reign which began more than thirty years ago. A few years after his accession he stood lonely in the spotlight at the League of Nations, seeking in vain aid against the Italian Fascist invaders of his country. But the Italians overran Ethiopia and the Lion of Judah was driven from his lair to spend five years in exile in Britain until Allied troops, mainly British, liberated Ethiopia in 1941. Thus ended Ethiopia's single brief experience of foreign domination in a 3,000-year-old history of independence which dwarfs that of any other African land.

For Ethiopia, the emperor's return meant a continuation of feudal autocracy. Haile Selassie has retained power tightly in his hands. He has no enthusiasm for political parties or the type of democratic reforms which might threaten his paternalistic rule.

In his Palace of the Prince of Paradise in the Ethiopian capital of Addis Ababa he sits regal as the royal lions which stalk the grounds outside. Court protocol is strict and formal morning dress is the requirement for visitors to the emperor's presence. By tradition the emperor's own subjects grovel at his feet. He rules by kingly decree and patronage and through his personal appointees. When his green Rolls-Royce purrs through the streets of the capital his subjects fling themselves to the ground in homage. Even diplomats and foreign residents alight from their cars and bow to the imperial figure riding with a cloak flung about his shoulders.

Yet, although Haile Selassie rules something after the fashion of a medieval monarch and there has been little apparent movement toward democratization in the political sphere, it is he who has sought to modernize his country and draw it into the twentieth century out of the dark ages. It is he who has encouraged economic and educational progress, sometimes against resistance from more conservative elements within the country.

With few skilled and highly educated men among Ethiopia's 20,000,000 people, this progress comes mainly through the labors of foreign specialists who have been invited by the emperor, or whose offers of service he has accepted. British and Swedish influence has long been considerable in Ethiopia and nationals of these countries have held prominent official posts. Canadian

Jesuits run a university college, the Norwegians are training a navy, and the French and the West Germans and the Israelis are involved in various projects of assistance. The United States has an aid program and Americans in their private capacities have been employed as advisers in various government departments. Ethiopian Airlines, which since World War II has linked Ethiopia by air with the outside world, and which perhaps more importantly has opened up communications within the country, is operated by Trans World Airlines.

Lately there has been a trend toward "disengagement" of Ethiopia from blatant involvement with the West, of which more later. Thus the Soviets have appeared on the scene and the Communist Chinese have been hovering in the background. Interestingly enough, Haile Selassie has struck up a warm personal friendship with Yugoslavia's President Tito and Yugoslavian aid to Ethiopia is becoming an important factor to the country.

For centuries Ethiopia has been a backward country. Addis Ababa itself, for example, has few outstanding modern buildings. It is a capital of humble houses with whitewashed mud walls and thatched roofs, and has a low sky line, for the Ethiopians have not mastered the art of building higher than one story. Eucalyptus wood is a staple fuel and smoke from the eucalyptus fires curls lazily over the town. The men wear traditional dress of white cotton jodhpurs with a cotton toga flung around their shoulders, while the women wear ankle-length white cotton dresses, also with a toga but with a colored border. Pack animals, mainly mules and donkeys, clatter through the streets, for Ethiopia discovered the wheel only latterly.

Further, progress has been hindered by the diversity of its peoples and the isolation of one tribe from another which has persisted even until recent times. Thus, although the Amharas are the ruling minority and their language of Amharic is the official tongue, there are the tribal factions of Galla and Gurage and of the ancient province of Tigre, and militant tribes such as the Danakil and the Karayu and the Issa. The presence of Somalis in the Ogaden region is a further complicating factor and, beside inherent tribal differences and occasional reluctance to submit to the authority of the central government, there are important religious differences. The Amharas, for example, are Christians of the ancient Coptic Church and have made this the state religion, but many of the tribesmen in outlying districts are Moslems or pagans.

To weld all these peoples together and uplift their living standards, Haile Selassie has looked to educational advance. He personally conducts Ethiopia's educational program and allocates somewhere between 11 per cent and 30 per cent of the nation's budget to education. The estimates vary with different observers and are difficult to confirm, for funds are dispensed at the emperor's direction and there is no budget in the orthodox sense. Some observers say the emperor has contributed some of his personal fortune to education and clearly he holds it in high regard.

Nevertheless only some 70,000 children have been attending government schools in recent years, with perhaps another 70,000 receiving private instruction, and this is a small percentage of the school-age population.

Promising young men have been selected for further tuition in the capital and the cream of these, as well as officers and administrators in government employ, have been dispatched to universities in the United States and Europe for advanced study.

Ironically it appears that it was from the seeds of these educational reforms planted by the emperor that sprang a revolution in late 1960 intended to overthrow him.

With the emperor absent on a visit to West Africa and South America, young Ethiopian intellectuals, frustrated at a pace of advance they considered too slow, attempted to seize power. Two of the ring leaders were Germame Newaye, governor of the province of Jigjiga who received his university education at Columbia University, and his elder brother Mengestu, commander of the emperor's elite Imperial Bodyguard.

In a radio broadcast to the world, the rebels declared: "The people of Ethiopia have waited for a long time with patience in the hope that they will be free some day of oppression, poverty and ignorance. In doing this they have amply demonstrated their abundant patience, but empty promises can no longer satisfy the people, who now want concrete action, aimed at improving their standard of living.

"Development plans have not been executed in practise and the long strides being made by the newly independent African states, who are making progress day by day, have made the peoples of Ethiopia realize that these new nations are advancing quite fast, leaving the people of Ethiopia behind. This has shattered the hopes of the Ethiopian people."

According to the rebels, Emperor Haile Selassie had been deposed in his absence and a new government had taken over, headed by the emperor's eldest son, Crown Prince Asfa Wassan, and supported by the armed forces, the police and "educated youngsters."

But the rebels were too optimistic. They had still to fight a pitched battle in the streets of Addis Ababa with troops loyal to the emperor. Hundreds were killed in the fighting and the rebels eventually lost the day. The emperor flew back to secure his throne and announce that his son had acted "under coercion." The Lion of Judah had not yet lost his roar.

At Ethiopian embassies abroad, where some incautious diplomats had welcomed the revolt without waiting until its success was assured, and at universities in the United States where some students from Ethiopia lit celebratory bonfires at the first news of upheaval, there was consternation at the emperor's return.

Yet the paradox underlying the revolt was illustrated by one Ethiopian student in the United States, critical of Haile Selassie. As he mourned the failure of the revolt, he added in the same breath: "The Emperor has done more for Ethiopia in the past thirty years than all his ancestors did during the past 3,000 years."

.   .   .

Although the rebels charged Haile Selassie with moving too slowly at home, in foreign affairs he has made determined efforts to end Ethiopia's isolation from the outside world.

His bitter experience at the hands of the League of Nations in 1935 has not lessened his faith in collective security nor impaired his support of the United Nations. Ethiopia was a founder member of the UN, and of the International Monetary Fund and the International Bank for Reconstruction and Development.

Haile Selassie dispatched Ethiopian troops to Korea to fight for the UN, and Ethiopian soldiers and technicians are at work with the UN in the Congo.

But the emperor scored a considerable diplomatic achievement when he persuaded the UN's new Economic Commission for Africa to make its headquarters in the Ethiopian capital of Addis Ababa, where he offered to build it a handsome palace on an imposing esplanade.

Perhaps this more than anything marked the end of Ethiopia's detachment from continental African affairs and its emergence in pan-African politics.

Siting of the UN's commission in Addis Ababa ensures a constant flow of African diplomats and delegates and officials from every country in the continent to and from Ethiopia. But Ethiopia's new interest in black Africa does not stop there. African leaders from Kwame Nkrumah to Tom Mboya are welcomed in the Ethiopian capital. African students have been offered scholarships at Addis Ababa's university college. Important African anniversaries and freedom days are celebrated with publicity in the capital.

The Ethiopians themselves are showing their flag in various parts of the continent beyond their own mountain land. Ethiopian delegations attend various pan-African conferences. They were at the important All-African Peoples Conference in Accra and other gatherings in different capitals. Haile Selassie has visited West Africa and on a state visit to Ghana decorated President Nkrumah with the Exalted Order of Sheba, Ethiopia's highest award. In return he was given Ghana's first state award, the Most Exalted Order of the Star of Africa.

The emperor has aligned himself with African states in condemnation of South Africa's apartheid policy and dedicated Ethiopia to assisting the achievement of independence of "our African brothers who are still under mandatory rule." Thus Ethiopia, with Liberia, decided to take South Africa to the International Court of Justice over its controversial administration of South-West Africa.

All this indicates that Haile Selassie is leading his country, with its longest history of independence in Africa, to what he hopes will be a position of stature and influence in the new black councils of the continent.

Although Ethiopia's increased contact with the Communist world recently has startled some Western circles, it is perhaps not too surprising when viewed against the background of Ethiopia's purpose in Africa.

In the past, Ethiopia has been on friendly terms with various Western countries and has largely been reckoned a Western ally. This, however, might be a compromising stand among the new black states of Africa, numbers of whom are pursuing a policy of nonalignment, and who might dismiss Ethiopia as a tool of the West.

Therefore behind Ethiopia's new association with the Soviet Union some observers detect a policy of "disengagement" from too-blatant cooperation with the West. This would surround Ethiopia with a more neutral aura perhaps more acceptable to other African states.

When Emperor Haile Selassie toured the Soviet Union in 1959, the Soviets obviously attached considerable importance to his visit. Mr. Khrushchev was waiting at the airport and whisked the emperor away to an apartment in the Kremlin. Truckloads of peasants were brought in from the country to swell the cheering crowds and banners bearing greetings in the Ethiopian language of Amharic fluttered across the road.

During his visit to Leningrad the emperor was escorted to the Museum of Anthropology and Ethnography to be shown drawings of himself with his father, together with pictures of nineteenth- and twentieth-century Russian and Soviet hospitals in Ethiopia, and a display of Ethiopian newspapers and a modern Ethiopian bible. There was even some talk of a merger between the Ethiopian Coptic Church and the Russian Orthodox Church which had first been mooted in czarist days.

The emperor paid handsome tribute to Soviet achievements and at the end of his visit it was announced that Mr. Khrushchev would pay a return visit to Ethiopia and that the Soviet Union would grant a long-term, low-interest loan to Ethiopia of $100,-000,000. The Soviet Union was to build a technical school in Addis Ababa, would send machinery and other items to Ethiopia in terms of a trade pact and would make the emperor a personal gift of an Ilyushin 14 aircraft. Since then the Soviets have followed up with an agreement to make a geological survey of Ethiopia for minerals, to establish gold-mining plants and to build a big oil refinery at Assab on the Red Sea.

On his way home the emperor also floated smaller loans from Czechoslovakia and Yugoslavia.

Ethiopia has long been the subject of scare stories about Communist penetration in Africa. For years a fanciful story has circulated that the Soviet Union's hospital maintained in Addis Ababa is a headquarters for Soviet intrigue and spying. But the hospital in fact dates back to czarist times and its activities have been innocuous.

With later developments, of course, it is evident that the Soviets now really do consider Ethiopia a worth-while target in their African offensive. But Haile Selassie is no inexperienced young leader. He has held on to his throne for a third of a century in the face of various challenges, and knows many tricks of maneuver. A more neutral stance is one thing, but it is difficult to believe that the Lion of Judah is inviting the Russian bear to share his lair.

The fluid stage in Ethiopian politics will likely come when the emperor, now nearing his seventies, passes from the scene.

It is widely believed that the emperor had passed over Crown Prince Wassan and selected as his successor his second, and favorite son, Masfen Makonnen, Duke of Harar. The duke was killed in an automobile accident, however. Even before the abortive 1960 coup, Prince Wassan's relations with his father were understood to be strained. Now it is thought that the emperor favors as his successor the schoolboy son of the late Duke of Harar. This little boy might still be a young man when called upon to mount the throne and exercise the same authority and wisdom as his grandfather.

· · ·

Like a craggy island in a flat sea, Ethiopia sits perched above the desert countries which flow below it and around it on all sides.

To the north there is Eritrea, federated with Ethiopia by the United Nations in 1952. Eritrea is virtually a self-governing province of Ethiopia, becoming more and more subject to central control. Formerly part of Italy's East African empire and for a while under British control during and after World War II, it gives Ethiopia a front on the Red Sea, and the ports of Massawa and Assab. Its capital is Asmara and sited there is a fair-sized American military telecommunications base.

To Ethiopia's west lies the Sudan, through which runs the cleaving line between Arab Africa and black Africa. The peoples of the northern Sudan are Arab in character, owing strict allegiance to Islam, but the tribes in the south, bordering on the Congo, Uganda, Kenya and parts of Ethiopia, are African, mixed pagans and Christians.

However, it is the Arab Sudanese who dominate the Sudan and are regarded with traditional wariness by the Christian Ethiopians, who have a deep-rooted fear of Moslem penetration.

To Ethiopia's south lies Kenya.

But Ethiopia's most troublesome borders lie in the southeast and east where the bloc of nomadic Somalis press in and over them.

The Somalis are strung all across the peninsula which juts out into the Indian Ocean like a rhino's horn, and which is sometimes called the Horn of Africa. There are between 2,000,000 and 3,000,000 of them. Some 500,000 of them live in Ethiopia itself and there are between 50,000 and 100,000 in northern Kenya. But the bulk are spread across what used to be three separate Somalilands administered by France, Britain and Italy (the latter as a United Nations trust territory) respectively. In 1960 the British and Italian territories became independent and fused as the new Somali Republic.

Ethiopia opposed the union, criticizing Britain and Italy for allowing it, and is against any further reunification of the Somalis. Many Somalis themselves envisage a new Greater Somalia, including their fellow Somalis from Kenya, French Somaliland and Ethiopia, as well as the existing Somali Republic.

The Ethiopians for religious and other reasons resent the creation of an Islamic Greater Somalia on their borders, while the

Somalis in turn suspect the Ethiopians of territorial designs on their country.

The question is inflamed by disputes over important border territories which both sides claim as theirs. Already the Ethiopians and Somalis have clashed in border skirmishes over these lands.

Thus Africa's most ancient lands and newest nations alike are swept by the tide of the African revolution.

CONCLUSION

CHAPTER XXIV

Africa: Curtain Up!

WHEN MY NEWSPAPER assigned me to Africa in 1955, my wife and I went down to the Brooklyn waterfront to arrange for the shipment of our car before we left.

"Where ya goin'?" queried one of the dock workers.

"South Africa," I told him.

"Jeeze," he exclaimed with new respect, "ya missionaries or somethin'?"

Such was the darkness of Africa to an ordinary citizen of the United States in 1955, a great dark void where only a missionary would voluntarily go.

When I arrived in Africa there were only two other American foreign correspondents stationed in my territory. For some while thereafter, the three of us, from the New York *Times, Time-Life,* and *The Christian Science Monitor,* were the sole full-time resident correspondents of the American press covering Africa south of the Sahara.

Nowadays the picture is a very different one. Africa is big news. The news agencies have bureaus in half a dozen African capitals. The reporters and the television cameramen have come flooding in. One American news magazine has a rumored budget of $100,000 a year for its main African bureau. More than 330 correspondents were accredited to the United Nations Congo operation at the peak of the crisis.

The great raw presence of Africa has come marching out of television sets in millions of homes from Pasadena, California, to Stockholm, Sweden. The name of Patrice Lumumba, who was a nonentity little more than a year before his death, quickly becomes a household word and his murder causes diplomatic shock and student riots in capitals around the world. Africa has been discovered. It still may be confusing, but there is no lack of interest in it. Sometimes the problem seems to be to keep it out of the headlines.

All this new interest is good to see, particularly in the United States. Inevitably the United States will bear heavy responsibilities on behalf of the West in Africa. It is the strongest of the Western nations. It has the wealth and the technological resources to solve many of Africa's economic problems. To many Africans it is the most acceptable spokesman for the West, for it has not itself been a colonizing power. Thus it is right and proper that the concern of its citizens for Africa should be awakened, that more American news organizations should send back an informative coverage of Africa, that the skimpy corps of American experts on Africa should be expanded, and that the long-neglected African operations of the State Department and other governmental agencies should be revitalized.

There are welcome signs that all this is taking place, yet there is some sadness in the fact that it should have taken the chaos of the Congo, and particularly the threat of communism's fist thrust deep into the heart of Africa, to really put the continent on the map.

It was primarily the threat of a Communist takeover in the Congo which jolted the United States out of its apathy toward Africa.

Previously the United States has not had much of an African policy that any African specialist could see or understand, but now the pace of events is forcing it to mold one. The main priority is that it should be a real African policy, geared by experts to the needs and realities and character of Africa, and not just a policy of stolid anticommunism transferred to an African battleground. If it is a program of anti-Communist hysteria, designed to block the Communists first, and maybe, if there is any energy left over, to help the Africans last, we will not make many friends in Africa. African states are not averse to playing Western and Communist worlds off against each other for aid. But, illogically and paradoxically, they are extremely sensitive to gestures motivated by

Cold War considerations, rather than by genuine respect and friendship. This is one of the contradictory facts of life in Africa today and a good example in itself of the type of conundrum with which the American policy maker must juggle.

. . .

None of this is meant to minimize the Communist threat in Africa. We should be under no delusions about the grim intentness with which the Soviets and the Communist Chinese are pursuing their ambitions in this continent

Until a few years ago, Moscow's opportunities for contact with black Africa were necessarily limited. Most of the continent was under the control of stoutly anti-Communist colonial powers like Britain, France and Belgium. The colonial security men kept a sharp eye on traffic to and from Communist lands and upon Communist attempts to infiltrate.

Some Africans studying in European capitals such as London and Paris were befriended by Communists and encouraged to visit Communist countries, sometimes with their expenses paid for them. Some students were offered trips on the understanding that their passports would not be visaed or otherwise stamped by the Communist authorities. This would enable them to keep their sorties behind the Iron Curtain a secret from their colonial rulers upon their return to Africa.

The Soviets also churned out their propaganda. In Eastern Nigeria, for example, British security men discovered several African bookstores selling literature supplied by the state publishing house in Moscow. The shopowners had been offered it on attractive terms, all free, and they could keep as profit whatever they sold it for. Much of the literature was straightforward. It included Russian classical works, novels, plays and so on, to which nobody could object. Slotted into the covers, however, were the latest Communist party pamphlets and policy statements and pronouncements on events of the day. The material had been flown from Moscow to Paris, then to a neighboring African country and smuggled across the border.

Meanwhile, the Soviets were doing their homework on Africa. Most of their African experts had never set foot there. But they worked with the latest books and newspaper articles, and even reports and statistics and publications from individual colonies. They wrote a *Study of African Languages* and produced dictionaries in the Hausa (Nigeria) and Swahili (East Africa) languages.

The procession of African colonies to independence, beginning with Ghana in 1957, gave the Communist nations their entrée to Africa. Now they could send independence delegations and ambassadors and cultural and trade and other missions to states which were sovereign and no longer under suspicious colonial eyes. In Ghana, smiling Soviet Minister Ivan Benediktov bustled hither and thither, asking interested questions and proffering good will and congratulations. In the press camp the men from *Pravda* and the Soviet newsreel industry clustered African journalists about them over bottles of vodka brought from Moscow. The delegations from Communist countries delivered their independence gifts, then pressed for trade and diplomatic ties.

Since then, the Communists have been among the first to give formal recognition and hearty good wishes to one new state after another, and there has been a steady increase in Communist activity in African affairs.

There has been a marked stepup in radio programs beamed at Africa, for example. Moscow now broadcasts to Africa in English for nineteen hours a week, with a further nineteen hours in French and three in Swahili. Peking is directing thirty-five hours a week of English broadcasts specifically to Africa, as well as another fourteen hours in English to Africa and other areas jointly.

Africans have a consuming passion for education and now that the colonial rulers have gone, the Communists can openly recruit students. Some 500 nonwhite students a year are getting a university education in Moscow's new Friendship University. The Soviets pay their traveling expenses, the cost of their tuition and living, and also give them a special allowance for warm winter clothing, a thoughtful gesture towards students from tropical lands.

Various cultural and literary conferences lure eager young

African writers and creative artists behind the Iron Curtain that used to be.

The Soviets' own African research program has been boosted. The Soviet Academy of Sciences has formed an African Institute with a faculty of their country's fifty leading experts on Africa. They are to prepare textbooks on Africa for Soviet schools and universities, conduct their own research programs and train a new crop of African experts.

Of the Communists' activities on the continent of Africa itself, we already know. The scale of effort in Guinea seemed to indicate an attempt to make this little West African land the first Communist foothold in black Africa. Ethiopia has been tempted with a $100,000,000 loan, but it will take much more than that to convert wily Emperor Haile Selassie to communism. In the Congo came the Soviets' biggest play for influence.

In the Congo lay the gravest danger, for there was the threat of physical intervention by the Soviets. Would the Soviets really have sent an army crashing through the Congo jungles? Do they relish the committal of Soviet troops to a difficult campaign in Africa so far from their homeland? These are dangerous questions on which to gamble an answer.

Yet communism does not always come in the shape of a Red Army uniform and a tommy gun. It is there in the shape of the Soviet ambassador who speaks the local language flawlessly and who just happens to be an admirer of precolonial African bronze work. It exists in the presence of the Communist Chinese rice expert who has just pioneered at home such a rice scheme as the Africans are launching. It arrives with the Communist technicians who move in unobtrusively without contracts or guarantees, while we are still negotiating diplomatic immunity for ours. It spreads a little every time the pro-Communist newspaper in South Africa gibes at the all-white exclusivity of American embassy parties, or the mellifluous voice of Peking Radio relays the latest, loaded account of race segregation in the American South. It rears its subtle head each time the Soviet Union forces the West onto the defensive on colonial topics at the United Nations.

Aid, trade, propaganda, sympathy—these are the weapons

which have dominated the Communist campaign to date in Africa.

If they win the propaganda war and convince the African that a Communist is a man's best friend, there is no need for a hot war in Africa. There is no reason why Soviet boots should scuff through the sands of Africa in a campaign of impossible physical conquest. There is no need even for bloody takeovers by diehard indoctrinated African Communists. A leader such as the Communists hope to make of Sekou Touré, or whom they might have made of Patrice Lumumba, will serve their purpose just as well for the moment.

For the Communists aim to convince Africans that they understand them best. It is as simple as that. By their account, they are the noncolonialists, the people who best understand African inferiorities, frustrations, ambitions and the passionate African devotion to the assertion of African independence.

Parallel to this goes Communist smearing of the United States, as the West's principal spokesman, with the tarbrush of Western colonialism, dollar imperialism, racial discrimination, and self-interest in Africa. If Africans are persuaded to believe this, there is no need for the Communists to fight any military battles. They will just as effectively orient Africa's trade toward the Communist world, swing the flow of African minerals away from the West, deny the West the support of Africa at the United Nations and produce an African neutralism highly tinged with anti-Western suspicion and hostility.

This then is the trap that yawns. We must be strong in defense of our principles, prepared even to defend them with force at the right time and right place. But we must recognize that Communist emissaries in Africa are another of the facts of African life. It is unrealistic to imagine that Africans will not establish relations with the Communist as well as the Western world. If we become obsessed with the Communist bogey in Africa we may leap into the trap with a program inspired by short-term political considerations rather than the desire to see the emergence of a strong and independent Africa. The Africans will see through that and the suspicions kindled by the Soviets will be fanned.

So much of it all is not a question of dollars and aid but
attitudes. If we are to help Africa, it ought to be for Africa's
sake. The sincerity ought to shine through. Americans, after all,
are the true revolutionaries. Theirs is the land of Jefferson and
Lincoln. They have been anticolonialists since 1776.

Education is one of Africa's dominant needs. This is a sphere
in which the United States might make a tremendous contribution, both by bringing African students to the United States
and sending American teachers to Africa.

Yet on the eve of the last American presidential election there
occurred an incident in connection with American educational
aid to Africa which dramatizes the pitfalls confronting American
policy.

After a squabble between the State Department and the
Kennedy Foundation, the latter provided $100,000 for a crash
program to airlift two or three hundred Kenya Africans to the
United States for study. This was the joint idea of Mr. John F.
Kennedy, then campaigning for the presidency, and Kenya
nationalist leader Tom Mboya, soon to face an election in his
own country. In the United States it was popular with Negro
voters, and in Kenya it was well received by Mr. Mboya's supporters. It recognized the great need and opportunity for African
study in the United States. But the way in which the scheme
was arranged, and the lack of proper mechanism for selecting
students most fitted for the opportunity, has drawn the criticism
of many leading American educators.

As Dr. Cornelis W. de Kiewiet, president of the University of
Rochester and an American specialist on Africa, wrote in the
New York Herald Tribune: "What was good politics for Mr.
Mboya and Mr. Kennedy sent a chill down the spine of thought-
ful educators."

Ironically, Dr. de Kiewiet was in Kenya on a mission to assess
Africa's educational needs with four other American university
presidents and educators when the news of the grant broke.

He wrote at the time: "It is significant that not a single
European official or African leader has spoken to us with approval of the announcement from Washington.

"From here the $100,000 grant has a shabby look. It is a

campaign maneuver and a by-product of the noisy and confusing business of electing an American president. It is no way to support the claim that America has a clear policy in Africa."

In citing this case it is not the intention to single out Mr. Kennedy or even his administration for criticism. The previous administration made its blunders. During the presidency of Mr. Eisenhower, Africans at an important international conference at Accra once held up publication of a message of greetings from the Soviet Union for three days until local American diplomats could get a similar message out of Washington to be read simultaneously with the Communist one. Indeed, in the early days of its office, there are indications that the Kennedy administration is paying much more attention to Africa than did Mr. Eisenhower's, and pursuing a more positive and perceptive line in African affairs.

The student airlift was not a bungle committed in the course of an attempt to counter the Communist presence in Africa. But it was an indication of the type of bungle which may be committed when short-term political considerations are the motivation.

To prevent this type of mistake, the United States needs more experts on Africa, more understanding of African problems, more informed thinking and better long-range planning on Africa.

For example, it must be assessing its attitude to the African forces which might emerge in South Africa after a possible upheaval there; it may be too late to tell them *then* that it has always supported their aspirations. What about the confused nationalist opposition groups emerging in Angola?

What about an African bid to take those American-financed copper mines of Northern Rhodesia out of the Rhodesian Federation dominated by whites and into a new, African-run East African federation?

Where would America stand in a clash between Liberia and Guinea? It is a hypothetical case, but rich ores straddling the common boundary conceivably could provide the spark. On the one hand there is the crisp, determined administration of Guinea, dealing with the Communists, supplied with Czechoslovakian arms, but headed by a dynamic young leader who might group an important sector of French-colonized Africa behind him. On the other hand there is Liberia, a ramshackle state shot through with much inefficiency, but a recipient of American aid, the site of American rubber plantations and tied to the United States with certain mutual defense agreements. Its amiable President Tubman has little stature with Africa's serious young nationalists. What stance would America adopt?

What if Dr. Nkrumah's army marched into little Togoland? What about Katanga's Mr. Tshombe, firmly opposed to communism, but whose pro-Belgian stance and connection with Patrice Lumumba's death prevent him setting foot in many African lands? Whose claim will we recognize to pan-African leadership? What if rival trade union movements develop in Africa, one tied to the anti-Communist International Confederation of Free Trade Unions, but the other seeking its own "African identity"? What about an African common market? What if Uganda breaks up? These are just a few hypothetical questions, but elementary ones compared with those that Africa may in fact toss at the rest of the world.

. . .

For one that has turned a whole continent upside down in three or four years, the African revolution has not fared too badly. There has been turmoil and disaster, and the explosion of the Congo and Angola sometimes gives the impression that all Africa is in flames.

There may be much more violence, but in fact the transition in which millions of Africans have overthrown their colonial rulers has been remarkably peaceful throughout enormous tracts of the continent. In many instances there lingers much respect and even affection between former colony and former overlord.

With the Congo a notable exception, there has not been widespread anarchy. The jungle has not crept back and covered everything. The administration has not collapsed. There is as much inefficiency as when the white men ruled, and in some countries maybe a little less. A white man is still probably safer in Accra at dead of night than in Central Park, New York. Africans have faced up to their international responsibilities. They pay their dues at the United Nations, and their armies have kept the United Nations Congo operation afloat. A delegate from Africa has yet to brandish his shoe at the General Assembly as did Mr. Khrushchev.

Africa has not become an appendage of the Asian or Western or Communist blocs. It has become a strikingly powerful diplomatic force of its own in international affairs.

It has not gone Communist, and Communist successes to date in Africa are minor. They too have their problems. The Soviets and the Communist Chinese may yet find themselves working against each other in Africa. The Communists' African men are good and we must not underrate them. Nor must we overrate them. The Soviet ambassador in Leopoldville looked just as harassed and confused by the postindependence chaos as any Western diplomat. Soviet aid rushed to the Congo included bananas and sugar—two of the Congo's exports. The wheat the Soviets shipped to Matadi could be milled only a thousand miles away in Katanga.

The driving force behind African diplomacy today is to eradicate the last outposts of foreign rule and to assert the African "personality," as Dr. Nkrumah calls it. But you might term it dignity.

Africans sizzle at attempts to make them pawns in the power struggle. They want to keep the Cold War out of Africa. As they see it, they are not fighting either communism or Westernism but their own intensely personal battle against poverty, backwardness and centuries of indignity. Africa is for Africans. They admire American progress and technology but they do not want to become imitation Americans. The tourist who says: "Why don't you do it the way we do back in Winnetka, Illinois?" may be losing a friend for his country. They are Africans and they have their own African way of doing things. It is just possible that their ways are sometimes better.

Thus they can be sharp with either side from time to time. For all his apparent procommunism, Guinea's President Touré has publicly rebuked the Communists in the United Nations General Assembly. Ghana's President Nkrumah has had angry private words to say about Communist Chinese incursions in Tibet.

Yet the African states will unleash their fury on the West for Western backing of the French in Algeria, or for Belgian chicanery in the Congo, or apartheid in South Africa. Sometimes Western statesmen are alarmed at the vehemence of these attacks. But they do not mean that the Africans are pro-Communist. They mean that they are pro-African.

Hysterical, hypersensitive to criticism, imperious, illogical, infuriating, even racially arrogant—all these things Africans may be in the future, just as white men have been before them.

There may be further outbreaks of barbarism, although Africa has yet to produce anything on the scale of the calculated savagery of Belsen and Buchenwald, or the Japanese war atrocities.

There may be victimization of whites, and perhaps racial discrimination by nonwhites against whites.

Democracy may be at a premium. There is a distinct trend already to one-party rule in many African lands. For the moment there is no buffering middle-class between the elite tier of intellectuals and the peasant masses. Autocracy may be the pattern.

Africans may not measure up very well by the standards of Western Christian civilization. But this is a strange yardstick to use on people who are not Western, not particularly Christian, and not necessarily civilized by a Western gauge of refinement.

This is Africa. We must try to understand it.

Of course, it all may end up as a terrible disappointment. Nobody pretends that independence has solved Africa's problems. Africa's leaders are confident and learn fast, but nobody can doubt the many pitfalls and challenges that lie ahead of them. In the economic sphere, for example, their problems are increased with independence, for the new states like Ghana, Guinea and Nigeria plan much more accelerated development than was their lot under colonialism.

There are dams to be flung across roaring rivers, ports to be constructed, shipping and air lines to be launched, armies and navies and diplomats to be trained, millions of homes and factories to be built and the living standards of the masses to be raised. The problems are awesome.

But take heart. This is not the end. It is just the beginning. The curtain is only going up.

Index

Date Due

JUL 6 '62			
JAN 25 '63			
NOV 6 '64			
MAR 1 2 '65			
APR 1 5 '66			
MAY 6 '66	T		
MAY 2 7 '66			
MAY 1 5 1970			
FEB 2 1975			
𝒢𝐵	PRINTED	IN U. S. A.	